Sass and Compass in Action

Sass and Compass
in Action

WYNN NETHERLAND
NATHAN WEIZENBAUM
CHRIS EPPSTEIN
BRANDON MATHIS

MANNING
SHELTER ISLAND

Manning Publications Co.
20 Baldwin Road
PO Box 261
Shelter Island, NY 11964

Development editor:	Scott Stirling
Technical proofreader:	Matt Martini
Copyeditor:	Andy Carroll
Proofreader:	Katie Tennant
Typesetter:	Dottie Marsico
Cover designer:	Marija Tudor

ISBN 9781617290145
Printed in the United States of America
1 2 3 4 5 6 7 8 9 10 – MAL – 18 17 16 15 14 13

*To those who craft the web
and delight in the work of their hands*

brief contents

contents

preface

Just a few short years ago, the idea of a book on Sass or Compass seemed absurd. As early adopters, we knew we had seen the future of stylesheet authoring, but we struggled to gain much traction outside the Ruby community in which Sass was born. Developers often didn't see the dichotomy of using frameworks to create dynamic web pages while still writing static CSS by hand. Yet others were distrustful of Sass's only syntax at the time, the original indented, whitespace-significant syntax. It felt too rigid, like too much of a departure from CSS.

In 2010, as we worked to evangelize the benefits of Sass to our designer friends across the industry (and making some converts, we should add), Sass and the idea of preprocessed CSS began to get a foothold in development and designer circles. When Sass introduced the SCSS syntax, many of the objections to adopting Sass began to fade away and we saw a real tipping point in projects using Sass for stylesheet authoring.

At the time, many other languages with a similar vision were emerging. Much like Sirius and XM validated the idea of satellite radio, healthy competition helped validate the idea of preprocessed CSS. It was in this environment of initial industry curiosity that Manning approached us to write a book about Sass and Compass. We agreed to write this book because we wanted to share Sass with a broader audience. While it's taken much longer to produce than we wanted due to career moves and major life events for each of us, we're excited to offer this book to the community that has grown up around Sass.

If you're new to Sass, we hope it provides a solid foundation for the language and opens your eyes to new techniques. Even if you've been writing Sass for many years, we're confident you'll deepen your understanding of advanced Sass and Compass features that you'll take back to your own projects.

acknowledgments

We couldn't write a book about Sass (and Compass by extension) without thanking Hampton Catlin. Sass has made CSS fun again for so many of us. Though the syntax has evolved, Sass has always kept to the spirit of CSS while extending it in powerful ways. Hampton's vision and hard work have made an indelible mark on the project and the community.

Chris Eppstein, we (your coauthors), would like to extend our sincere appreciation to you. Without your tireless efforts extending and maintaining Sass and Compass over the last few years, we can say with certainty that the community would not be what it is today.

We'd like to thank the folks at Manning for sticking with us during a long, long journey to get this book published. Writing a book about fast-moving open source is always difficult, as the landscape is constantly shifting. We're excited to put this book in the hands of designers and developers wanting to level up their front-end tools.

Finally, special thanks to our technical proofreader, Matt Martini, for his careful reading of the final manuscript shortly before it went into production, and to the following reviewers, who read our chapters several times at different stages during development and offered invaluable feedback: Adam Michela, Adam Yonk, Andrea Ferretti, David A. Mosher, David Landau, Ezekiel Templin, Graham Ashton, Jacob Rohde, Jake Stutzman, James Hafner, Jason J. W. Williams, Jeremiah Stover, Jeroen van Dijk, Ken Paulsen, Kerrick Long, Kevin Sylvestre, Kyle Wild, Ron Chloupek, Ryan Kelln, and William Dodson.

WYNN NETHERLAND

I would like to thank my wife Polly for dealing with the stress and deadlines of yet another manuscript. Thanks for loving this crazy person.

I'd also like to thank Jason J. W. Williams, another Manning author, for sharing his polyglot authoring toolchain and countless hours of technical support.

about this book

So many of us pick up techniques from the community, learning stylesheet hacks and other tricks in short-form blog posts or screencasts. This book aims to present a top-down survey of two tools—Sass and Compass—to expand your CSS toolkit and make you a better stylesheet author. While focusing on practical application, we take a systematic approach to teaching Sass syntax and applying the patterns in the Compass framework. Hopefully, the reader will walk away with a more complete understanding of both Sass and Compass.

Audience

This book is designed for two main audiences. First, we want to reach out to web designers, those who write a lot of CSS but might not have considered ways to automate parts of the stylesheet authoring process. Second, we want to show full stack developers how to treat stylesheets, images, and fonts like any other project asset and how to handle them throughout the lifecycle of a project from development to production.

Roadmap

If you're new to Sass and Compass, you might find yourself jumping to appendixes A and B as you begin the book. Those appendixes provide setup instructions and other prerequisites you'll need for the book.

Chapter 1 dives right into the powerful features of the Sass language. You'll discover not only exciting features, but hopefully a renewed joy for CSS when the tedium of static stylesheets disappears. We'll also give you a taste of the Compass framework in examples that provide practical application of Sass's features.

Chapter 2 goes deeper into Sass and covers variables, mixins, and other language features that provide the building blocks for the rest of the book.

Chapter 3 jumps right into one of the most common uses for CSS, building grid systems. As you'll see, with Sass, there's far less math involved.

Chapter 4 takes a step back to give a broader view of how the Compass framework can reduce the mundane tasks that come with stylesheet authoring.

In Chapter 5, we take a survey of Compass's CSS3 module and how it provides vendor-independent implementation of the most commonly used aspects of CSS3.

Chapter 6 is a fun experiment with CSS sprites, an advanced technique every designer should know.

Chapter 7 demonstrates how to optimize your stylesheets for both development debugging and production deployment using Compass's compile features. Chapter 8 builds on this theme and shows advanced techniques to compress and minify your stylesheet assets for deployment.

Chapter 9 is aimed at the advanced developer who would like to use Sass's advanced scripting techniques. Chapter 10 expands on this topic and walks you through creating your own Compass plugin.

Code conventions and downloads

Source code in listings or in text appears in a `fixed-width font like this` to separate it from the ordinary text. Code annotations accompany many of the listings, highlighting important concepts. In some cases, numbered cueballs link to additional explanations that follow the listing.

Source code for the examples in this book can be downloaded from the publisher's website at www.manning.com/SassandCompassinAction. Updates to code will be available at https://github.com/pengwynn/sass-and-compass-in-action.

Author Online

Purchase of *Sass and Compass in Action* includes free access to a private web forum run by Manning Publications where you can make comments about the book, ask technical questions, and receive help from the authors and from other users. To access the forum and subscribe to it, point your web browser to www.manning.com/SassandCompassin-Action. This page provides information on how to get on the forum once you're registered, what kind of help is available, and the rules of conduct on the forum.

Manning's commitment to our readers is to provide a venue where a meaningful dialog between individual readers and between readers and the author can take place. It's not a commitment to any specific amount of participation on the part of the authors, whose contribution to the AO remains voluntary (and unpaid). We suggest you try asking the authors some challenging questions lest their interest stray!

The Author Online forum and the archives of previous discussions will be accessible from the publisher's website as long as the book is in print.

about the authors

WYNN NETHERLAND has been building the web for nearly twenty years. He's authored or contributed to several books on topics from web development to open government. When he's not shipping at GitHub, you can find him speaking at industry conferences, hanging out at developer meetups, or picking his guitar on the back porch.

CHRIS EPPSTEIN is an engineering graduate from the California Institute of Technology and has more than ten years of experience building websites and applications for Silicon Valley startups. He has a passion for front-end engineering and is currently working on front-end architecture and developer relations at LinkedIn. An active member of the Ruby open source community, Chris created the Compass Stylesheet Authoring Framework, is a member of the Sass core team, maintains many open source projects, and has contributed to dozens of others.

NATHAN WEIZENBAUM is a graduate of the University of Washington, majoring in Computer Science and Philosophy, and has been the lead developer for Sass since it was first conceived. He's currently a software engineer working on Gmail at Google.

BRANDON MATHIS is on the Compass core team and creator of Octopress, a beautifully extensible blogging framework for hackers based on Jekyll. He currently is a designer at MongoHQ.

about the cover illustration

The figure on the cover of *Sass and Compass in Action* is captioned "Silanka," a woman from a Slavic tribe that lived in the Gail River Valley. The river, called Zilja in Slovene, originates in southern Austria and flows through some of the most picturesque landscapes of the Julian Alps. This illustration is taken from a recent reprint of *Balthasar Hacquet's Images and Descriptions of Southwestern and Eastern Wenda, Illyrians, and Slavs* published by the Ethnographic Museum in Split, Croatia, in 2008. Hacquet (1739–1815) was an Austrian physician and scientist who spent many years studying the botany, geology, and ethnography of many parts of the Austrian Empire, as well as the Veneto, the Julian Alps, and the western Balkans, inhabited in the past by peoples of many different tribes and ethnicities. Hand-drawn illustrations accompany the many scientific papers and books that Hacquet published.

The rich diversity of the drawings in Hacquet's publications speaks vividly of the uniqueness and individuality of the eastern Alpine and northwestern Balkan regions just 200 years ago. This was a time when the dress codes of two villages separated by a few miles identified people uniquely as belonging to one or the other, and when members of a social class or trade could be easily distinguished by what they were wearing. Dress codes have changed since then and the diversity by region, so rich at the time, has faded away. It is now often hard to tell the inhabitant of one continent from another, and today the residents of the picturesque towns and villages in the Slovenian Alps or Balkan coastal towns are not readily distinguishable from the residents of other parts of Europe.

We at Manning celebrate the inventiveness, the initiative, and the fun of the computer business with book covers based on costumes from two centuries ago brought back to life by illustrations such as this one.

## Part 1

Getting acquainted with Sass and Compass

The first part of this book introduces you to Sass and Compass, looking at Sass's core and covering some of the principles behind writing dynamic stylesheets. In chapter 1, we look at what it means to author stylesheets dynamically and discuss development principles to help wield this power wisely. You'll see how Sass simplifies stylesheet authoring by helping you avoid repetition with selector nesting and variables, and how you can intelligently reuse common styles and patterns using @extend and mixins. We discuss the Compass framework and how it provides patterns and tools to make styling websites smooth and efficient.

Chapter 2 helps you get acquainted with the Sass syntax and its many powerful features. We discuss how to use variables in Sass and how scoping works. You'll learn how nesting selectors and subproperties can make your stylesheets cleaner and easier to read. You'll see how Sass has improved CSS's @import to let you combine many stylesheets into one, allowing you to break up your styles into smaller, more manageable files. We look at using mixins to easily share common styles while avoiding repetition, and how to pass arguments and use variables in mixins, making it easy to customize the styles while preserving patterns. You'll learn to use selector inheritance with @extend, another way to reduce repetition, when to use inheritance and when to use mixins, and best practices.

After reading the first two chapters, you should feel comfortable with the Sass syntax and have some great ideas for how to improve your stylesheets. You'll have a good grasp of what it means to think dynamically about stylesheets. In the next part, we move from the principle to the practical, and solve some real-world problems using Sass and Compass.

Sass and Compass make stylesheets fun again

This chapter covers

- Getting started with Sass and dynamic stylesheets
- Writing stylesheets more efficiently with Sass features
- A quick introduction to Compass
- Compass solutions to real-world stylesheet challenges

Sass is an extension of CSS3 that helps you create better stylesheets with less effort. Sass frees you from repetition and gives you tools to be creative. Since you can implement changes much faster, you'll be free to take risks in your designs. Your stylesheets will be able to keep pace with changing colors and changing HTML markup, all the while producing standards-based CSS you can use in any environment. The Sass processor is written in Ruby, but unless you want to hack the language itself, you need not care.

Throughout this book, we speak to two sets of readers, hoping to find some common ground with each camp. If you find yourself in both groups, even better.

To our web designer friends: You have all the Adobe app keyboard shortcuts memorized. You choose complementary colors based on RGB values alone. You may or may not sport a pair of dark-rimmed glasses, but chances are you start your day with coffee or tea and the latest from *Smashing Magazine*. By your own admission, you know enough jQuery to be dangerous and don't know why your developer friends chuckle when you talk about CSS as a language.

We'll set you free from the tedious and let you do what you do best—be creative. We know you have opinions on resets, typographic scales, color palettes, and layouts. We'll show you how to create stylesheets faster with less repetition. You'll start doing less in graphics software and more in your stylesheets.

To our front-end developer pals: You take pride in your ability to slice-and-dice a Photoshop comp into semantically sound HTML and CSS, but there's a problem. Your server templates are DRY because you *Don't Repeat Yourself,* but your stylesheets are as soggy as a doorbell-interrupted Raisin Bran breakfast. As the project grows, you also find that organizing your stylesheets is a challenge. If only you could author stylesheets in the same way you write the other code in your software project—with variables, reusable parts, and control flow. Take heart, have we got a project for you!

In this chapter, we'll look at powerful Sass features such as nested rules, variables, mixins, and selector inheritance, and how Compass leverages these into reusable patterns to free you from mindless repetition and let you focus on your design instead of your styles. If you don't already have Sass installed, go ahead and jump to appendix A and follow the steps outlined there. If you're reading this at the coffee shop on your iPad, you can still run these basic examples online at the Sass website: http://sass-lang.com/try.html.

1.1 Getting started with Sass

Before we jump into some examples, it's important to nail down some keys to success with Sass. Sass isn't a silver bullet or pixie dust. It won't instantly help your color, typography, or layout choices, but it can help you implement your ideas faster, with less friction. Before we get into syntax and features, let's take a look at the big picture. When using Sass, the Sass engine compiles your stylesheet source files into 100% pure CSS during your development workflow, as shown in figure 1.1.

Though there are many options for running the Sass engine, ranging from the command line to server framework integration to GUI tools, the key takeaway is that Sass produces CSS during your *development* workflow. You deploy *static* CSS as you normally would; you just benefit from Sass language features to write that CSS much faster and maintain it more easily.

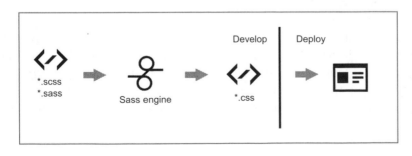

Figure 1.1 The Sass authoring and compilation workflow

1.1.1 *From CSS to Sass*

If you're skilled in creating CSS, you'll find the on-ramp to using Sass a short one. Sass focuses on *how* to create awesome stylesheets, not *what* goes into them. We'll cover tools like Compass that provide you with CSS best practices, but ultimately you'll benefit from this book if you have a firm grasp of CSS. As with anything in computing, *garbage in, garbage out*. If you need a CSS primer, you might want to check out another Manning title, *Hello! HTML5 and CSS3*.

Sass supports two syntaxes. The original *indented syntax* has a .sass extension and is whitespace aware, so instead of surrounding properties with braces, you indent them underneath their selector. Rather than using semicolons, each property is separated by a new line:

```
h1
  color: #000
  background: #fff
```

SCSS, or *Sassy CSS*, was introduced in Sass 3.0 and is a superset of CSS3. SCSS files have a .scss file extension and are chock-full of familiar braces and semicolons:

```
h1 {color: #000; background: #fff}
```

This demonstrates the primary differences between the two syntaxes, but there are other differences which are discussed in appendix C.

Sass will continue to support both syntaxes. You can even mix and match each syntax within the same Sass project (just not within a single file). It's important to choose a syntax that's right for you and your team. If you work in a Python or Ruby environment, perhaps the whitespace-aware indented syntax will fit nicely. If your team deals with outside design agencies, then Sassy CSS provides a lower barrier to entry.

In addition to sound CSS skills and a grasp of Sass syntax, it's important to take a dynamic view of stylesheets.

1.1.2 *Think dynamic*

Outside of basic brochure sites, who really writes much static HTML anymore? You take your HTML and carve it up for your blog engine, CMS, or application framework to *preprocess*, mixing markup and dynamic content. These tools give life to your HTML and it's crazy to imagine the web without them. So *why do you still write static stylesheets?* You'll see how the concepts you use in creating static markup, *dynamically*, can be applied to creating static stylesheets, *dynamically*. What does it mean to write dynamic stylesheets? It means that when you author Sass stylesheets, you're no longer limited by how the browser thinks about CSS. With conditional logic, reusable snippets, variables, and various other tools, you can bring your stylesheets to life. Changing a website's layout and color scheme can be as simple as tweaking a few variables. Of course, though Sass lets you write stylesheets in a dynamic fashion, the output is still 100% pure static CSS. Once you're working with dynamic stylesheets, you can now listen to that inner voice that keeps shouting *Don't Repeat Yourself*.

1.1.3   Don't Repeat Yourself

Sass gives stylesheet authors powerful tools that remove the tedium from many CSS tasks you do over and over and over. Many features of Sass embrace the familiar programming axiom *Don't Repeat Yourself*, letting you *DRY* up your stylesheets. As you create your stylesheets, repetition should be a red flag. Constantly ask yourself, *how can I work smarter, not just harder?* In the next few sections, we'll show you how to let Sass squeeze more reuse out of your stylesheets.

1.2   Hello Sass: DRYing up your stylesheets

We've been harping on DRY-DRY-DRY up to this point. So what does a soggy stylesheet look like? Consider the following CSS.

> **Listing 1.1   A soggy stylesheet in need of DRYing**

```
h1#brand {color: #1875e7}

#sidebar { background-color: #1875e7}

ul.nav {float: right}
ul.nav li {float: left;}
ul.nav li a {color: #111}
ul.nav li.current {font-weight: bold;}

#header ul.nav {float:right;}
#header ul.nav li {float:left;margin-right:10px;}
#footer ul.nav {margin-top:1em;}
#footer ul.nav li {float:left;margin-right:10px;}
```

Even in this extremely simplified example, the duplication is apparent. What happens if the marketing team wants to tweak that lovely shade of blue from #1875e7 to #0f86e3? Sure, two occurrences is manageable, but when it's a dozen or more across several stylesheets, find-and-replace seems archaic, don't you think? Eight instances of ul.nav in a 10-line stylesheet also seems excessive.

In the next few sections, you'll discover a cool breeze of syntactic sugar that will DRY up this stylesheet and blow you away, including variables, mixins, nested selectors, and selector inheritance. If we seem to move fast, don't fret. We dig deeper into each of these concepts in chapter 2.

1.2.1   Reuse property values with variables

Are you using search-and-replace to swap hex code values and manage color palette changes in your stylesheets? With Sass, you can assign values to *variables* and manage colors, border sizes, and virtually any stylesheet property value in a single location:

```
$company-blue: #1875e7;

h1#brand {
color: $company-blue;
}

#sidebar {
background-color: $company-blue;
}
```

Sass variables start with the $ symbol and can contain any characters that are also valid in a CSS class name, including underscores and dashes. In this simple example, if you want to tweak the shade of blue, you can update it in one spot and the rest of your stylesheet falls in line.

If you come from a development background, variables should feel natural. If you're coming to Sass from a design background, variables may seem intimidating at first glance. But they're really nothing new. You already use named values in CSS such as blue, green, inherit, block, inline-block, serif, and sans-serif. Think of variables as your own special values. Next up, using nested selectors to create deep descendant CSS selectors with less typing.

1.2.2 *Write long selectors more quickly with nesting*

Did you ever hear about the Texan who went to work for the state painting dashed center lines on the highway? He was a top performer his first week, painting 10 miles of road. Production tailed off quickly, as he covered five miles in his second week, and only two in the third. When he rounded out the last week of the month with only a single mile, his supervisor asked him what seemed to be the problem. "Well," the worker remarked, "it keeps getting farther and farther back to the bucket."

That's exactly how it can feel working with deep descendant CSS selectors. Consider the following CSS:

```
ul.nav  {float: right}
ul.nav li {float: left;}
ul.nav li a {color: #111}
ul.nav li.current {font-weight: bold;}
```

Sass lets you *DRY* that up a bit. Find the file 1.1.2.nesting.scss in the code examples folder for chapter 1 or create your own by saving a text file with the following contents.

Listing 1.2   Nesting CSS selectors

```
ul.nav {
  float: right;

  li {
    float: left;
    a {
      color: #111;
    }
    &.current {
      font-weight: bold;
    }
  }
}
```

From your terminal, run the sass command and pass it the path to the file:

```
sass 1.2.nesting.scss
```

You should get the following CSS results in your terminal output.

Listing 1.3   Resulting CSS after using nested selectors

```
ul.nav {
  float: right; }
  ul.nav li {
    float: left; }
    ul.nav li a {
      color: #111; }
    ul.nav li.current {
      font-weight: bold; }
```

Other than some formatting differences, that's the same CSS we started with. (Don't sweat the format just yet. We'll discuss more about Sass's output options a bit later.)

Using Sass, you can *nest* rules and avoid duplicating the same elements in your selectors. Not only does this save time, the added benefit is that if you later change ul.nav from an unordered list to an ordered list, you only have one line to change. This is especially true with the last selector in the example. The & is a *parent selector.* In this case &.current evaluates to li.current. If the markup were to change to using the current class on some other element, this line in the stylesheet would just work. Now that you've seen how to reuse values with variables and write longer selectors with nesting, let's put the ideas together and look at Sass mixins.

1.2.3   *Reuse chunks of style with mixins*

Variables let you reuse *values*, but what if you want to reuse large blocks of rules? Traditionally in CSS, as you see duplication in your stylesheets, you factor common rules out into new CSS classes.

Listing 1.4   Traditional CSS refactoring

```
ul.horizontal-list li {
  float: left;
  margin-right: 10px;
}

#header ul.nav {
  float: right;
}

#footer ul.nav {
  margin-top: 1em;
}
```

You then need to give your ul.nav elements an additional class of horizontal-list. This works fine, but what if you wanted to keep your classes more semantic and still get the reuse?

Let's open or create 1.1.2.mixins.scss, our second example.

Listing 1.5   Reusing code with @mixin and @include

```
@mixin horizontal-list {
  li {
```

```
      float: left;
      margin-right: 10px;
   }
}

#header ul.nav {
   @include horizontal-list;
   float: right;
}

#footer ul.nav {
   @include horizontal-list;
   margin-top: 1em;
}
```

Just as the name suggests, Sass mixins *mix in* rules with other rules. You've extracted the rules for the horizontal list into an aptly named mixin using the @mixin directive. You then *include* those rules into other rules using the @include directive. You no longer need the .horizontal-list class, since those rules are now mixed into your ul.nav rules in your resulting CSS.

Listing 1.6 Mixins help you remove redundant styles

```
#header ul.nav {
   float: right;
}

#header ul.nav li {
   float: left;
   margin-right: 10px;
}

#footer ul.nav {
   margin-top: 1em;
}

#footer ul.nav li {
   float: left;
   margin-right: 10px;
}
```

As handy as this is, the real power of Sass mixins comes from combining them with variables to make reusable, parameter-driven blocks of styles. For example, let's suppose you wanted to vary the item spacing in your horizontal list. Find the next code example, 1.1.2.2.mixins-parameters.scss, and consider the following changes.

Listing 1.7 Mixins with variables

```
@mixin horizontal-list($spacing: 10px) {
   li {
      float: left;
      margin-right: $spacing;
   }
}
```

```
#header ul.nav {
  @include horizontal-list;
  float: right;
}

#footer ul.nav {
  @include horizontal-list(20px);
  margin-top: 1em;
}
```

You've updated the mixin and added a $spacing parameter with a default value of 10px. Parameters are no different than the variables we looked at earlier. In this case, you've specified a default value so that in the case of the navigation list in the header, you get the default spacing. In the footer, you now can pass in a value of 20px to get more spacing between the list elements, as you can see in the CSS output.

Listing 1.8   Final CSS output after using mixins

```
#header ul.nav {
  float: right;
}

#header ul.nav li {
  float: left;
  margin-right: 10px;
}

#footer ul.nav {
  margin-top: 1em;
}

#footer ul.nav li {
  float: left;
  margin-right: 20px;
}
```

Sass mixins save you a lot of time, letting you reuse chunks of properties, but the astute reader might notice that what you've gained in productivity, you may have given back in stylesheet weight, since mixin styles are duplicated in each instance where they're included. Fear not: with Sass, you always have options. Selector inheritance deals with just this issue.

1.2.4   *Avoid property duplication with selector inheritance*

As you've seen, Sass mixins can be a powerful way to avoid duplication when writing your stylesheets. Bur since rules are mixed into other classes in the compiled CSS, you're not avoiding duplication entirely. Because CSS file size is important, Sass includes another slightly more complex way of avoiding duplication altogether. Selector inheritance instructs a selector to *inherit* all the styles of another selector without duplicating the CSS properties. Take, for instance, the styles for a set of form error messages.

Listing 1.9 Some CSS for error messages

```css
.error {
  border: 1px #f00;
  background: #fdd;
}

.error.intrusion {
  font-size: 1.2em;
  font-weight: bold;
}

.badError {
  @extend .error;
  border-width: 3px;
}
```

Using selector inheritance, you can instruct `.badError` to inherit from the base `.error` class, yielding the results shown next.

Listing 1.10 Reducing redundancy with selector inheritance

```css
.error, .badError {
  border: 1px #f00;
  background: #fdd;
}

.error.intrusion,
.badError.intrusion {
  font-size: 1.2em;
  font-weight: bold;
}

.badError {
  border-width: 3px;
}
```

In this case, it makes sense to have both the error and badError classes, since you expect to use both of them in your HTML, but occasionally your base class isn't something you expect to use in your markup. In Sass 3.2, the placeholder selector was introduced to allow you to use selector inheritance without creating throwaway base classes.

Listing 1.11 Selector inheritance with the placeholder selector

```css
%button-reset {
  margin: 0;
  padding: .5em 1.2em;
  text-decoration: none;
  cursor: pointer;
}

.save {
  @extend %button-reset;
  color: white;
```

```
  background: #blue;
}

.delete {
  @extend %button-reset;
  color: white;
  background: red;
}
```

As the name *placeholder* implies, the classes that extend %button-reset take its place in the generated CSS.

Listing 1.12   Resulting CSS after using selector inheritance

```
.save, .delete {
  margin: 0;
  padding: .5em 1.2em;
  text-decoration: none;
  cursor: pointer;
}

.save {
  color: white;
  background: #blue;
}

.delete {
  color: white;
  background: red;
}
```

Placeholders give you a safe way to store common styles without worrying that they'll interfere with any of your class names. Also, if a placeholder is never extended, the styles inside of it are never compiled to CSS, keeping your stylesheets light and free from the bloat of unused styles.

With a little planning, selector inheritance is a nice way to keep your Sass DRY and your CSS lean. Now that you've seen how Sass helps you avoid repeating yourself, in the next section you'll see what Compass brings to the table.

1.3   *What is Compass?*

Compass helps Sass authors write smarter stylesheets and empowers a community of designers and developers to create and share powerful frameworks. Put simply, Compass is a Sass framework designed to make the work of styling the web smooth and efficient. Much like Rails as a web application framework for Ruby, Compass is a collection of helpful tools and battle-tested best practices for Sass.

Compass is made up of three main components. It includes a library of Sass mixins and utilities, a system for integrating with application environments, and a platform for building frameworks and extensions. Expanding the big picture diagram from earlier in this chapter, let's see how Compass fits into your development workflow in figure 1.2.

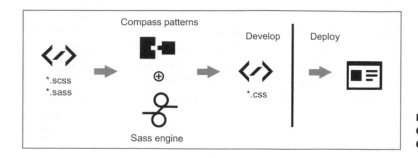

Figure 1.2
Compiling with
Compass

1.3.1 The Compass library

Compass comes with a host of Sass mixins and functions that are organized into modules, all of which are thoroughly documented with examples on the Compass website. This library insulates you from cross-browser quirks and provides a great set of proven design patterns for resets, grid layouts, list styles, table helpers, vertical rhythm, and more. Compass also comes with helpers for CSS3, handling vendor prefixes and abstracting away different browser implementations of emerging CSS3 features, making it much easier to write cutting-edge stylesheets.

Compass can do some really handy tasks like measuring images from the filesystem and writing them into your stylesheets. Asset URL functions are available that make it easy to move assets around in a project or even switch to a content delivery network (CDN) without having to rewrite your stylesheets. Compass can even combine a directory of images into a single sprite image and do the otherwise tedious task of calculating coordinates and writing the spriting CSS for you.

These are tasks you could tackle yourself, and sometimes will, but Compass bundles proven solutions from the design community, letting you focus on getting more done in less time.

The Compass Core stylesheet framework isn't going to make your website pretty. In fact, all features in the core framework are *design agnostic* so that they can be used with any website design. Website design aesthetics, like all fashions, come and go. So the task of providing well-designed website features is left to the Compass community of front-end developers and designers through the use of plugins.

1.3.2 Simple stylesheet projects

Both Sass and Compass are written in Ruby and have their origins in the Ruby on Rails community, but Compass provides tools and configuration options to make it easy to write Sass stylesheets outside of Ruby-based projects. Whether you need to simply build an HTML mockup or to integrate Sass into a large application framework like Django, Drupal, or .NET, Compass makes it a snap (see figure 1.3).

Compass understands that you aren't building stylesheets. You're building a design. As such, Compass wants to know where you keep things like image, font, and JavaScript files so that it can simplify the management of and references to those files from within your stylesheets. For example, Compass will help you construct sprite maps and refer to those within your stylesheets; Compass will warn you if you reference an image that doesn't exist via the `image-url()` helper; and Compass can embed an image or font into your CSS so that the browser doesn't have to make another round trip to get that asset.

1.3.3 Community ecosystem

If you've been in web development for a while, you might remember the dark ages before JavaScript frameworks. It was truly a terrible world—the smallest quirk in the DOM might send you on a bug hunt for hours. These days, JavaScript frameworks isolate you from the browsers' inconsistencies and give you a foundation for sharing your code through plugins that others can easily drop into their projects. Thanks to the hard work of the web development community at large, developing with JavaScript is actually enjoyable these days.

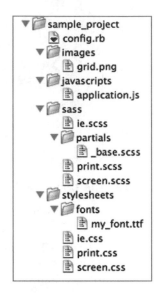

Figure 1.3   A standalone compass project

As a framework for Sass, Compass is a foundation for designers and developers to share their libraries and frameworks, empowering you to participate in an ecosystem of open source stylesheet development. Fading quickly are the days when sharing a bit of CSS wizardry meant embedding code snippets and demo files in a blog post. This strategy leaves each user owning their code without a way for the original developer to fix bugs and provide additional enhancements over time. With Compass, stylesheet libraries can be distributed like other software, which means fixing a bug or getting support for the latest browsers may just be a simple matter of upgrading and recompiling your stylesheets.

Many community members package up their bag of tricks into Compass extensions for others to begin using immediately, without requiring them to rewrite a nasty nest of static stylesheets. (See chapter 10 to learn how to write your own Compass extension.) Responsive layouts, typographic scales, custom animations, fancy buttons, icon sets, and color palettes can all be made into Compass extensions written in Sass. Compass extensions get you past the drudgery of building the basics so you can focus on what's unique and special about your website. As you progress from Sass novice to Sass assassin, if you're grateful for all the time Sass, Compass, and the community save you, you'll be able "pay it forward" by sharing your hard work with others.

1.4   Create a Compass project

If you haven't installed Compass already, go ahead and jump to appendix A and follow the instructions outlined there. After you have the bits installed, you'll be ready to start using Compass. Your first task will be creating a Compass project.

Like any good command-line interface (CLI), Compass provides substantial help messages for its many options. Let's check your Compass install. Open a terminal window in the root of a new stylesheet project. Now, run `compass help`. If you're greeted with help text and command-line options, you're good to go. If not, circle back to appendix A one more time and we'll see you on the flip side.

Let's start by creating a new Compass *project*, which is a configuration file and folders for your Sass source and CSS output. We'll call it *sample*:

```
compass create sample
```

Now list the contents of your new folder:

```
total 8
drwxr-xr-x  6 wynn   staff  204 Jan  3 12:11 .
drwxr-xr-x  3 wynn   staff  102 Jan  3 12:12 ..
drwxr-xr-x  4 wynn   staff  136 Jan  3 12:11 .sass-cache
-rw-r--r--  1 wynn   staff  315 Jan  3 12:11 config.rb
drwxr-xr-x  5 wynn   staff  170 Jan  3 12:11 sass
drwxr-xr-x  5 wynn   staff  170 Jan  3 12:11 stylesheets
```

Using the defaults, Compass has unfurled a `config.rb` configuration file, a `sass` folder for your Sass source, and a `stylesheets` folder for your CSS output. For a full list of Compass configuration options, please consult appendix B. For now, we'll work with the default settings and set out to tackle some real-world CSS problems using Compass.

1.5 Solve real-world CSS problems with Compass

Now that you've seen how to create a skeleton Compass project, let's take a look at how Compass can help solve some stylesheet challenges you probably face every day. In the next few sections you'll apply Compass's built-in modules (which are only nice bundles of Sass mixins and other features) to CSS resets, grid layouts, table formatting, and CSS3 features.

1.5.1 Clear the canvas with resets

Made popular by Eric Meyer and other standards advocates, adding a *CSS reset* has become the first task for designers when creating a stylesheet. If you've ever used a CSS grid framework, you've used a CSS reset, perhaps without even knowing it. A CSS reset simply removes all intrinsic browser styling from all elements, providing a common blank canvas to add back the styling you want.

Eric's classic reset looks like this.

Listing 1.13 Classic CSS reset

```
/* v1.0 | 20080212 */

html, body, div, span, applet, object, iframe,
h1, h2, h3, h4, h5, h6, p, blockquote, pre,
a, abbr, acronym, address, big, cite, code,
del, dfn, em, font, img, ins, kbd, q, s, samp,
```

```
small, strike, strong, sub, sup, tt, var,
b, u, i, center,
dl, dt, dd, ol, ul, li,
fieldset, form, label, legend,
table, caption, tbody, tfoot, thead, tr, th, td {
  margin: 0;
  padding: 0;
  border: 0;
  outline: 0;
  font-size: 100%;
  vertical-align: baseline;
 background: transparent;
}
body {
  line-height: 1;
}
ol, ul {
  list-style: none;
}
blockquote, q {
  quotes: none;
}
blockquote:before, blockquote:after,
q:before, q:after {
  content: '';
  content: none;
}

/* remember to define focus styles! */
:focus {
  outline: 0;
}

/* remember to highlight inserts somehow! */
ins {
  text-decoration: none;
}
del {
  text-decoration: line-through;
}

/* tables still need 'cellspacing="0"' in the markup */
table {
  border-collapse: collapse;
  border-spacing: 0;
}
```

You might have noticed from the default Sass file, screen.css, that Compass ships with its own reset based on Eric's, allowing you to put all browsers on equal footing with a single line in your Sass file:

```
@import "compass/reset"
```

There's a lot going on in this one line, so let's break it down. You use the Sass @import rule to import the Compass Reset module. A module is a standalone portion of the

Compass framework that can be added independently to your project. With this one line, the contents of your CSS output file include your CSS reset.

Listing 1.14   CSS output file, including CSS reset

```
html, body, div, span, applet, object, iframe,
h1, h2, h3, h4, h5, h6, p, blockquote, pre,
a, abbr, acronym, address, big, cite, code,
del, dfn, em, font, img, ins, kbd, q, s, samp,
small, strike, strong, sub, sup, tt, var,
dl, dt, dd, ol, ul, li,
fieldset, form, label, legend,
table, caption, tbody, tfoot, thead, tr, th, td {
  margin: 0;
  padding: 0;
  border: 0;
  outline: 0;
  font-weight: inherit;
  font-style: inherit;
  font-size: 100%;
  font-family: inherit;
  vertical-align: baseline;
}

body {
  line-height: 1;
  color: black;
  background: white;
}

ol, ul {
  list-style: none;
}

table {
  border-collapse: separate;
  border-spacing: 0;
  vertical-align: middle;
}

caption, th, td {
  text-align: left;
  font-weight: normal;
  vertical-align: middle;
}

q, blockquote {
  quotes: "" "";
}
q:before, q:after, blockquote:before, blockquote:after {
  content: "";
}

a img {
  border: none;
}
```

It should be noted that adding styles to your stylesheet isn't the default behavior of most Compass modules, but since the usual use case is to apply the CSS reset, the Compass Reset module goes ahead and applies the `global-reset` mixin upon import. Let's take a look at that mixin.

Listing 1.15   CSS `global-reset` mixin

```
@mixin global-reset {
  html, body, div, span, applet, object, iframe,
  h1, h2, h3, h4, h5, h6, p, blockquote, pre,
  a, abbr, acronym, address, big, cite, code,
  del, dfn, em, font, img, ins, kbd, q, s, samp,
  small, strike, strong, sub, sup, tt, var,
  dl, dt, dd, ol, ul, li,
  fieldset, form, label, legend,
  table, caption, tbody, tfoot, thead, tr, th, td {
    @include reset-box-model;
    @include reset-font; }
  body {
    @include reset-body; }
  ol, ul {
    @include reset-list-style; }
  table {
    @include reset-table; }
  caption, th, td {
    @include reset-table-cell; }
  q, blockquote {
    @include reset-quotation; }
  a img {
    @include reset-image-anchor-border; } }
```

Note that Compass is using the Sass `@mixin` and `@include` features we looked at earlier to build the reset. In addition to the `global-reset`, the Reset module includes a number of more surgical reset mixins, including one for HTML5 elements. By adding `@include reset-html5` to your Sass file, you get an additional CSS rule in your output for all the HTML5 elements that need some basic styling.

Listing 1.16   Resulting code after HTML5 reset

```
article, aside, canvas, details, figcaption, figure,
footer, header, hgroup, menu, nav, section, summary {
  margin: 0;
  padding: 0;
  border: 0;
  outline: 0;
  display: block;
}
```

For additional Compass Reset module mixins, be sure and check out the Compass online docs. Now that you have a handle on resets, let's look at how Compass can help you more effectively use CSS grid frameworks.

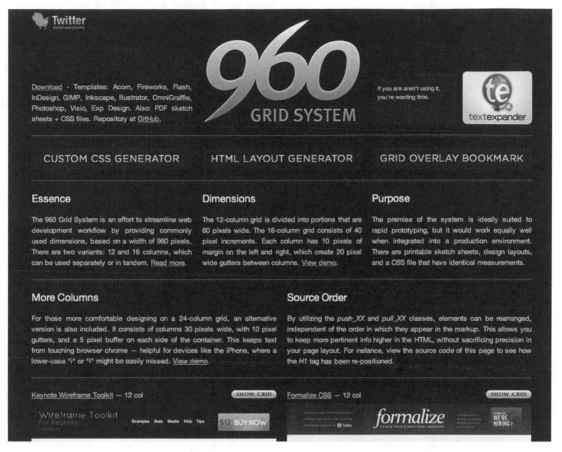

Figure 1.4   960.gs—the 960 Grid System CSS framework

1.5.2   *Create layouts without a calculator*

One of the major trends in CSS in the last couple of years has been the emergence of popular CSS grid frameworks such as Blueprint and 960 Grid System (see figure 1.4). Grid layouts, which have long been a cornerstone of good print design, have made their way online as the medium has matured. Grid frameworks allow you to allot a certain number of columns for your layout and then apply a column-based layout with uniform gutters to your content.

Basically, grid frameworks reduce the math needed to create a nice column layout. They do this with CSS rules that set the layout and widths for a container element as well as for each possible column width in the grid. Let's look at a snippet from Blueprint.

Listing 1.17   Blueprint grid layout

```
.container {
  width: 950px;
  margin: 0 auto;
}

/* Sets up basic grid floating and margin. */
.column, .span-1, .span-2, .span-3, .span-4, .span-5,
.span-6, .span-7, .span-8, .span-9, .span-10, .span-11,
.span-12, .span-13, .span-14, .span-15, .span-16,
.span-17, .span-18, .span-19, .span-20, .span-21,
.span-22, .span-23, .span-24 {
  float: left;
  margin-right: 10px;
}

/* The last column in a row needs this class. */
.last { margin-right: 0; }

/* Use these classes to set the width of a column. */
.span-1 {width: 30px;}

.span-2 {width: 70px;}
.span-3 {width: 110px;}
.span-4 {width: 150px;}
.span-5 {width: 190px;}
.span-6 {width: 230px;}
.span-7 {width: 270px;}
.span-8 {width: 310px;}
.span-9 {width: 350px;}
.span-10 {width: 390px;}
.span-11 {width: 430px;}
.span-12 {width: 470px;}
.span-13 {width: 510px;}
.span-14 {width: 550px;}
.span-15 {width: 590px;}
.span-16 {width: 630px;}
.span-17 {width: 670px;}
.span-18 {width: 710px;}
.span-19 {width: 750px;}
.span-20 {width: 790px;}
.span-21 {width: 830px;}
.span-22 {width: 870px;}
.span-23 {width: 910px;}
.span-24 {width:950px; margin-right:0;}
```

With these CSS rules in place, you can create a 16-column layout simply by adding the container class to a container element and a span-xx class to each element you want to place on the grid. Laying out content in this way also lets you prototype more quickly by not having to remember the multiples of 40 between 30 and 950.

So how does Compass improve upon CSS grid frameworks? First, Compass provides support for grid framework styles as mixins, allowing you to pull in just the features you want to use while avoiding littering your HTML markup with extra classes. The second, and perhaps most important, way Compass supports grid frameworks is in the way it changes how you create these frameworks, as you'll see in chapter 4.

Let's create a Compass project using Blueprint. Run the following in a terminal window:

```
compass create my_grid --using blueprint
```

Just as in section 1.4, you should find a freshly stamped Compass project in a folder called my_grid, only this time the screen.scss file has more content. The file is well annotated and provides a quick survey of most of the Blueprint modules at your disposal along with a set of styles for a basic layout. The first thing to notice here is that column layouts can be *mixed in* to a set of styles. So instead of setting a class of span-8 in your HTML, you use the column Sass mixin:

```
@include column($sidebar-columns);
```

Also note the variable $sidebar-columns. This is extremely powerful because now, thanks to Sass, you can make your layouts variable-driven. You can rapidly prototype and play with different layouts including number of columns, gutter width, and sidebar sizes all by changing a few variables at the top of your Sass file. To do this in traditional CSS grid frameworks, you'd have to do the math to create those CSS layouts, and then change the CSS classes in your markup as well.

We won't go into all the aspects of the Blueprint grid here. We jump into using Blueprint with Compass later in chapter 6. We'll continue our survey of real-world Compass applications by taking a look at the Compass table helper.

1.5.3 *Zebra-stripe like a pro with table helpers*

Continuing our overview of Compass features, let's look at the Compass table helpers, a set of Sass mixins that make prettifying your HTML tables easier. Let's look at an example.

Listing 1.18   Compass table helpers

```
@import "compass/reset"
@import "compass/utilities/tables";

table {
  $table-color: #666;
  @include table-scaffolding;
  @include inner-table-borders(1px, darken($table-color, 40%));
  @include outer-table-borders(2px);
  @include alternating-rows-and-columns($table-color,
              adjust-hue($table-color, -120deg), #222222); }
```

Now let's break this down. You import the table helpers using the @import rule. This provides four mixins for your use. The table-scaffolding provides base styles for your th and td elements that you stripped with your CSS reset, as well as an often-used pattern of right alignment for numeric columns. Here's the source for this mixin.

Listing 1.19   Table helper mixin

```scss
@mixin table-scaffolding {
  th {
    text-align: center;
    font-weight: bold; }
  td,
  th {
    padding: 2px;
    &.numeric {
      text-align: right; } } }
```

The inner-table-borders and outer-table-borders mixins work as advertised, adding borders to the table and to cells within the table.

Lastly, the alternating-rows-and-columns mixin is an easy way to add some zebra-striping to your HTML table. You might ask why you wouldn't use the :nth-child, :even, or :odd CSS pseudo selectors for this task, and you'd be right to ask. That's exactly what Compass is doing under the hood. But this mixin provides some additional support for class-name-based striping as well as color intersections. Let's look at the source.

Listing 1.20   A mixin for alternating colors by row or column

```scss
@mixin alternating-rows-and-columns(
        $even-row-color,
        $odd-row-color,
        $dark-intersection,
        $header-color: white,
        $footer-color: white) {

  th {
    background-color: $header-color;
    &.even, &:nth-child(2n) {
    background-color: $header-color - $dark-intersection; }
  }
  tr.odd {
    td {
      background-color: $odd-row-color;
      &.even, &:nth-child(2n) {
        background-color: $odd-row-color - $dark-intersection; }
    }
  }
  tr.even {
    td {
      background-color: $even-row-color;
      &.even, &:nth-child(2n) {
        background-color: $even-row-color - $dark-intersection; }
    }
  }
    tfoot {
      th, td {
        background-color: $footer-color;
        &.even, &:nth-child(2n) {
          background-color: $footer-color - $dark-intersection; }
      }
    }
```

Note that the color values are not only variables; they're employing a bit of math to ensure proper contrast for readability. You'll learn more about how Sass deals with variables and math in the next chapter. Let's keep moving with a look at how Compass means never having to write vendor prefixes again.

1.5.4 *Easy CSS3 without vendor prefixes*

When CSS3 started gaining adoption by modern browsers, designers were excited to start using CSS for tasks that used to require stupid stylesheet tricks. We were so excited that we could now make those glorious rounded corners with a few lines of CSS that we didn't mind the vendor prefixes that came with them very much. *Vendor prefixes* are those -webkit and -moz bits that browsers add on to CSS features that have experimental support. In its simplest form, this means that to give a <div> a set of rounded corners with a 5px border radius, you have to resort to CSS like this:

```
.rounded {
  -webkit-border-radius: 5px;
  -moz-border-radius: 5px;
}
```

As usual, Compass can save you from the repetition with a set of border radius mixins found in the Compass CSS3 module. Import the module into your Sass file and include the mixin:

```
@import "compass/css3";
.rounded {
  @include border-radius(5px);
}
```

This will yield the following CSS:

```
.rounded {
  -moz-border-radius: 5px;
  -webkit-border-radius: 5px;
  -o-border-radius: 5px;
  -ms-border-radius: 5px;
  border-radius: 5px;
}
```

Not only did you save your fingers from the common repetition of -webkit and -moz but you're also being good designers and supporting the other common vendor namespaces as well. Though that bit of repetition isn't horrible, what if you only want one of the four corners to be rounded? Well, the Mozilla folks don't yet see eye to eye with the rest of the field on the best way to make that happen, so you're left with this:

```
.rounded-one {
  -moz-border-radius-topleft: 5px;
  -webkit-border-top-left-radius: 5px;
}
```

That's where Compass shines. You can target a single corner for a border radius with the border-corner-radius mixin:

```
.rounded-one {
  @include border-corner-radius(top, left, 5px);
}
```

This will give you the CSS you want, Mozilla quirk included:

```
.rounded-one {
  -moz-border-radius-topleft: 5px;
  -webkit-border-top-left-radius: 5px;
  -o-border-top-left-radius: 5px;
  -ms-border-top-left-radius: 5px;
  border-top-left-radius: 5px;
}
```

That's just the tip of the tip of the tip of the CSS3 iceberg in Compass. We take a deeper look at all the time-saving features in chapter 9.

1.6   Summary

In this first chapter, we've looked at the case for CSS preprocessing. We took a quick look at four key features of Sass: variables, nested selectors, mixins, and selector inheritance. We also looked at some real-world applications of Sass included in the Compass framework, including CSS resets, grids, table styling, and CSS3 rounded corners.

In the next chapter, we'll dive deeper into Sass syntax, including color functions and scripting support. After you get a bit more Sass under your belt, we'll take a deeper look at Compass.

Basic Sass syntax

This chapter covers

- Reusing colors, lengths, and other values with variables
- Adding structure to your CSS by nesting rules
- Writing maintainable stylesheets by distributing them among multiple files
- Reusing entire styles with mixins and inheritance

Sass's SCSS syntax is a superset of the syntax of CSS3. This means that if can read and write CSS, you already know the basics of how to read and write Sass.

On top of CSS, Sass adds new features and new syntax that let you express more styles more clearly with less writing. Some Sass additions are designed to be easy to understand for people who understand CSS, even without having seen Sass before. Most of them require some explanation, though, which is what this chapter is for.

When reading a Sass file for the first time, you begin by just looking at the part you're familiar with: the CSS. The fundamental purpose of any Sass file is to style a website, just like CSS, so the style being defined is still the most important part of the file.

After you understand the styles, you look at the Sass features being used. If there are any you don't recognize, you can look them up in this book. Then, for the ones you do, you ask yourself, *how might these be helping to express the style?*

Writing Sass is similar to reading it in that you start with CSS, just the same as you would if you weren't using Sass at all. Then you consider which features of Sass can improve your CSS. Are you using the same color (or variants of it) all over the place? Do all of your selectors start with the same ID? Sass can help.

The first chapter gave a brief overview of the main features of Sass. This chapter goes into more depth, explaining the ins and outs of those features. We start by talking about variables, the simplest and most fundamental form of reuse in Sass. Then, we talk about different things you can do with nested selectors to keep your stylesheets lean and easy to read. Next, we'll look at how to spread out your stylesheet into multiple files to make it easy to work with large numbers of styles. We'll take a detour into silent comments, which are a great way of keeping notes in a file without exposing them for all the world to see. Finally, we'll look at two ways of reusing entire chunks of style: mixins, which make it easy to use a pattern over and over, and inheritance, which makes it possible to express relationships between classes.

First let's talk about variables, the most basic form of reuse in Sass.

2.1   Working with variables

One of the major benefits of Sass is the variables it brings to CSS. Variables allow you to name CSS values that you use repeatedly and then refer to them by name rather than repeating the value over and over. You can also name values you only use once in order to make it more clear what they're for.

Sass uses $ to distinguish variables (such as $highlight-color, $sidebar-width). The dollar sign was chosen because it's visually distinctive, it's aesthetically pleasing,[1] and it's not used elsewhere in CSS and thus doesn't come into conflict with any present or future CSS syntax.

The most basic aspect of variables is how they're declared in the first place; naturally, this is what we'll focus on first.

2.1.1 Declaring

A Sass variable is declared a lot like a CSS property:

```
$highlight-color: #abcdef;
```

This means that $highlight-color is now #abcdef. Any value that could be used for a CSS property can also be used as a variable, including multiple values separated by spaces ($basic-border: 1px solid black;) or commas ($plain-font: "Myriad Pro", Myriad, "Helvetica Neue", Helvetica, "Liberation Sans", Arial, sans-

---

[1] Older versions of Sass used ! instead of $ for variables. The change was made largely because !highlight-color just looked ugly.

serif; sans-serif;). This doesn't have any effect until you refer to the variable, which you'll learn to do shortly.

Unlike CSS properties, variables can appear outside any CSS rule. If they do appear in a CSS rule, then the variable can only be used in that rule (or its descendants; see section 2.2). The same is true if they appear in any other sort of { ... } block, like @media or @font-face blocks:

```
$nav-color: #abcdef;

nav {
  $width: 100px;
  width: $width;
  color: $nav-color;
}
```

The $nav-color variable is declared outside any CSS rule, so it can be used anywhere in the stylesheet, such as in the nav rule. The $width variable was declared within the { and } of the .nav rule, so it can only be used within that rule. This means that it's safe to use $width again elsewhere in the stylesheet without fear of affecting this use.

Just declaring variables isn't very interesting—you want to use them, too. You've already seen $width and $nav-color used in the example, so let's look in more depth at the ways variables can be used.

2.1.2 Referencing

Variables can be placed anywhere in a property that a normal CSS value like 1px or bold can. They're simply replaced by their value when the CSS is generated. Then, if you need a different value later, you can change the variable's value, and everywhere it's referenced the value will change as well:

```
$highlight-color: #abcdef;

.selected {
  border: 1px $highlight-color solid;
}
```

Here the $highlight-color variable, when it's used in the border property, is replaced by the color #abcdef when the code is compiled to CSS. This gives elements with the selected class a one-pixel, solid, #abcdef-colored border.

Variables can even be used when declaring other variables. This is useful when you have different levels of granularity in the values you want to name. The following example has one variable at the level of granularity of individual color value, and another at the level of a more-complex border value:

```
$highlight-color: #abcdef;
$highlight-border: 1px $highlight-color solid;

.selected {
  border: $highlight-border;
}
```

Here the value of the `$highlight-border` variable is set using the `$highlight-color` variable. This works just like it did when you were setting the `border` property directly: the value of `$highlight-border` becomes `1px #abcdef solid`. This is then used as the value for the `border` property.

We'll wrap up our examination of variables by looking at a useful quirk in the way variable names work.

2.1.3   Variable names: dashes or underscores?

Variable names in Sass allow the same characters as property and selector names in CSS, including dashes and underscores. Different people prefer different styles; some use dashes to separate words within variables (`$highlight-color`), and some use underscores (`$highlight_color`). The dash style is more widely used, including in Compass and in this book.

Sass doesn't want to force anyone to use either dashes or underscores, though. To that end, the two are completely compatible. A variable declared using dashes can be referenced using underscores, and vice versa. This means that someone using Compass can use underscores throughout their stylesheets, even though Compass uses dashes everywhere:

```
$link-color: blue;

a {
  color: $link_color;
}
```

In this example, `$link-color` and `$link_color` both refer to the same variable. In fact, dashes and underscores are interchangeable most places in Sass, including mixins (see section 2.5) and Sass functions (section 11.3). They aren't interchangeable in the plain-CSS parts of Sass like class, ID, or property names, though.

Although variables are useful on their own, they're the most basic tool Sass has to offer. Their full potential is only unlocked when they're used alongside other features of Sass. One of those features is the ability to nest rules within one another, which we'll look at next.

2.2   Nesting CSS rules

One of the most annoyingly repetitive aspects of CSS is writing selectors. When you're writing a bunch of styles that all target the same section of the page, you often need to write the same ID over and over again:

```
#content article h1 { color: #333 }
#content article p { margin-bottom: 1.4em }
#content aside { background-color: #eee }
```

Sass can save a lot of typing in these situations, and be easier to read as well. In Sass, you can put rules within rules, like Russian nesting dolls. Sass will unpack these nested rules into CSS for you, saving all that retyping:

```
#content {
  article {
    h1 { color: #333 }
    p { margin-bottom: 1.4em }
  }
  aside { background-color: #eee }
}
```

Sass will take this and translate it into the same CSS you saw earlier. It does this in two
steps, one for each of the levels of nesting but the last, like opening up the nesting
dolls. First, it takes #content (the *parent*) and sticks it onto the beginning of article
and aside (the *children*):

```
#content article {
  h1 { color: #333 }
  p { margin-bottom: 1.4em }
}
#content aside { background-color: #eee }
```

Then, since #content article still has more rules nested, Sass does the same thing
again and sticks the new selector onto its nested rules:

```
#content article h1 { color: #333 }
#content article p { margin-bottom: 1.4em }
#content aside { background-color: #eee }
```

A given rule can contain both properties, like in normal CSS, and other nested rules.
This is useful when you need special styling for a container element and child elements contained within:

```
#content {
  background-color: #f5f5f5;

  aside { background-color: #eee }
}
```

The container rule is kept around, and the nested rules are unpacked just like they
would be if the container didn't have any properties:

```
#content { background-color: #f5f5f5 }
#content aside { background-color: #eee }
```

Plain old nesting works for most cases, but sometimes it's not enough. What if you
want to apply a pseudo-class like :hover that needs to be nestled right up against the
selector? Sass has a special construct, &, for that and other purposes.

2.2.1 &, the parent selector

Normally, when Sass unpacks a nested rule, it connects the parent (#content) to the
children (article and aside) with a space (#content article and #content aside).
This is known in CSS as the *descendant combinator*, since it selects the article and aside
elements contained within (descendants of) the element with ID content. But there
are times when you don't want Sass to use the descendant combinator to make this
connection.

The most common case where the descendant combinator is undesirable is when you're writing `:hover` styles for something like a link. For example, this Sass won't work properly:

```
article a {
   color: blue;
   :hover { color: red }
}
```

This means that `color: red` should apply to `article a :hover`—all the descendants of links within `article` that are being hovered over. That's not right! You want the style to apply to the link itself, and the descendant combinator can't do that for you.

Instead, you use a special Sass selector called the *parent selector*. The parent selector is used in nested rules to give finer control over how the nesting is unpacked. It's a single `&` and it can go anywhere in the selector that an element name like h1 could:

```
article a {
  color: blue;
  &:hover { color: red }
}
```

When the selector for a nested rule that contains a parent selector is unpacked, the parent isn't combined using a descendant combinator like it normally would be. Instead, the `&` is replaced by the parent itself:

```
article a { color: blue }
article a:hover { color: red }
```

This is useful for adding pseudo-classes like `:hover` to the parent. It also allows you to add a selector *before* the rest of the parent selector. For example, if you use JavaScript to add an `ie` class to the `<body>` tag when the user is using Internet Explorer, you can easily target it with `&`:

```
#content aside {
  color: red;

  body.ie & { color: green }
}
```

Sass is smart about selector nesting even beyond the parent selector. When it encounters selector groups—multiple selectors separated by commas—it figures out what it has to do to nest them correctly.

2.2.2 *Nesting selector groups*

In CSS, the selector h1, h2, h3 matches h1 elements, h2 elements, *and* h3 elements. Similarly, `.button, button` matches button elements *and* elements with class `.button`. These are known as *selector groups*. A rule with a selector group applies to all the elements that match some selector in the group:

```
.button, button {
  margin: 0;
}
```

This is a welcome relief from repetition in CSS, but the relief is short-lived. Eventually, you need to have a selector group that only applies within a container. CSS makes you repeat the container's selector for each selector in the group:

```
.container h1, .container h2, .container h3 { margin-bottom: .8em }
```

Luckily, Sass's nested rules can help here too. When Sass unpacks a rule nested inside a selector group rule, it unpacks it for each of the selectors in the group:

```
.container {
  h1, h2, h3 {margin-bottom: .8em}
}
```

First, it combines .container and h1, then .container and h2, and then .container and h3. Finally, it puts all three selectors together in a new group, and pops out the repetitive CSS you saw earlier. It'll do the same thing for rules nested within a selector group rule:

```
nav, aside {
  a {color: blue}
}
```

First, it combines nav and a, and then aside and a. Then it puts the two new selectors together in a new group:

```
nav a, aside a {color: blue}
```

Handling nested selector groups is one of the bigger wins that Sass offers in terms of saving on typing. Especially when you have selectors nested two or three levels deep, having even a single group can really explode the amount of typing you'd need to do in normal CSS.

The other side of the same coin is that you need to be mindful of the CSS that will be generated when using nested selector groups. Although Sass may make it seem like a small amount of text, if your styles end up producing a large amount of CSS, they can slow down your site.

The final aspect of selector nesting that we'll look at is how it works with selector *combinators*, a fancy word for >, +, and ~. It turns out that it just works: you don't even need to use the parent selector.

2.2.3 *Child and sibling combinators: >, +, and ~*

These are called combinators because they're used in combination with other selectors to instruct the browser to only select those elements in a specific context:

```
article section   { margin: 5px }
article > section { border: 1px solid #ccc }
```

The child combinator, >, allows you to select elements that are immediate children of another element. The first selector will style all section elements within an article element. The second selector uses the child combinator to select only the section elements that are immediate children of an article element.

In this example, the adjacent sibling combinator, +, lets you select the paragraph that immediately follows a header element:

```
header + p { font-size: 1.1em }
```

Here, the general sibling combinator, ~, selects every article that comes after another article regardless of any elements that may be between them:

```
article ~ article { border-top: 1px dashed #ccc }
```

These combinators can be used with nested rules with no extra effort. Just leave them dangling at the end of the parent, or at the beginning of the child:

```
article {
  ~ article { border-top: 1px dashed #ccc }
   > section  { background: #eee }
  dl > {
    dt { color: #333 }
    dd { color: #555 }
  }
  nav + & { margin-top: 0 }
}
```

Sass will expand these nested styles, joining selectors on the combinators just like you'd expect:

```
article ~ article { border-top: 1px dashed #ccc }
article > footer  { background: #eee }
article dl > dt { color: #333 }
article dl > dd { color: #555 }
nav + article { margin-top: 0 }
```

CSS rules aren't the only things that can be nested in Sass. Properties also benefit from this reduction in repetition.

2.2.4   *Nested properties*

CSS selectors aren't the only things that can be nested in Sass. Properties can be nested, too. Although the problem of repetition isn't as bad for properties as it is for selectors, it can still get annoying to type border-style, border-width, border-color, and all sorts of border-nonsense. In Sass, you only need to type border once:

```
nav {
  border: {
    style: solid;
    width: 1px;
    color: #ccc;
  }
}
```

To nest properties, you split them at the -, add a : after the root property, and nest the subproperties in a block beneath the root property. Like nested CSS selectors, Sass will unpack your subproperties and join the parent and the children at the -, yielding the CSS properties that would be repetitive to write by hand:

```
nav {
  border-style: solid;
  border-width: 1px;
  border-color: #ccc;
}
```

You can even write styles for shorthand properties followed by nested exceptions:

```
nav {
  border: 1px solid #ccc {
    left: 0px;
    right: 0px;
  }
}
```

This is nicer than writing the equivalent CSS:

```
nav {
  border: 1px solid #ccc;
  border-left: 0px;
  border-right: 0px;
}
```

Property and selector nesting are great features, and not just because they reduce the amount of typing you have to do. They also simultaneously make your stylesheets easier to read and work with, because the visual, indented structure mirrors the structure of the styles that are being written.

But sometimes even this isn't enough for keeping track of a large stylesheet. Sometimes the only way to deal with a massive amount of styles is to split them up into multiple files. Sass supports this directly by adding built-in support for CSS's @import rule.

2.3 *Importing Sass files*

One of the seldom-used features of CSS is the @import rule. This rule allows one CSS file to include all the styles defined in another. Unfortunately, in order to do this, the browser has to download another CSS file, which usually makes the page load too slowly for CSS's @import to be practically useful.

Sass has an @import rule as well, but Sass does its importing when it's compiling to CSS. That means that all the styles end up in the same CSS file, so no extra download is needed. In addition, all the variables and mixins (see section 2.5) defined in the imported file are made available to the importer.

Sass's @import also doesn't require you to specify the full name of the imported file. You can leave off the .sass or .scss extension (see figure 2.1). This is so that you, or people whose Sass styles you're importing, can switch between the Sass and SCSS syntaxes without breaking your stylesheet. For example, the line @import "sidebar"; will include all the styles from sidebar.scss into the current stylesheet.

In this section, you'll learn how to use @import to manage many Sass files at once. First, we'll cover making Sass files that are only ever going to be imported, since these are actually the most common sort of file you'll write in a large Sass project. Then, we'll look at several ways to use imported files to make your styles more reusable,

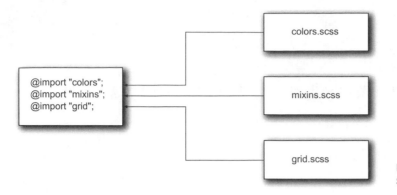

Figure 2.1   Importing Sass files

including declaring customizable variables and importing within the scope of a single selector. Finally, we'll wrap up by explaining how to use the plain CSS @import directive in Sass.

Usually you don't want to make a CSS file for each Sass file you're importing. Sass has a special convention for dealing with this.

2.3.1   Using Sass partials

When you're splitting up your Sass styles among many files using @import, usually you only want to generate a few CSS files. The Sass files that are only meant for @importing and don't need their own individual CSS files are known as *partials*, and Sass has a special convention for naming them.

The convention for Sass partials is to begin the filenames with _. This tells Sass that it shouldn't generate an individual CSS file for the partial, and should only use it for imports. Sass will also let you omit the _ when @importing a partial. For example, to include the variables from the themes/_night-sky.scss partial, you'd just have to add @import "themes/night-sky"; to your stylesheet.

Partials can be included by multiple different files. This can be useful for having a shared set of styles across multiple pages or even projects. Sometimes it's useful to allow the importing stylesheet to tweak those styles. Sass has a feature just for that: default variable values.

2.3.2   Default variable values

Normally, if you declare a variable multiple times, the last declaration is the final value of the variable. For example:

```
$link-color: blue;
$link-color: red;

a {
  color: $link-color;
}
```

In this example, the anchor's color will be set to red. This isn't always what you want. If you're writing a Sass library that will be @imported by someone else, you may want to allow the @importer to customize some of the values in your file. This is what Sass's !default flag is for. It's sort of like the opposite of !important, but for variables. It means, *if this variable is already declared, leave it alone, but otherwise use this value.*

```
$fancybox-width: 400px !default;

.fancybox {
  width: $fancybox-width;
}
```

If a user sets $fancybox-width before @importing your Sass partial, then your declaration of 400px is ignored because of the !default flag. If the user hasn't set the value of $fancybox-width it'll *default* to 400px.

Next we'll look at nested imports, which allow a partial to be imported within the scope of a single selector.

2.3.3 *Nested imports*

Unlike plain CSS, Sass allows @imports to appear inside CSS rules. The styles in the imported document are unpacked as though they were nested within the rule themselves. So if one file, named _blue-theme.scss, contained this,

```
aside {
  background: blue;
  color: white;
}
```

and then another imported it, like so,

```
.blue-theme {@import "blue-theme"}
```

the result would be the same as if you had written the contents of _blue-theme.scss inside the .blue-theme rule to begin with:

```
.blue-theme {
  aside {
    background: blue;
    color: #fff;
  }
}
```

Any variables or mixins (see section 2.5) defined in the @imported file are also available in the rule. They aren't available outside it, though, which makes nested @imports useful for applying color themes or other styles configured with variables to a specific section of your site.

Sometimes it can be useful to use CSS's own @import mechanism, which is performed in the browser. Sass provides several ways to fall back on this.

2.3.4 *Plain CSS imports*

Since Sass is compatible with plain CSS, it also supports normal CSS @imports. Although in general Sass will try to find a Sass file to import, there are three things that will tell it to forget that and send a simple CSS @import, despite the additional download:

- The imported filename ends with .css.
- The imported filename is a URL (such as "http://sass-lang.com/stylesheets/ application.css"). This allows Sass files to use services like Google's Font API.
- The imported filename is a CSS url() value.

This means you can't directly import a plain CSS file without having Sass think you want a plain CSS @import as well. But since Sass is compatible with CSS, you can rename the file to .scss and import it that way.

Imports are an important part of keeping Sass code maintainable and easy to understand. Another less-impressive but still important aspect of this is comments. Comments help style authors keep track of what they were thinking when they first wrote some Sass. In plain CSS, comments are all visible to users, but Sass provides support for some comments that are never seen in the CSS output.

2.4 Silent comments

Comments in CSS are useful for organizing your styles, reminding your future self why you did something, and similar purposes of stylesheet annotation. But you don't always want your comments to be visible to everyone who cares to view source on your website.

Sass provides an alternative form of comments called *silent* in addition to the standard CSS /* ... */ comments that aren't part of the CSS output. These comments have the same form as single-line comments in languages like JavaScript, Java, and other C-like languages. They begin with // and last until the end of the line:

```
body {
  color: #333; // This won't appear in the CSS
  padding: 0; /* This will appear in the CSS */
}
```

It's actually also possible for CSS-style /* ... */ comments to be silent too. If they show up in tricky places (basically, places where a full CSS property or selector wouldn't be allowed) Sass can't figure out how to slot them back into the CSS output, and they're discarded:

```
body {
  color /* This won't appear in the CSS */: #333;
  padding: 1em; /* Nor will this */ 0;
}
```

Now that you've got comments down, you understand the three basic ways to keep your Sass organized and readable: nesting, importing, and commenting. That means it's time to move on to features that not only help you keep your styles organized, but help you write altogether better styles. The first of these features is the ability to abstract out repetitive styles with mixins.

2.5 *Introducing mixins*

When you have a few small stylistic similarities throughout your site—colors and fonts that you use consistently—variables are a great way to keep track of them. But when your styles get more complicated, you need to be able to reuse more than just individual values. You need to reuse whole chunks of style. In Sass, you do this with mixins.

A mixin is defined using the @mixin rule. This looks just like any other CSS @-rule, like @media or CSS3's @font-face. It gives a name to a bunch of styles, so that those styles can be easily reused throughout the stylesheet. The following Sass code defines a simple mixin for adding cross-browser rounded corners to a CSS rule:

```
@mixin rounded-corners {
  -moz-border-radius: 5px;
  -webkit-border-radius: 5px;
  border-radius: 5px;
}
```

The mixin can then be used anywhere in the stylesheet using the @include rule. This takes all the styles in the mixin and puts them wherever it was @included. When you write this,

```
.notice {
  background-color: green;
  border: 2px solid #00aa00;
  @include rounded-corners;
}
```

Sass turns it into this:

```
.notice {
  background-color: green;
  border: 2px solid #00aa00;
  -moz-border-radius: 5px;
  -webkit-border-radius: 5px;
  border-radius: 5px;
}
```

The border-radius, -moz-border-radius, and -webkit-border-radius properties in .notice all came from the rounded-corners mixin. In this section, you'll learn to use mixins to avoid repetition. With the use of arguments, mixins will even allow you to abstract out common patterns in your styles, so that they can be reused easily elsewhere. In fact, mixins are so useful, it's tempting to overuse them. Overuse can result in a large amount of generated CSS that's slow to download. As such, we'll start by discussing which situations call for the use of mixins.

2.5.1 *When to use mixins*

Mixins allow you to easily share styles among different parts of the stylesheet. Any style you find yourself repeating from rule to rule would make a good mixin, especially when that style seems like a logical unit: a good group of properties that make sense to set together.

A good rule of thumb for determining whether a group of properties would make sense as a mixin is whether you can come up with a good name. If you can find a nice short name that describes the style those properties bestow (like `rounded-corners`, `fancy-font`, or `no-bullets`), then they'd probably make a good mixin. If you can't, maybe a mixin isn't called for.

In some ways, mixins are a lot like CSS classes. Both let you name chunks of style, so it can be confusing when to use which. The most important distinction is that classes are meant to be used in your HTML, whereas mixins share styles within the stylesheets. This means that classes should be *semantic*, not *presentational*: they should describe the meaning of an HTML element, not how it looks. Mixins, on the other hand, *should* be presentational: they're designed to describe how a CSS rule should look.

In the preceding example, `.notice` is a semantic class name. When an HTML element has `class="notice"`, that describes the meaning of the element: it's some sort of message for the user. The `rounded-corners` mixin is presentational. It describes the visual style (specifically, the corners) of whatever rule includes it.

Using mixins and classes together allows you to write clean HTML and CSS using semantic classes, while still avoiding repetition using mixins. In addition to making your HTML and CSS easier to read and maintain, sticking to this distinction makes it easier to think about your styles as you're writing them.

Sometimes it's useful to put more than just properties into a mixin. Luckily, Sass allows you to put rules in mixins as well.

2.5.2   *CSS rules in mixins*

Mixins can contain more than just properties. They can also contain CSS rules, with selectors and properties of their own.

Listing 2.1   A mixin containing rules

```
@mixin no-bullets {
  list-style: none;
  li {
    list-style-image: none;
    list-style-type: none;
    margin-left: 0px;
  }
}
```

When a mixin containing CSS rules is `@included` in a parent rule, the rules in the mixin become nested within the parent. As an example, look at the following Sass code, which uses the `no-bullets` mixin:

```
ul.plain {
  color: #444;
  @include no-bullets;
}
```

Sass's @include directive expands the mixin, replacing it with the contents. Effectively, the previous example becomes the following.

Listing 2.2   Resulting code from including no-bullets in ul.plain

```
ul.plain {
  color: #444;
  list-style: none;
}
ul.plain li {
  list-style-image: none;
  list-style-type: none;
  margin-left: 0px;
}
```

The rules within the mixin can even use the Sass parent selector, &. Just like when it's used outside of mixins, it's replaced by the parent selector when Sass unpacks the nested rules.

   If a mixin contains only CSS rules and no properties, it can be included at the top level of the document, outside of any CSS rule. This isn't very useful when you're only writing mixins for yourself, but if you're using a library like Compass, this is a good way of providing styles in such a way that you can choose whether to use them.

   Next, you'll learn how to make mixins more flexible and reusable by allowing them to take arguments.

2.5.3   *Passing arguments to a mixin*

Mixins don't have to always produce the exact same style. A mixin can take arguments that allow the @includer to customize the exact style the mixin produces. Arguments are just variables that are assigned to CSS values provided when the mixin is @included. If you've used JavaScript, this works just like a function:

```
@mixin link-colors($normal, $hover, $visited) {
  color: $normal;
  &:hover { color: $hover; }
  &:visited { color: $visited; }
}
```

When the mixin is @included, arguments are passed just like they would be to a CSS function. When you write this,

```
a {
  @include link-colors(blue, red, green);
}
```

Sass turns it into this:

```
a { color: blue; }
a:hover { color: red; }
a:visited { color: green; }
```

When you're @includeing a mixin, it can sometimes be hard to keep track of which argument means what and which order they go in. Because of this, Sass allows the arguments to be explicitly named using the syntax $name: value. Named arguments can go in any order, as long as they're all present:

```
a {
  @include link-colors(
    $normal: blue,
    $visited: green,
    $hover: red
  );
}
```

Although it's good to allow customizability for mixins with arguments, sometimes arguments can be a pain when you don't need to customize. Thus Sass allows mixins to declare default values for their arguments.

2.5.4   *Default argument values*

Arguments can also have default values, which are used if the mixin isn't passed enough arguments when it's @included. Default arguments take the form $name: default-value. The value can be any normal CSS value, including other arguments.

Listing 2.3   Setting default values for arguments

```
@mixin link-colors(
  $normal,
  $hover: $normal,
  $visited: $normal
  ) {
  color: $normal;
  &:hover { color: $hover; }
  &:visited { color: $visited; }
}
```

Now if someone does @include link-colors(red), $hover and $visited will automatically be red too.

Mixins are only one of the features Sass has for making styles reusable. You've learned that mixins should be used for reusing presentational styles, but what happens when you want to reuse semantic classes as well? For this, you have the other main reuse feature in Sass: selector inheritance.

2.6   *Trimming CSS with selector inheritance*

The final major method for reducing repetition when using Sass is known as *selector inheritance*. Based on the idea of object-oriented CSS pioneered by Nicole Sullivan, selector inheritance is the ability to tell Sass that one selector should inherit all the styles defined for another selector. This is declared using the @extend-rule.

Listing 2.4 Extending styles with selector inheritance

```
.error {
  border: 1px red;
  background-color: #fdd;
}
.seriousError {
  @extend .error;
  border-width: 3px;
}
```

This means that `.seriousError` will inherit all the styles for `.error` defined anywhere in the stylesheet. HTML elements with `class="seriousError"` will be styled as though they had `class="seriousError error"`. They'll not only have a three-pixel border, but that border will be red and the elements will have a light red background as well, since that was the style defined for `.error`.

`.seriousError` won't just inherit the style for `.error` itself. Any CSS rule that has to do with `.error` will work with `.seriousError` as well.

Listing 2.5 `.seriousError` inherits from `.error`

```
.error a {
  color: red;
  font-weight: bold;
}
```
◁ **Applies to
.seriousError a**

```
h1.error {
  font-size: 1.3em;
}
```
◁ **Applies to
h1.seriousError**

Links within an element with `class="seriousError"` will also be red and bold.

In this section, we'll look at situations when inheritance is appropriate to use, as opposed to mixins. Then we'll cover advanced ways to put inheritance to work, before examining how inheritance works in detail. Finally, we'll look at some of the potential pitfalls of using inheritance, and how to avoid them.

Inheritance and mixins are, in some ways, very similar in what they do. It's important to know when each of them is the right tool to use, so that's what we'll go over first.

2.6.1 When to use inheritance

In section 2.5.1, we said that mixins should be "presentational" and share style, whereas classes should be "semantic" and convey meaning. Since inheritance is a relationship between *classes* (and sometimes other sorts of selectors), that relationship should be on the level of semantics. When an element having one class (such as `.seriousError`) *means* that it should have another (such as `.error`), you should use inheritance.

This is high-concept, so let's look at it from a different perspective. Imagine you're designing a page and adding classes, and you find that one of your classes (.seriousError) is a more specific version of another (.error). What do you do?

- You could write the same styles for both of them, but that would be a lot of repetition. You shouldn't have to repeat yourself when using Sass.
- You could use a selector group (.error, .seriousError) to write the same rule to both selectors. This is great if you have all the styles for .error in one place, but if .error is used a lot in your stylesheet, this becomes much more difficult.
- You could use a mixin to provide the same styles for both classes. This would work fine, but it has the same problem as the selector group when .error is used all over the stylesheet. And it's not like the two classes just *happen* to have the same style. You should be able to express the relationship more clearly.
- So you use @extend. Having .seriousError inherit from .error makes the relationship between the two clear. More important, everywhere you use .error in your stylesheet will work for .seriousError as well.

Now that you have a better idea of when inheritance should be used and what it's particularly good for, it's time to look at some advanced uses.

2.6.2   *Advanced inheritance*

Any CSS rule can use @extend, and almost any CSS rule can be @extended. Most of the time you just want to use it with single classes, but occasionally you'll want something more. The most common advanced use is to inherit an HTML element. Although the default browser styles won't be inherited since they aren't part of the stylesheet, any of the styles you write will.[2]

The following style defines a class called disabled that will make elements look like grayed-out links. It does so by extending a, the link element:

```
.disabled {
  color: gray;
  @extend a;
}
```

If a rule @extends a complex selector, it'll only inherit styles that would apply to elements matching that selector. So if .seriousError @extended .important.error, it would inherit styles for .important.error and h1.important.error, but not for .important or .error. In this case, you'd probably want .seriousError to @extend .important and .error separately.

If a selector sequence (#main .seriousError) @extends another selector (.error), only elements matching #main .seriousError inherit the style of .error (just like with a single class). Elements with class="seriousError" outside of .main are unaffected.

---

[2]   This is a moot point if you're using a CSS reset, since the element will be completely styled by your stylesheet anyway.

Only selector sequences like `#main .error` can't be `@extend`ed. This is because the styles that would be inherited for `#main .error` will almost always be nearly identical to the styles for plain `.error`, and the distinction could get confusing.

Now that you understand what inheritance does, it's time to explore what Sass is doing to the CSS to make it work.

2.6.3 *How inheritance works*

Unlike variables and mixins, inheritance isn't as simple as replacing `@extend` with some CSS styles. It's important to have a basic understanding of what's going on under the hood so that you aren't surprised by the generated CSS.

The basic idea behind `@extend` is that if `.seriousError @extend`s `.error`, then every time `.error` appears in the stylesheet, it's replaced with `.error, .seriousError`. This means that the CSS rule applies to both `.error` and `.seriousError`, just as desired. The details get complicated when `.error` appears in complex selectors like `h1.error` or `.error a` or `#main .sidebar input.error[type="text"]`, but Sass will worry about those for you.

There are two important practical consequences of this that you should know:

- Unlike mixins, inheritance generates relatively little additional CSS. Since it only repeats the selector, not the properties, using inheritance can result in far less CSS than using mixins. This can be important if you worry a lot about the speed of your site.
- Inheritance works with the *cascade*. When two different CSS rules apply to the same HTML element, and they each have different values for the same property, the cascade is how CSS decides which one applies. It's pretty intuitive: usually the more specific selector wins, and failing that, the rule that comes last in the stylesheet.

Though mixins sidestep the cascade by putting their styles right in the CSS rule, with inheritance the cascade matters. The styles being inherited are defined wherever they were defined for the `@extend`ed selector, and at the same level of specificity. Usually this doesn't pose a problem, but it's important to be aware of nonetheless.

2.6.4 *Best practices when using inheritance*

Usually, using inheritance will keep your CSS nice and trim since it's only copying selectors, not bunches of CSS properties. But if you're not careful, you can put Sass into a position where it has to copy a huge number of selectors.

The best way to avoid this is to never use `@extend` in CSS rules with descendant selectors like `.foo .bar` (`.foo.bar` is safe, though). If you do, *and* `@extend` is also used in a descendant selector, the size of your selectors can quickly get out of hand:

```
.foo .bar { @extend .baz; }

.bip .baz { a: b; }
```

In this example, Sass has to make sure that the styles that apply to .baz also apply to .foo .bar (an element with class="bar" within an element with class="foo"). Then you have a CSS rule that applies to .bip .baz (an element with class="baz" within an element with class="bip"). Notice the three separate cases where this rule might apply to .foo .bar.

Listing 2.6   Inheritance can quickly get complicated

```html
<!-- Case 1 -->
<div class="foo">
  <div class="bip">
    <div class="bar">...</div>
  </div>
</div>

<!-- Case 2 -->
<div class="bip">
  <div class="foo">
    <div class="bar">...</div>
  </div>
</div>

<!-- Case 3 -->
<div class="foo bip">
  <div class="bar">...</div>
</div>
```

Sass has to generate three new selectors for this. If either rule were longer, the number would become much greater. Sass won't always generate *all* possible selector combinations, but the number can still get pretty big, so better to avoid it if possible.

It's worth noting that it's completely safe to use @extended selectors with as many descendant selectors as you want, as long as there aren't any descendant selectors @extending them as well.

2.7   *Summary*

This chapter introduced the fundamental building blocks of Sass and Compass. Using the tools explained here, you can go off and use Sass to write wonderfully clear, repetition-free, semantic CSS. You have a reasonably deep understanding of the tools Sass provides, and some good rules of thumb for when to use each one.

Variables are the most basic tool provided by Sass. They allow individual CSS values to be reused, either throughout the stylesheet or locally within a single rule. Variables, along with mixins and even Sass filenames, can use either - or _ interchangeably.

Similarly basic is the Sass nesting facility. Nesting allows CSS rules to be laid out within one another, reducing the repetition of typing out common selectors and making it easy to see the structure of a stylesheet at a glance. Sass also provides the special parent-reference character, &, which allows for even more powerful nesting.

You've also learned about Sass's stylesheet importing, another important feature. This allows a single CSS file to be generated by many separate Sass files, making it easier to work on large amounts of CSS without the performance penalty of CSS `@import`. With nested imports and default variable values, importing also enables more powerful, customizable stylesheets.

Mixins allow Sass users to write semantic stylesheets while still avoiding repetition of presentational styles. You learned not only how to use mixins to reduce repetition, but when to use them so that your stylesheets and CSS are as maintainable and semantic as possible.

Finally, we looked at selector inheritance, the other side of the same coin as mixins. Inheritance allows you to declare relationships between semantic classes and use those relationships to keep your CSS lean and easy to maintain.

If you were to use just what you've learned in this chapter, you could write fine Sass, but soon you'd start to wonder if there were ways you could make it even better. You'd think your mixins could be more reusable, and wish you could have Sass do some math for you. You'd start to wonder if it would be possible to theme your entire site using only one color variable, and if you could write stylesheets so reusable you could share them among your sites and with your friends.

In the next chapter, we'll explore Sass's scripting features, which enable you to do all of these things.

Part 2

Using Sass and Compass
in practice

In the first two chapters, you got acquainted with Sass and Compass, and we covered the core features of the Sass syntax. In the next three chapters, you'll see the practical value of Sass and Compass, how they help you tackle previously tedious tasks, and how they help you write powerful stylesheets with far less effort.

In chapter 3, you'll see how Compass simplifies one of the most fundamental elements of web design, layout. In this chapter, we discuss the principles behind grid layouts and cover the tools Compass provides to make them incredibly simple and flexible. Whereas traditional CSS grid systems require you to litter your markup with stacks of presentational class names, in this chapter you'll see how Compass lets you use Blueprint and 960 Grid System without imposing upon your markup. You'll see how the dynamic nature of Sass allows you to set up a grid framework and easily change it by changing a few variables. Finally, you'll learn how to maintain vertical rhythm with Compass's typography helpers.

In chapter 4, we dig deeper into the Compass tool chest and look at Compass mixins, which help you eliminate the drudgery of authoring repetitive stylesheets. Compass provides a fantastic set of style patterns wrapped up in dynamic mixins. You'll learn how you can reset browser styling defaults and help older browsers catch up with HTML5 resets. We look at mixins for styling links, horizontal and inline lists, and other helpful patterns for typography and layout.

Chapter 5 shows how Compass mixins take the headache out of writing cross-browser CSS3. You'll see how easy it is to write cutting-edge stylesheets with box shadows, rounded corners, and gradients without the hassle of managing vendor prefixes or having to keep track of varying browser implementations. We look at how Compass simplifies `@font-face` and even helps you support some CSS3 features in older versions of IE with easy CSS PIE integration.

When you've completed this part, you should have a good understanding of how Compass fits into your stylesheet workflow and solves your everyday problems. You should also have a more tangible sense of the power of dynamic stylesheets and how you can write better stylesheets with less effort. In the next part, we take a look at ways to use Compass's brilliant automatic CSS spriting, how to take your stylesheets from prototype to production, and how to optimize your stylesheets for better performance.

3

CSS grids
without the math

This chapter covers

- Basic grid theory and when you might use a grid
- CSS grid framework options when using Compass
- Maintaining vertical rhythm in your layouts using typography helpers

3.1 *What is a grid?*

Whitespace is a powerful, yet often underutilized aspect of great web design. Whitespace (or negative space) is the area between "the other stuff" in your layouts and content. Whitespace can create separation between types of information, helping you to visually scan content or calling your attention to items of greater importance.

A *grid* is a layout framework that helps you make efficient use of whitespace in your web pages, providing uniform dimensions for columns and rows of content, as well as other whitespace elements like margins and gutters. Though grids have been common in print since the invention of the printing press, they became popular in web design only a few short years ago. In addition to providing some best practices for whitespace use in your designs, CSS grids also allow for rapidly prototyping new layouts, since you can more quickly adjust the width of content areas.

3.1.1   *Without CSS grids, or designing without a net*

Uniform whitespace isn't just a matter of aesthetics; it helps you scan and read content. Our eyes are drawn to the space between objects on a page, and uneven amounts of whitespace draw attention. This can be either good or bad, but too much attention leads to cognitive noise.

Compare a paragraph written on lined paper to a note inside of a greeting card and the value of those lines becomes obvious. Without a consistent baseline, your handwriting suffers and its legibility declines sharply. In the same way, designing without a grid leaves you with inconsistent sizes and arbitrary alignment, dramatically reducing the impact of your design. CSS grid frameworks lay down a groove of consistent measurements so you're not left to the peril of "eyeballing" your layouts. Let's look at a simple grid example.

3.1.2   *What is a grid system or framework and how does it work?*

In case you haven't worked with grids before, let's look at some grid layouts in action. If you happen to have an internet connection handy, you may want to follow along online. We'll take a look at Geoffrey Grosenbach's excellent PeepCode blog (http://blog.peepcode.com/archives), shown in figure 3.1, which makes effective use of a CSS grid layout.

Take a look at figure 3.1. How many columns are in the grid? If you said four, you'd be partially correct. There are indeed four columns of thumbnails, but take a look at the footer. There are six columns of links down there. If you press Ctrl+G, you'll see that Geoffrey has wired up a nice little Easter Egg to reveal the underlying grid layout (see figure 3.2).

Figure 3.1 The PeepCode blog uses a CSS grid.

As figure 3.2 reveals, there are actually 12 columns. Each thumbnail is three columns wide (4 x 3 = 12) and each column in the footer is only two columns wide (6 x 2 = 12). This kind of layout makes it easy to distribute images in an eye-pleasing arrangement, but it does so much more. If you click through to any of the articles in Geoffrey's archives (and hit Ctrl+G), you'll see the same grid at work (see figure 3.3).

Figure 3.2 The grid revealed

The article in figure 3.3 is only five columns wide. The layout uses seven columns of negative space to provide a background image of a business card, a design that supports the content of the article.

So you can see the value that grids provide, but where do Sass and Compass come in?

Figure 3.3 Grid layouts are for text, too.

3.1.3 Grids with Sass and Compass

At their core, grids are simple mathematical divisions which define a structure for content and containers. Compass (and Sass) step in and handle all the math, freeing you from the tedium of rolling your custom grid width classes by hand. You can use either CSS classes or Sass mixins to construct your grid layout. Using Sass variables, you can configure your grids easily, trying new settings simply by changing a few variables.

Next we'll look at what grid systems are made of and how Sass and Compass help you master them.

3.2   *Getting started with grids*

In this section, we'll cover some advanced features of CSS grid frameworks. If you're already familiar with using CSS grids, this will be a review. If this is your first foray into the world of CSS grids, this section will serve as a quick primer. Now, let's define some terms.

3.2.1   *Terminology*

Though all CSS grid frameworks have their own internal names for grid elements, there are some concepts which they all share (see table 3.1).

Table 3.1   **Grid framework terms**

Term	Definition	In markup
Column	Vertical unit of measurement of content	No
Container	HTML element wrapping a grid layout	Yes
Gutter	Uniform space between columns in a grid	No

The items in table 3.1 are core to any CSS grid, but as you'll see, only the grid container is represented in your markup.

COLUMNS

Columns are at the heart of grid frameworks. In print media, if "Content is King," then columns are the power behind the throne. Authors are called *columnists*. Classified ads are sold in units of *columns* and inches. In web design, we've advanced beyond our slate-gray, center-justified Stone Age wrought with red, blue, and purple links. But, as a medium, the web still trails print in many ways. CSS has long had the ability to adjust how content is rendered horizontally, but vertical layout has been a challenge. Native support for column-based layout is only now making its way into the CSS spec and it will be years before you can reliably depend on it. This vacuum gave rise to CSS grid frameworks and column-based layouts.

Take another look at figure 3.2. Those vertical shaded items are *columns*. You can observe that they're each 30 pixels wide and share a uniform spacing. There are many techniques for achieving columns in CSS. We'll look at a few in the context of several grid systems throughout section 3.2. For now, it's only important to know that all CSS grids have the notion of columns and those columns have an equal width within a container. We'll explore containers in the next section.

CONTAINERS

Looking back at the Blueprint example in figure 3.2, you might get the impression that CSS grids turn the whole page into a column-based layout, much like a newspaper page. On the web, since you have no control of a user's screen size and resolution, you don't know how big "the page" actually is. In CSS grids, you enable a column-based layout within a *container*. A grid may have just one container, or it might include a number of containers. In some cases, you might enable different containers with differing column widths and column counts, as you'll see later when we cover the 960 Grid System. In CSS grid frameworks, a container is merely a wrapping element, usually a <div> that scopes the CSS selectors used to implement the grid.

Now that you know that CSS grids all have columns in one or many containers, let's look at another linchpin of grid-based layouts, the gutter.

GUTTERS

Just like gutters on a house take rainfall and move it efficiently off a roof and into the storm drain, gutters help our eyes efficiently notice the boundaries of areas of content. Consider again the Blueprint example in figure 3.2. Those gaps in between the shaded columns are the *gutters*. Note that, just like the columns, the gutters have a uniform width, in this case 10 pixels. Different grid layouts employ different math to achieve their column layouts, but they're all based on number of columns, column width, and gutter width.

Up until now, we've looked only at fixed-sized, pixel-based columns and gutters. In the next section, we'll look at alternative CSS grid layouts.

3.2.2 Choosing a grid style, semantic versus pragmatic

Most technologies are not without detractors. CSS grid frameworks are no different. Critics claim that using CSS classes to specify grid layout couples presentation with content. Folks in this semantics camp argue that markup should be about content and data, and not indicate anything about presentation of that data. Pragmatists counter that semantic meaning resides in the markup and not in class names.

Fortunately, Compass gives you the choice of using CSS classes or including grid layout styles in your own selectors with mixins.

3.2.3 Fixed versus fluid grids

Given the wide range of user screen sizes on the web, designers have two choices: choose a reasonable, *fixed* layout size for most users (and constrain the content to that layout), or implement a flexible or *fluid* layout and let the content adapt to the user's screen, even when the browser is resized.

Figure 3.4 shows a quick example of a fluid grid from Stephen Bau based on Nathan Smith's popular 960 Grid System. In this composite image, you can see how the same 16-column grid can grow as the user's browser window changes sizes.

Though fluid layouts might sound appealing (after all, who likes to be inflexible?), the nature of dynamic content, including images and copy, makes fluid layouts more difficult to implement and maintain. We'll look at a few of those later in the chapter when we discuss the 960 Grid System and others.

Now that we've covered the basics of CSS grid frameworks, in the next section we'll take an in-depth look at four popular grid systems and how to use them with Compass.

Figure 3.4   960 fluid grid

3.3   *Using Blueprint*

Originally developed by Olav Bjørkøy in 2007, Blueprint CSS is now maintained by Joshua Clayton and a team of contributors. Blueprint packages common CSS techniques for grid layout, typography, and form styling into a framework that can be used from project to project. You can use Blueprint whole or à la carte, choosing only those modules you like. Most designers who use Blueprint initially do so for the grid layout features, so let's start there.

As you saw in section 3.1, CSS grid layouts consist of containers, columns, and gutters. As you're about to see, columns and gutters are virtual, meaning you won't see any items in your markup for actual columns and gutters. Instead, you indicate how many column widths (and gutter space between them) your content should consume. Let's look at an example of using Blueprint with static CSS.

3.3.1   *Blueprint with plain CSS*

First, you need to download and unarchive Blueprint's CSS and supporting assets into your project and reference them in the <head> of your document.

Listing 3.1   Adding Blueprint to a page

```
<link rel="stylesheet" href="css/blueprint/screen.css">
<link rel="stylesheet" href="css/blueprint/print.css">
<!--[if lt IE 8]>
  <link rel="stylesheet" href="css/blueprint/ie.css">
<![endif]-->
```

In this basic example, you add the stylesheets for both screen and print media types, as well as a conditional stylesheet to handle all of Internet Explorer's lovely quirks. This is the kitchen-sink approach: enable all of Blueprint's features, including its reset, grid, typography, and forms support. You could choose to include just the Blueprint modules you want, but this example will suffice for now. We'll take a look at how to optimize Blueprint in Compass in section 3.3.3.

Now that you've included Blueprint on your page, you're all set to create your grid system. Let's look at a basic layout.

Listing 3.2   A basic Blueprint layout

```
<section class="container">                          ◄—① Create grid layout
  <header class="main span-24">         ◄─┐
    Header                                  ② Full-width header
  </header>
  <section class="content span-20">    ◄─┐
    Content                                 ③ Main content area
  </div>
  <aside id="sidebar" class="span-4 last">  ◄─┐
    The last column                          ④ Sidebar
  </aside>
  <footer class="main span-24">
    Footer
  </footer>
</section>
```

In this basic example, you've created a simple two-column, blog-style layout with full-width header and footer. You begin by adding the container class to the element to wrap your grid ①. You make your header and footer elements take up the full width of your grid (24 columns in this case) with the span-24 class ②. Since you want a vertical split between your main content and sidebar, you assign the span-20 ③ and span-4 classes, respectively. Note the last class for your sidebar ④. This class eliminates the gutter on the right side of this column, since it's the last column in a row.

We don't have the space to dive into the complete source of Blueprint, but it's important to understand a few things in the CSS before we jump into a Compass example. Consider the following listing.

Listing 3.3   Selected CSS for Blueprint example

```
.container {width:950px;margin:0 auto;}          ◁━❶ Set grid width
.column,
.span-1,
.span-2,
.span-3,
.span-4,
...                                                  ❷ Float columns
.span-24 {float:left;margin-right:10px;}         ◁    left; add gutter
.last {margin-right:0;}
.span-1 {width:30px;}
.span-2 {width:70px;}
.span-3 {width:110px;}                             ❸ Sidebar
.span-4 {width:150px;}                            ◁
...                                               ❹ Main
.span-20 {width:790px;}                           ◁  content
.span-21 {width:830px;}
.span-22 {width:870px;}
.span-23 {width:910px;}                            ❺ Full width
.span-24 {width:950px;margin-right:0;}           ◁    implies no gutter
```

In this abridged listing from the Blueprint grid module, we get a look at how the grid is implemented. The container has a width of 950 pixels and is centered in the page ❶. Next, all possible column widths (indicated with the span-x classes) are floated to the left and have a right gutter of 10 pixels via a right margin ❷. Next, the width of the sidebar and main content are set via span-4 ❸ and span-20 ❹. Finally, the full-width header and footer elements share the same width as the container ❺.

If this is your first exposure to CSS grids, you can see that the math isn't difficult. Blueprint provides classes for each column width from 1 to 24 in 40-pixel increments: 30-pixel columns with 10-pixel gutters. In addition to basic span-x classes, Blueprint also provides similar classes named append-x, prepend-x, pull-x, and push-x for leading or trailing column padding or nudging columns horizontally on the grid, as well as other classes for adding borders and other niceties. Now that we've explored a bit of the theory and CSS behind Blueprint, let's look at how Compass makes implementing Blueprint grids even easier.

3.3.2   *Blueprint grids with Compass*

Now that you've seen how to implement a simple layout using CSS, let's take a look at how to do the same Blueprint layout in Compass. Let's get started by generating a new Compass project.

Listing 3.4   Generating a basic Blueprint project

```
compass create simple --using blueprint/basic

directory simple/
directory simple/images/
directory simple/sass/
directory simple/sass/partials/
```

Grid settings

```
directory simple/stylesheets/
    create simple/config.rb
  ❷ create simple/sass/screen.scss
  └▷ create simple/sass/partials/_base.scss
    create simple/sass/print.scss
    create simple/sass/ie.scss
    create simple/images/grid.png
    create simple/stylesheets/ie.css
    create simple/stylesheets/print.css
    create simple/stylesheets/screen.css
...
```

❶ **Main stylesheet**

In addition to the basic project structure, it's important to note a couple of things. First, Compass creates a main stylesheet, screen.scss, and imports Blueprint ❶. Next Compass creates a _base partial that contains the math for your grid ❷. In this case, it matches the (30 + 10) x 24 setup from the static CSS example, so you'll leave it alone for now. You might be wondering why you'd used blueprint/basic. Compass provides a few options for implementing Blueprint, which we'll look at in a moment. For the sake of this example, we'll look at the basic pattern first.

Let's take a look inside your generated screen.scss stylesheet starting point.

Listing 3.5   Default screen.scss for Blueprint basic pattern

```
// This import applies a global reset to any page that imports
// this stylesheet.
@import "blueprint/reset";                          ❶ Default Blueprint reset

// To configure blueprint, edit the partials/_base.sass file.
@import "partials/base";                             ❷ Grid settings

// Import all the default blueprint modules so that we can access
// their mixins.
@import "blueprint";                                   Make Blueprint
                                                       modules
// Import the non-default scaffolding module.        ❸ available
@import "blueprint/scaffolding";

// Generate the blueprint framework according to your
// configuration:
@include blueprint;                                 ❹ Generate grid

@include blueprint-scaffolding;                     Forms and other
                                                  ❺ Blueprint niceties
```

In this generated file, you gain the Blueprint reset ❶, import your grid settings from the partial ❷, and make the Compass-powered Blueprint mixins available ❸. Now you're ready to generate your grid ❹ and add some additional Blueprint features for handling forms ❺. The real magic happens when you generate the grid with @include blueprint. Let's take a look at what that line is doing by looking at the Compass source.

Listing 3.6   Compass-powered Blueprint grid generation

```
@mixin blueprint-grid {
  ...
  // Use these classes (or mixins) to set the width of a column.
  @for $n from 1 to $blueprint-grid-columns {            ◁┐  Generate span-xx
    .span-#{$n} {                                          ❶  classes
      @extend .column;
      width: span($n); } }
  .span-#{$blueprint-grid-columns} {                     ◁┐  Last column
    @extend .column;                                         class needs
    width: span($blueprint-grid-columns);                ❷  no gutter
    margin: 0; }
  ...
```

Inside Compass's Blueprint module, a couple of mixins deep lies the `blueprint-grid`
mixin, which does most of the heavy lifting for your grid. This mixin handles the math
for your grid, based on the values you specified in your _base.scss partial. It loops
through the number of columns and generates the CSS classes you expect ❶. Just like
in the static CSS example from earlier in the chapter, it treats the last column class differently, omitting the gutter ❷. As you can see, if you were to modify the math in your
base partial, you'd get a new grid system with minimal effort. We only highlight this
mixin to demonstrate *how* Compass supports Blueprint classes. The beauty is that you
never have to deal with this sort of code at all if you don't want to. You can use the
Blueprint classes without any thought as to how they're created. But as with all things
Compass, it's important to understand what's going on under the hood.

Now that you've seen how Compass makes quick work of creating class-based Blueprint grids, let's look at some other options available.

3.3.3   *Blueprint in Compass without the classes*

In the previous example we used the Compass blueprint *basic* pattern:

```
compass create simple --using blueprint/basic
```

Compass also ships with a couple of other options. If you'd like to not use classes and
prefer to mix grid styles into your other selectors, use `blueprint/semantic`:

```
compass create simple --using blueprint/semantic
```

If you compare the generated files from both patterns, you can see not only some
additional files, but also some additional imports at the bottom of screen.scss:

```
// Combine the partials into a single screen stylesheet.
@import "partials/page";
@import "partials/form";
@import "partials/two_col";
```

Using this pattern, Compass doesn't generate those span-xx classes. Instead, you use
the `@column` mixin. Compass is nice enough to provide an example in the two_col
partial.

Listing 3.7 Default two-column Blueprint layout using Compass

```
#container {                              ❶ Set up grid
  @include container; }                      container        ❷ Full-width
#header, #footer {                                              header
  @include column($blueprint-grid-columns); }                  and footer
#sidebar {
  // One third of the grid columns, rounding down. With 24 cols,
  // this is 8.
  $sidebar-columns: floor($blueprint-grid-columns / 3);    ❶ Use a third of
  @include column($sidebar-columns); }                        columns for
#content {                                                  ❸ sidebar
  // Two thirds of the grid columns, rounding up.
  // With 24 cols, this is 16.
  $content-columns: ceil(2 * $blueprint-grid-columns / 3);
  // true means it's the last column in the row
  @include column($content-columns, true); } }
```

This listing is short but chock-full of Compass techniques that make working with grids faster (especially when you're refactoring later). To set up the grid, you need a container. Here, you mix in that behavior to your #container selector ❶. Your header and footer elements get set to full width via a mixin as well ❷. The most magical part of the code is when Compass calculates the number of columns for your sidebar and main content based on a one-third, two-thirds split for sidebar and content, respectively ❸. Using the floor and ceil methods, you can employ some basic rounding to ensure the proper split. Again, if you change the number of columns in your grid in your _base.scss partial, the code in this listing will just work.

Now that we've taken a drive-by look at Blueprint grids in Compass, let's explore some other popular CSS grids with Compass. Next up, we'll take a look at the 960 Grid System.

3.4 *Using 960.gs*

Another popular CSS grid framework is Nathan Smith's 960 Grid System (shown in figure 3.5). The power of the framework lies in its flexibility. Its 960-pixel width is ideal for a long-popular 1024-pixel screen width, and is a value that's divisible by 2, 3, 4, 5, 6, 8, 10, 12, 15, 16, 20, 24, 30, 32, 40, 48, 60, 64, 80, 96, 120, 160, 192, 240, 320, and 480.

Figure 3.5   960 Grid System

For the most part, the 960 Grid System functions much like the Blueprint CSS framework we've just explored, with a couple of key differences. First, gutters in 960 are split across both sides of each column, meaning both the first and last columns share a gutter on their outside edges. Second, 960 comes with scoped containers, supporting grids with different column counts and widths on the same page. 960 ships with 12-, 16-, and 24-column grids out of the box. See figure 3.6.

With this background, let's revisit our example from section 3.3.

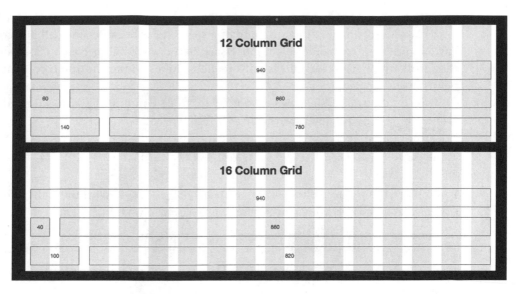

Figure 3.6　An example of 960.gs

3.4.1　*A basic 960 layout*

Let's recast the grid from earlier in the chapter from Blueprint CSS to the 960 Grid System. Begin by adding 960 to your page:

```
<link rel="stylesheet" href="css/reset.css" />
<link rel="stylesheet" href="css/text.css" />
<link rel="stylesheet" href="css/960.css" />
```

By default, you'll need to include 960's reset, optional text stylesheet, and the grid system to use either the default 12- or 16-column layouts.

Listing 3.8　A basic 960 Grid System 12-column layout

```
<section class="container_12">            ◁─❶ Create a grid layout
  <header class="grid_12">            ◁┐
    Header                             ❷ Full-width header
  </header>
  <section class="content grid_10">        ◁─❸ Main content area
    Content
  </div>
  <aside id="sidebar" class="grid_2">      ◁─❹ Sidebar
    The last column
  </aside>
  <footer class="grid_12">
    Footer
  </footer>
</section>
```

Note that the markup required for the 960 Grid System is very similar to the Blueprint example. Your container class becomes container_12 ❶ and your span-x classes become grid_x ❷, ❸, ❹. Astute readers will notice that the sidebar doesn't have a last class indicating you're at the end of a row. This is because since all 960 columns have a gutter on each side, it's unnecessary. 960 does have an omega class similar to Blueprint's last class, but this is only needed when you want to force content into a new row on the grid.

You could just as easily convert your layout to 24 columns. First, you'll need to reference the 24-column grid stylesheet:

```
<link rel="stylesheet" href="css/reset.css" />
<link rel="stylesheet" href="css/text.css" />
<link rel="stylesheet" href="css/960_24_col.css" />
```

You replace the reference to 960.css with 960_24_col.css. With the right grid CSS in place, you can modify your markup for the 24-column version.

Listing 3.9   A basic 960 Grid System 24-column layout

```
<section class="wrapper container_24">           ←❶  Create a grid layout
  <header class="main grid_24">
    Header
  </header>                              ❷  Full-width header
  <section class="content grid_20">      ←❸  Main content area
    Content
  </div>
  <aside id="sidebar" class="grid_4">    ←❹  Sidebar
    The last column
  </aside>
  <footer class="main grid_24">
    Footer
  </footer>
</section>
```

As expected, you adjust your container ❶ and columns ❷, ❸, ❹ to accommodate the change in math. Though this may seem obvious to those who've worked with 960 in the past, it's important to understand the grid options in 960 before we bring Compass to the party. In the next section, we'll show the true power of using the 960 Grid System in Compass.

3.4.2   *Using the 960 Grid System with Compass*

Support for the 960 Grid System isn't bundled with Compass, so you'll need to begin by installing the Compass plugin. You'll recall from chapter 3 that you do this via Ruby Gems:

```
gem install compass-960-plugin
```

Now you're ready to create your Compass project.

Listing 3.10   Generating a new 960 Grid System Compass project

```
compass create -r ninesixty twelve_col --using 960     ←❶  Require the plugin and
directory twelve_col/                                       apply 960 pattern
directory twelve_col/sass/
```

```
directory twelve_col/stylesheets/
   create twelve_col/config.rb
   create twelve_col/sass/grid.scss          ◁─❷  Grid settings
   create twelve_col/sass/text.scss
   create twelve_col/stylesheets/grid.css
   create twelve_col/stylesheets/text.css
```

When you unfurl a new 960 Grid System project using Compass, you need to require the plugin ❶ and apply the pattern, telling Compass which templates to unpack for you. Note that by default the plugin creates two stylesheets for you, the grid settings ❷ and the basic typography module that comes with 960. You'd most likely convert these to partials and reference them in one screen.scss stylesheet to cut down on network hops. But for the purposes of this example, let's explore the grid settings Compass gives you.

Listing 3.11   Default grid settings for Compass 960

```
@import "compass/reset";
@import "960/grid";

// The following generates the default grids provided by the css
// version of 960.gs
.container_12 {                          ◁─┐    Set up the 12-column
  @include grid-system(12); }             ❶   grid classes

.container_16 {                          ◁─┐    Set up the 16-column
  @include grid-system(16); }             ❷   grid classes

// But most compass users prefer to construct semantic layouts
// like so (two column layout with header and footer):

$ninesixty-columns: 24;                  ◁─┐    Set up the 24-column
                                          ❸   grid using mixins
.two-column {
  @include grid-container;
  #header, #footer {
    @include grid(24); }
  #sidebar {
    @include grid(8); }
  #main-content {
    @include grid(16); } }
```

You'll recall the semantic versus pragmatic debate from section 3.2.2. By default, the 960 Grid System Compass plugin supports three grids out of the box. It includes the class-based 12- and 16-column grids ❶, ❷ as well as the mixin-based (semantic) grid for 24 columns ❸. This means you have a choice of either using classes or mixing in the grid styles to your existing selectors. Let's fix up this stylesheet to match your markup.

Listing 3.12   Modifying 960 for your simple grid

```
@import "compass/reset";
@import "960/grid";

// The following generates the default grids provided by the css
// version of 960.gs
.container_12 {                              ❶ Remove 16-column
  @include grid-system(12); }                   grid; you don't need it

// But most compass users prefer to construct semantic layouts
// like so (two column layout with header and footer):

$ninesixty-columns: 24;                      ❷ Set up
                                                24-column grid
.wrapper {
  @include grid-container;
  header.main, footer.main {
    @include grid(24); }
  #sidebar {
    @include grid(4); }
  .content {
    @include grid(20); } }
```

To adapt the grid to your needs, you can remove the 16-column version, since you don't need it ❶. Since your 12-column grid works out of the box, you only need to set up your 24-column grid ❷. If you did prefer to use classes for the 24-column version, you could make another call to the grid-system mixin:

```
.container_24 {
  @include grid-system(24); }
```

Powerful and simple. For more about usage and features of the 960 Grid System plugin for Compass, please visit the project source, hosted on GitHub: https://github.com/chriseppstein/compass-960-plugin.

Up until now, our discussion of grid frameworks has focused on the vertical alignment of content in a grid. You've seen how to use containers to set up a grid layout. We looked at how to easily arrange content on the grid using both CSS class and Sass mixins. We also explored how to download Compass plugins that offer even more Grid support. In the next section, we'll look at an often-overlooked aspect of great grid design—typographical vertical rhythm.

3.5   *Vertical rhythm with Compass*

In the previous section, we looked at how CSS grids help you manage whitespace between vertical columns of content. Many designers stop there, without considering whitespace down the page, in and between rows of content. This content is usually text, but also includes images, videos, tables, and any other elements of your designs. Just as a grid places content in well-defined vertical columns with uniform gutters, a good grid also maintains *vertical rhythm*, uniformity of horizontal whitespace. So what does vertical rhythm look like? Let's go back to the PeepCode blog that we visited at the beginning of the chapter; see figure 3.7.

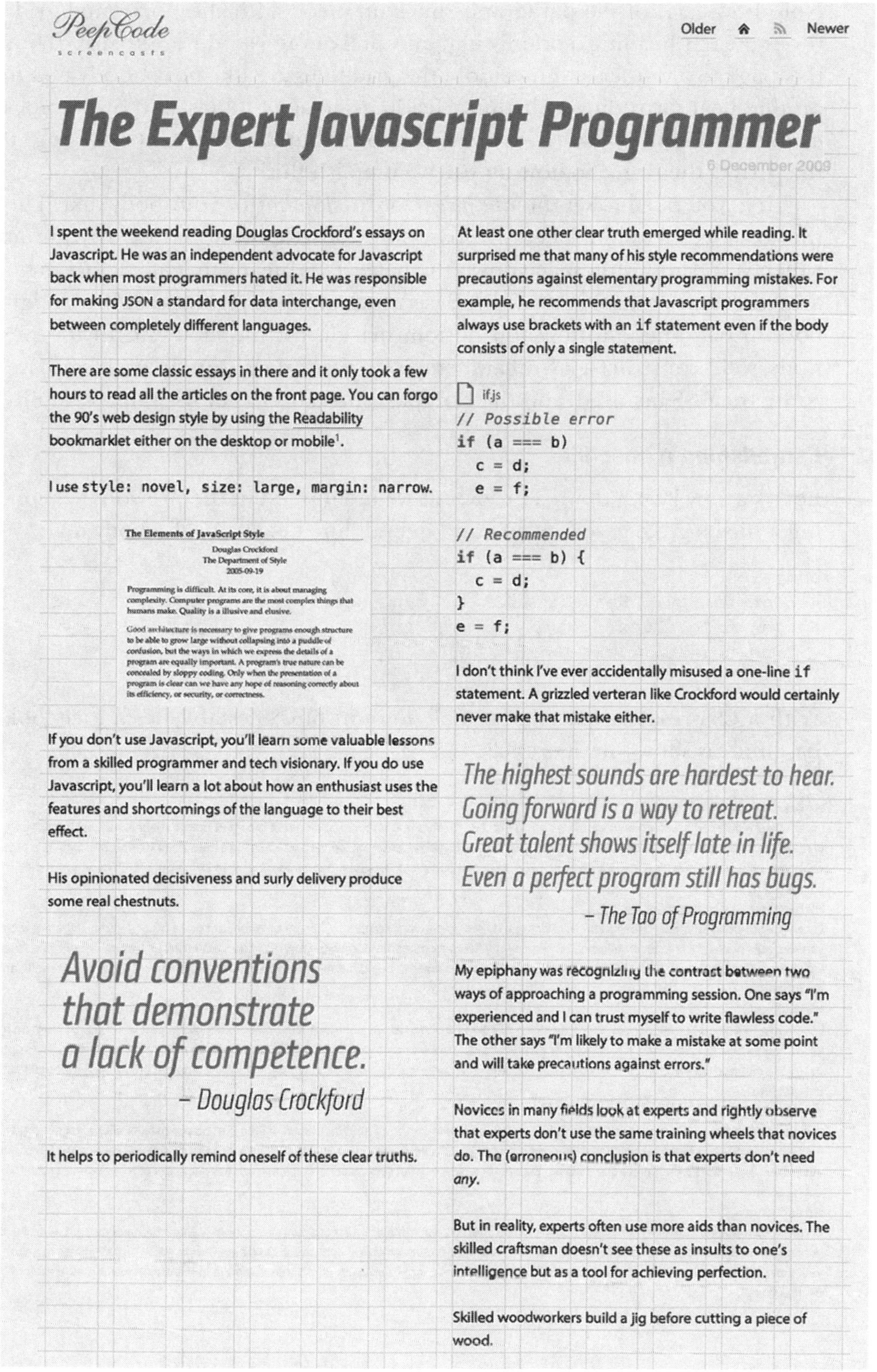

PeepCode
screencasts

Older   🏠   📶   Newer

The Expert Javascript Programmer

6 December 2009

I spent the weekend reading Douglas Crockford's essays on Javascript. He was an independent advocate for Javascript back when most programmers hated it. He was responsible for making JSON a standard for data interchange, even between completely different languages.

There are some classic essays in there and it only took a few hours to read all the articles on the front page. You can forgo the 90's web design style by using the Readability bookmarklet either on the desktop or mobile[1].

I use style: novel, size: large, margin: narrow.

The Elements of JavaScript Style

Douglas Crockford
The Department of Style
2005-09-19

Programming is difficult. At its core, it is about managing complexity. Computer programs are the most complex things that humans make. Quality is a illusive and elusive.

Good architecture is necessary to give programs enough structure to be able to grow large without collapsing into a puddle of confusion, but the ways in which we express the details of a program are equally important. A program's true nature can be concealed by sloppy coding. Only when the presentation of a program is clear can we have any hope of reasoning correctly about its efficiency, or security, or correctness.

If you don't use Javascript, you'll learn some valuable lessons from a skilled programmer and tech visionary. If you do use Javascript, you'll learn a lot about how an enthusiast uses the features and shortcomings of the language to their best effect.

His opinionated decisiveness and surly delivery produce some real chestnuts.

Avoid conventions that demonstrate a lack of competence.
— Douglas Crockford

It helps to periodically remind oneself of these clear truths.

At least one other clear truth emerged while reading. It surprised me that many of his style recommendations were precautions against elementary programming mistakes. For example, he recommends that Javascript programmers always use brackets with an `if` statement even if the body consists of only a single statement.

📄 if.js
```
// Possible error
if (a === b)
    c = d;
    e = f;
```

```
// Recommended
if (a === b) {
    c = d;
}
e = f;
```

I don't think I've ever accidentally misused a one-line `if` statement. A grizzled verteran like Crockford would certainly never make that mistake either.

The highest sounds are hardest to hear. Going forward is a way to retreat. Great talent shows itself late in life. Even a perfect program still has bugs.
— The Tao of Programming

My epiphany was recognizing the contrast between two ways of approaching a programming session. One says "I'm experienced and I can trust myself to write flawless code." The other says "I'm likely to make a mistake at some point and will take precautions against errors."

Novices in many fields look at experts and rightly observe that experts don't use the same training wheels that novices do. The (erroneous) conclusion is that experts don't need any.

But in reality, experts often use more aids than novices. The skilled craftsman doesn't see these as insults to one's intelligence but as a tool for achieving perfection.

Skilled woodworkers build a jig before cutting a piece of wood.

Figure 3.7   Vertical rhythm on the PeepCode blog

Note how each of the paragraphs lines up nicely with the horizontal grid lines even though each heading, code listing, and pull-quote is a different size. If you compare this page to a musical composition, the grid lines are like beats. Body text hums along on that beat, providing a rhythm. Headings, images, tables, and other block elements can enter on the up, down, or even back beat, but the body text returns to the rhythm that drives the page. So how do you accomplish this?

First, you need to set the *line height,* or the *leading* for your body text. The leading is the distance between successive base lines of text, your vertical rhythm and unit by which you'll add whitespace down the page. This means that all elements need to have a height that's a multiple of this base unit, adding up font size, line height, top and bottom padding, and top and bottom margin for the element. In the next few sections, we'll construct a layout and employ a vertical rhythm. In each step, we'll demonstrate the CSS involved, and the Compass shortcuts to get the same result in less time.

3.5.1   Establishing a baseline

Let's start by laying down a groove, as we mentioned in the previous section, by choosing a nice legible base font size and default line height for the body text:

```
body {
    font-family: 'Helvetica Neue', sans-serif;
    font-size: 16px;
    line-height: 24px;
}
```

With a CSS reset in place, this small amount of CSS establishes a nice-looking 1.5em baseline, as shown in figure 3.8.

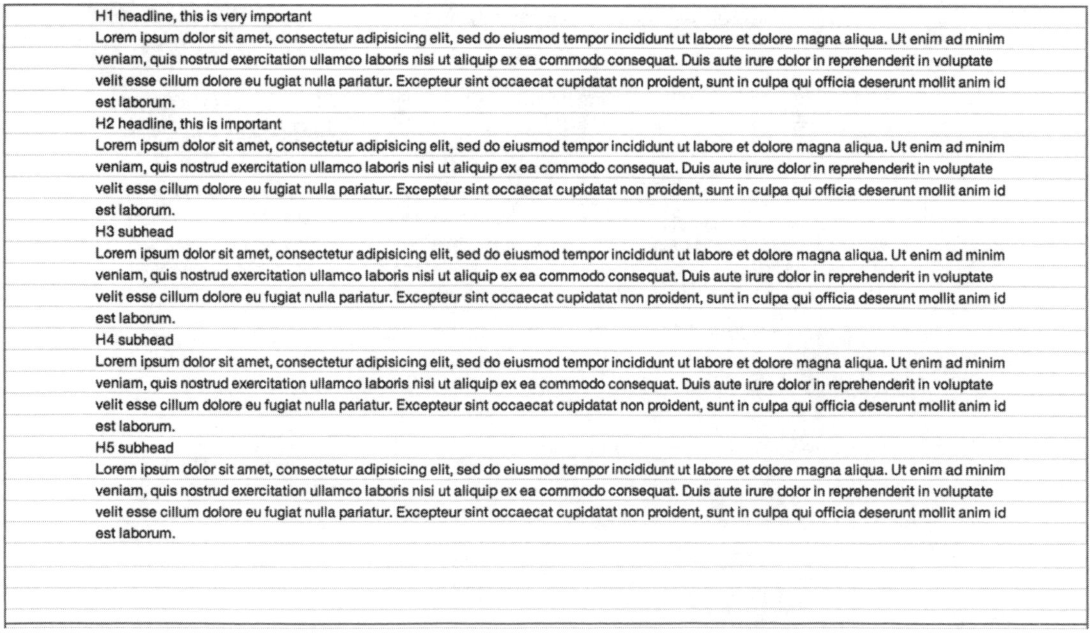

H1 headline, this is very important
Lorem ipsum dolor sit amet, consectetur adipisicing elit, sed do eiusmod tempor incididunt ut labore et dolore magna aliqua. Ut enim ad minim veniam, quis nostrud exercitation ullamco laboris nisi ut aliquip ex ea commodo consequat. Duis aute irure dolor in reprehenderit in voluptate velit esse cillum dolore eu fugiat nulla pariatur. Excepteur sint occaecat cupidatat non proident, sunt in culpa qui officia deserunt mollit anim id est laborum.
H2 headline, this is important
Lorem ipsum dolor sit amet, consectetur adipisicing elit, sed do eiusmod tempor incididunt ut labore et dolore magna aliqua. Ut enim ad minim veniam, quis nostrud exercitation ullamco laboris nisi ut aliquip ex ea commodo consequat. Duis aute irure dolor in reprehenderit in voluptate velit esse cillum dolore eu fugiat nulla pariatur. Excepteur sint occaecat cupidatat non proident, sunt in culpa qui officia deserunt mollit anim id est laborum.
H3 subhead
Lorem ipsum dolor sit amet, consectetur adipisicing elit, sed do eiusmod tempor incididunt ut labore et dolore magna aliqua. Ut enim ad minim veniam, quis nostrud exercitation ullamco laboris nisi ut aliquip ex ea commodo consequat. Duis aute irure dolor in reprehenderit in voluptate velit esse cillum dolore eu fugiat nulla pariatur. Excepteur sint occaecat cupidatat non proident, sunt in culpa qui officia deserunt mollit anim id est laborum.
H4 subhead
Lorem ipsum dolor sit amet, consectetur adipisicing elit, sed do eiusmod tempor incididunt ut labore et dolore magna aliqua. Ut enim ad minim veniam, quis nostrud exercitation ullamco laboris nisi ut aliquip ex ea commodo consequat. Duis aute irure dolor in reprehenderit in voluptate velit esse cillum dolore eu fugiat nulla pariatur. Excepteur sint occaecat cupidatat non proident, sunt in culpa qui officia deserunt mollit anim id est laborum.
H5 subhead
Lorem ipsum dolor sit amet, consectetur adipisicing elit, sed do eiusmod tempor incididunt ut labore et dolore magna aliqua. Ut enim ad minim veniam, quis nostrud exercitation ullamco laboris nisi ut aliquip ex ea commodo consequat. Duis aute irure dolor in reprehenderit in voluptate velit esse cillum dolore eu fugiat nulla pariatur. Excepteur sint occaecat cupidatat non proident, sunt in culpa qui officia deserunt mollit anim id est laborum.

Figure 3.8   Simple vertical rhythm example

To keep you honest, there's a repeating image as the background for the page which is 24 pixels tall, the same as the baseline. Now let's continue to develop your design. You need some contrast in size between your headlines and your body content. Let's establish your typographic scale for your <h1> through <h5> headlines.

Listing 3.13 Setting line height

```
h1 {font-size: 48px;}
h2 {font-size: 36px;}
h3 {font-size: 24px;}
h4 {font-size: 20px;}
h5 {font-size: 18px;}
h1,h2,h3,h4,h5 {line-height: 1.5em;}          ⊲─❶
p {margin: 1.5em 0;}
```

Now you've graduated the heights of your headlines ❶ and given them and the paragraphs a bit of breathing room, as shown in figure 3.9.

As you can see in the figure, you've got a nice range of headline sizes, but your body copy is no longer in sync with your desired vertical rhythm. To fix this, you need the height of your headlines and other elements to be multiples of your baseline. In the example, this means a headline's font size, line height, vertical margin, and

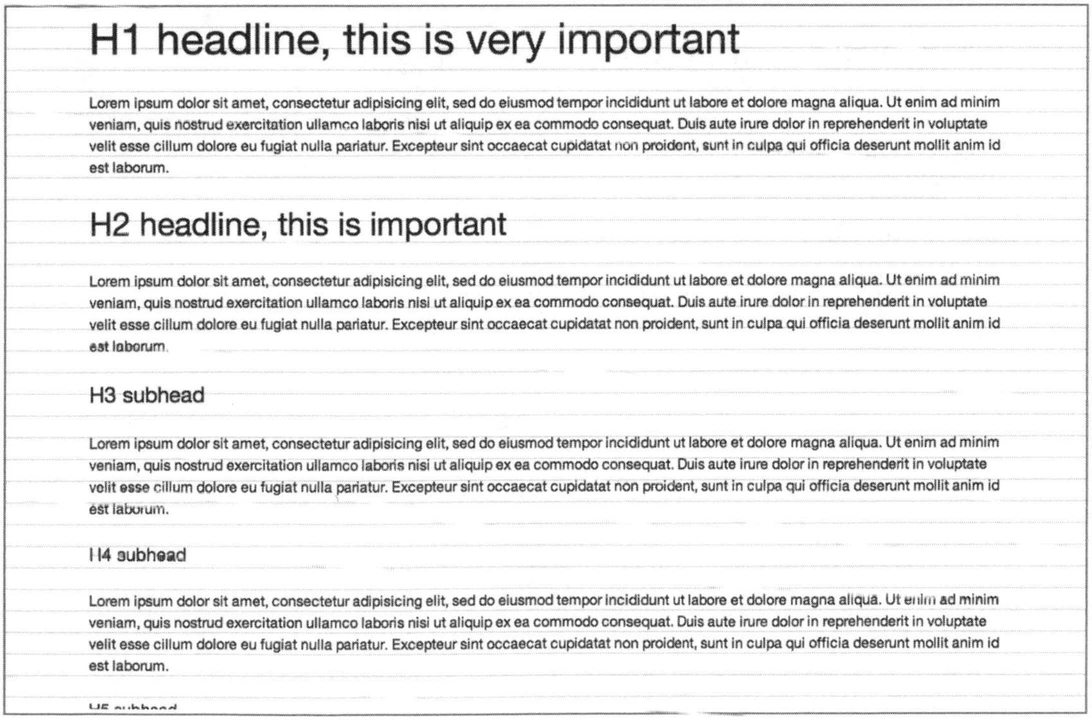

Figure 3.9 Setting up a typographic scale

vertical padding all added together need to be a multiple of 24, your baseline unit. Let's adjust your headline styles and get back in rhythm. The math for adjusting the line height to accommodate varying font sizes in order to stay on your baseline is this:

```
(baseline unit/ font-size) = line height
```

Since your <h1> is already a multiple of your baseline, let's take the <h2> in the example. The calculation would be this:

```
   (24px / 36px) = .6666667 em
h1 {font-size: 48px; line-height: 1.5em}
h2 {font-size: 36px; line-height: .666667em}
h3 {font-size: 24px; line-height: 1em}
h4 {font-size: 20px; line-height: 1.2em}
h5 {font-size: 18px; line-height: 1.33333em}
p {margin: 1.5em 0}
```

Adjusting the line height for each headline style gets you back on your vertical rhythm, as shown in figure 3.10.

As you can see, the body text is again rocking to your groove. Now this isn't hard math, mind you, but math is math. Why not let the computer do the heavy lifting, freeing you from calculating the line heights for each of these elements and allowing

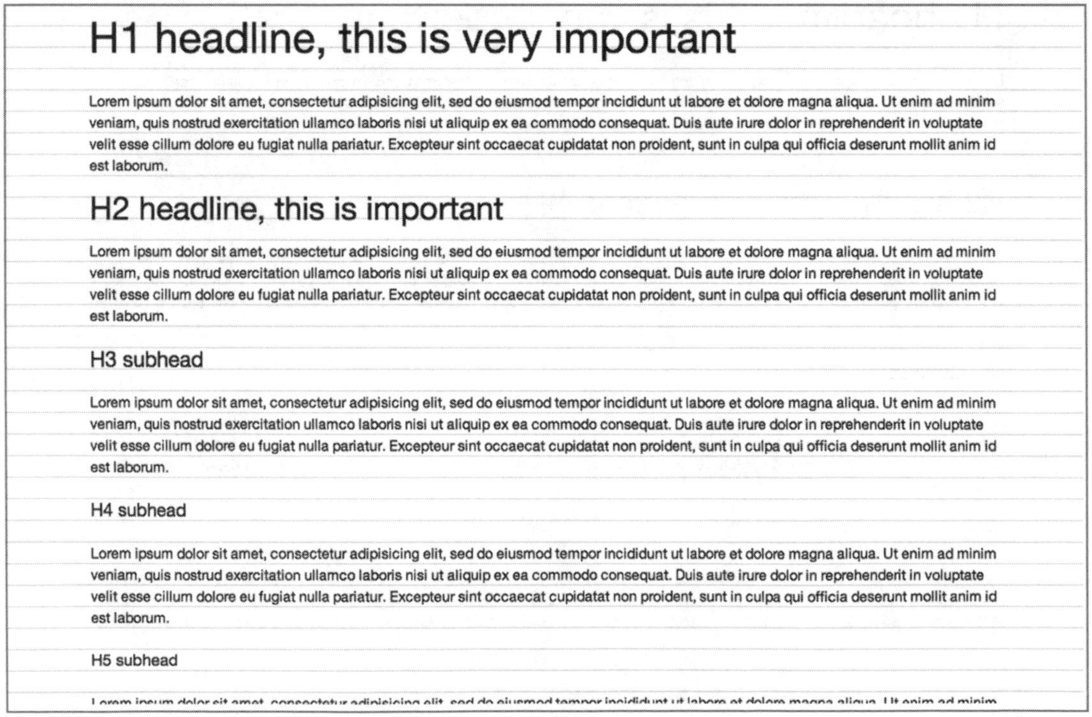

Figure 3.10   Vertical rhythm with typographic scale

you to experiment with different font sizes, letting the stylesheet *cascade* with your changes? Let's take a look at a Compass version of your stylesheet so far.

Listing 3.14   Vertical rhythm using Compass

```
@import "compass/typography";                ◁──❶ Import typography module

$base-font-size: 16px;                       ◁─┐
$base-line-height: 24px;                        │  Declare
@include establish-baseline;                  ❷ │  font size

body {
  font-family: 'Helvetica Neue', sans-serif;
  @include debug-vertical-alignment("../images/debug.png");   ◁─┐ Include
}                                                                │  debug
                                                              ❸  │  mixin
h1 {@include adjust-font-size-to(48px)}
h2 {@include adjust-font-size-to(36px)}
h3 {@include adjust-font-size-to(24px)}
h4 {@include adjust-font-size-to(20px)}
h5 {@include adjust-font-size-to(18px)}
p {margin: 1.5em 0;}
```

For your Compass version, you begin by importing Compass's typography module ❶. Next, you declare your base font size and base line heights as variables ❷. Compass includes a mixin to add your grid debug image to the page ❸. Finally, you can use the adjust-font-size-to mixin to set the font size and line height. Compass uses the same calculation as earlier in this section. The true power in this example lies in the flexibility. Now you can experiment with any of the values for base font size, base line height, or element font sizes and the appropriate math is worked out at compile time. Now that you've seen a quick example for establishing a baseline, let's look at additional helpers Compass provides for adding extra whitespace when you need it.

3.5.2   Leading and trailing whitespace

Compass's establish-baseline and adjust-font-size-to mixins make it super easy to lay down a vertical rhythm for your copy, but how do you keep that rhythm when you need to add extra space, without getting out your calculator? Fortunately, Compass provides helpers for those scenarios, too. Let's look back at the paragraph styles of the previous CSS example:

```
p {margin: 1.5em 0;}
```

You used top and bottom margins to give your paragraphs some separation, making it easier to scan the page. What if you wanted to do the same thing with an important headline?

```
h2.important {margin: 1.5em}
```

The problem is that unless the font size for this element is a perfect multiple of your baseline rhythm, you'll hit some sour notes in your design as your body copy will get off-rhythm. Compass provides some helpers to add leading (before) or trailing (after) whitespace to your elements and maintain your rhythm. You could style each of the preceding elements in this way:

```
p {@include leader; @include trailer;}
h2.important {@include leader(2); @include trailer(2)}
```

The `leader` mixin adds one baseline unit of margin before the element, whereas the `trailer` adds one baseline unit of margin after the element. Need more? You can pass the desired baseline units to the mixin. If you need padding instead of margin, Compass also provides `padding-leader` and `padding-trailer` variants of these mixins, which use padding instead of margin to add whitespace.

3.6   *Summary*

In this chapter, we looked at how popular CSS grid frameworks make it easy to manage whitespace and quickly prototype designs. Simply by adding a few CSS classes, you can create vertical columns of content with uniform spacing in between. You also saw how Compass makes using and creating grid frameworks much easier than using static CSS alone. Finally, you learned to manage whitespace down the page using Compass's vertical rhythm helpers in the typography module. In the next chapter, we'll take a deeper look at other Compass helpers that make quick work of typical CSS tedium.

Eliminate the mundane using Compass

This chapter covers

- Using Compass to reset default browser styles
- Compass helpers for better typography in your stylesheets
- Using Compass to create sticky footers, style tables, and floats

Now that we've taken a first pass at Sass syntax and looked at how Compass fits into your stylesheet workflow, let's dive deeper. In this chapter, we'll look at some everyday easy, yet mundane (read: not fun), tasks and how Compass can save you time and effort while taking advantage of community-vetted approaches. If you haven't made the jump to dynamic stylesheets and are still writing CSS by hand, you know that certain stylesheet tasks seem like death by a thousand paper cuts. Things like providing a CSS reset, styling list elements into horizontal navigation, setting link colors, and swapping headline text with images can get repetitive with each new project. In this chapter, we'll show you some helpers Compass provides to make these tasks quicker, easier, and more adaptive to your project.

4.1 *A better blank slate with targeted resets*

In chapter 1, we looked at CSS resets and how just by adding `@import "compass/reset"` to your Compass project, you can take advantage of Eric Meyer's Reset v2.0. Though convenient, there are times when a such a global reset can be heavy-handed. Fortunately, Compass offers more fine-grained approaches. To determine which approach to use, it's important to contrast the global and à la carte reset options.

4.1.1 *Global resets*

If you've used a CSS reset before, chances are it's a global reset that employs a scorched earth policy to eliminate most inherent styling that browsers apply to HTML elements. These resets became popular as a way to provide a consistent blank canvas for web applications. A global reset makes sense if you're building a traditional web app and you need to support a wide range of browsers including older versions of Internet Explorer. Compass provides a global reset, aptly named `global-reset`, based on Eric Meyer's classic. As with any Compass mixin, it's important to understand the internals of the `global-reset` mixin before you use it.

Listing 4.1 The Compass `global-reset`

```
@mixin global-reset {                                          ◁── Define
  html, body, div, span, applet, object, iframe,                   global
  h1, h2, h3, h4, h5, h6, p, blockquote, pre,                      reset
  a, abbr, acronym, address, big, cite, code,
  del, dfn, em, img, ins, kbd, q, s, samp,
  small, strike, strong, sub, sup, tt, var,
  b, u, i, center,
  dl, dt, dd, ol, ul, li,
  fieldset, form, label, legend,
  table, caption, tbody, tfoot, thead, tr, th, td,
  article, aside, canvas, details, embed,
  figure, figcaption, footer, header, hgroup,
  menu, nav, output, ruby, section, summary,
  time, mark, audio, video {                                  ◁── Includes
                                                                  individual
    @include reset-box-model;                                     mixins
    @include reset-font; }
  body {
    @include reset-body; }
  ol, ul {
    @include reset-list-style; }
  table {
    @include reset-table; }
  caption, th, td {
    @include reset-table-cell; }
  q, blockquote {
    @include reset-quotation; }
  a img {
    @include reset-image-anchor-border; }

  @include reset-html5; }
```

Note that `global-reset` is just a wrapper, applying several additional reset mixins internally. All together, the preceding mixins (included with Sass's `@include`) not only address browser inconsistencies in box models, typography, list styles, and table styles, but also add default styles for new HTML5 elements. We'll look at some of these specific mixins in the next section, but before we leave the `global-reset` mixin, it's worth noting that this Compass reset is unique in that it's applied simply by importing `compass/reset`. To understand why, let's look at the source of `compass/reset`:

```
@import "reset/utilities";

@include global-reset;
```

That's it, just two lines. In the first line, `@import` makes available the `global-reset` mixin as each of its mixins in turn. In the second line, `@include` includes the global reset. In the next section, we'll look at how to implement targeted resets without using the global reset.

4.1.2 Gain more control with targeted resets

Suppose you have a mobile interface where the global reset brings a lot of unnecessary weight. Perhaps your page doesn't use <tables>, <blockquotes>, or lists. Since page weight is critical, trimming the fat from your mobile application's stylesheets more proportionately affects the user experience than in a desktop browser. If you're writing plain CSS, you might have a snippet that you carry with you from project to project with a favorite global reset. If you want only a portion of that for your new project, you'd start carving it up in your text editor, trimming out what you don't need or want. Thankfully, Compass lets you pick and choose which of its resets you want to apply. To take advantage of these without using the global reset, use `@import "compass/reset/utilities"`. Let's take a look at a few of the mixins comprising the global reset we looked at in the previous section.

FUTURE-PROOF WITH RESET-HTML5

One of the exciting new features of HTML5 is the introduction of new markup tags. You can cut back on a diet of <div>s and use more meaningful tags like <header>, <footer>, and <nav> where appropriate. Unfortunately, not all browsers agree on how to handle these new tags. Suppose you want to list each of the new tags and apply `display: block` for each. You could memorize the list. You might even save a snippet of code to reuse from time to time. If you're using Compass, you can just use the `reset-html5` mixin to make quick work of this task. Let's look at Compass's `reset html5` mixin.

Listing 4.2   HTML5 reset

```
@mixin reset-html5 {
  article, aside, details, figcaption, figure,
  footer, header, hgroup, menu, nav, section, summary {
    display: block; } }
```

Now, by applying the mixin using `@include reset-html5` in your SCSS file, you don't have to remember all 11 tag names.

MORE RESETS IN THE COMPASS DOCS
The global reset and the HTML5 reset will most likely cover 90% of the use cases in your stylesheets, but we encourage you to check out the full list of resets in the Compass documentation. Table 4.1 provides a quick overview.

Table 4.1 Resets available in Compass

Reset mixin	Purpose
`reset-box-model`	Removes margin, padding, and borders on elements
`reset-font`	Resets the font size and baseline
`reset-focus`	Removes browser-supplied outlines (like `<input>` elements in Safari)
`reset-table` and `reset-table-cell`	Resets table borders and alignment
`reset-quotation`	Adds stylesheet-only quotation marks for `<blockquotes>`

Now that you've seen how to remove browser styles, let's take a look at how you can *add* your own styles in common scenarios using Compass helpers

4.2   *Utilities for faster, better-looking typography*

Perhaps nothing impacts your design more than typography. Typography is more than just choosing a typeface and a size. Styling lists and handling text wrapping have long been part of the job for print designers. Since the web is an interactive, data-driven medium, web designers have picked up new chores like styling hyperlinks and truncated text as well. Dealing with typography in your stylesheets is part choosing what the design outcome should be and part implementing those choices. Compass is here to help with that last part, letting you quickly knock out the tedium of styling links, lists, and other elements, and letting you focus on your design. In the next section, we'll look at some mixins that help you style your hyperlinks, the first of these typography helpers. For all of these examples, you'll need to be sure to `@import "compass/typography"` to use Compass's typography module.

4.2.1   *Anchors away: link helpers*

Good designs make effective use of contrast. Styling links to stand out from body copy isn't just good aesthetics; it's good user experience. Therefore, when creating a new stylesheet (just after setting up a reset), good designers will often define base colors for text and links—a simple task that Compass makes even simpler.

EASY COLORING WITH LINK-COLORS

Many of the patterns we take for granted in the CSS community were forged over years of trial and error with a dream of creating designs that worked reliably across several browsers. One such pattern was the suggested stylesheet order of hyperlink pseudo elements such as :hover and :visited to deal with *link specificity*, a fancy way of describing the precedence browsers give to the anchor tag pseudo elements. For instance, if you hover over a link that has been previously visited, which style wins?

Best practice suggests you include pseudo element selectors in the following order:

1 <a>
2 :visited
3 :focus
4 :hover
5 :active

This means your CSS would look something like the following.

> **Listing 4.3   CSS for setting link colors according to browser specificity**

```
a {color: #333}
a:visited {color: #555}
a:focus {color: #f00}
a:hover {color: #00f}
a:active {color: #f00}
```

It still can be tedious to remember this order and create additional pseudo elements just to change colors for your links. Sass's & parent selector doesn't buy you much. Fortunately, Compass provides an easy mixin to handle the job:

```
a { @include link-colors(#333, #00f, #f00, #555, #f00); }
```

Astute readers will note that the order of the colors in this Compass example doesn't match those in the CSS example. This is because Compass has chosen to optimize for stylesheet author productivity instead of browser precedence. The order of the color arguments for link-colors is the order in which you're most likely to use them in your stylesheets. Table 4.2 shows the order of the complete set of link-colors arguments as well as the order in which they're applied for browser link specificity.

Table 4.2   Arguments for link-colors

link-colors order	Browser order
<a>	<a>
:hover	:visited
:active	:focus
:visited	:hover
:focus	:active

If you're the attention-to-detail type who prefers readability over terseness, you can pass your arguments as named parameters:

```
a { @include link-colors(
        #333,
        $hover: #00f,
        $active: #f00,
        $visited: #555,
        $focus: #f00);
}
```

The unnamed syntax has its advantages. Following Pareto's famous 80/20 rule (in this case, 20% of the code will cover 80% of the use cases), since link-colors arguments are optional, you could specify default and :hover state colors simply by passing the first two arguments:

```
a { @include link-colors(#333, #00f); }
```

Now that you've seen how to add color to links, let's take a look at other ways Compass makes it easy to visually distinguish links in your designs.

HOVER WITH STYLE USING HOVER-LINK

Some usability experts say you should always add underlines to your links to cue users that an item is clickable. But there are times when, due to line height, adding underlines might actually degrade readability. Suppose you decide to add an underline only when a user mouses over a link with the following CSS:

```
a { text-decoration: none}
a:hover { text-decoration: underline }
```

Compass makes it easy to underline links just on the :hover state with the hover-link mixin:

```
a {@include hover-link}
```

Note how easy it is to grok what's going on with this mixin. You don't have to parse the properties in the stylesheets to see what's going on; it's right there in the name: hover-link.

INCOGNITO LINKS WITH UNSTYLED-LINK

Now imagine you want to hide a link altogether, removing any styling that would tip the user that a hyperlink lies within a paragraph of text. You could write something along the lines of the following CSS:

```
p.secret a {
  color: inherit;
  cursor: inherit;
  text-decoration: inherit
}
```

This would strip away any color, cursor, or underlining, letting your text blend in with any containing text. But what about the :hover and :focus states? Let's update the CSS:

```
p.secret a,
p.secret a:hover,
p.secret a:focus {
  color: inherit;
  cursor: inherit;
  text-decoration: inherit
}
```

This approach works, but Compass makes it much easier with the `unstyled-link` mixin:

```
p.secret a { @include unstyled-link }
```

Again, Compass mixin names make the stylesheet more descriptive. Now that you've seen how Compass makes styling links incredibly easy, let's look at how it makes dealing with lists easier.

4.2.2 *Creating versatile lists*

List element treatment is an often-overlooked aspect of great web typography. As a designer in a medium where short, clear communication is key, the `<ul>` is your friend. In this section, we'll take a look at some Compass helpers (Sass mixins) to make quick work of dealing with common tasks in designing great lists.

DRESSING UP LISTS WITH PRETTY-BULLETS

Image-based bullets (see figure 4.1) can add impact to your list elements. But IE support for `list-style-image` has been buggy since the property was first supported in version 5.5. For instance, prior to version 8, floated list elements won't display a list item image in Internet Explorer. In order to find a cross-platform solution, designers will often use background images as list item "bullets":

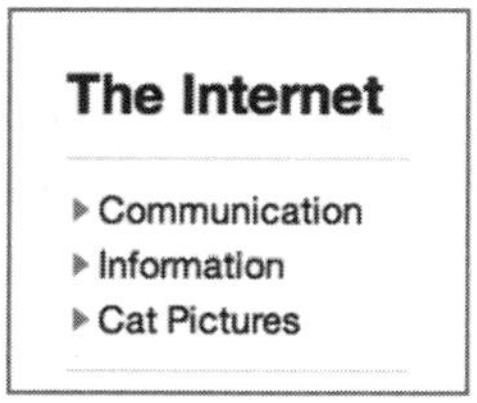

The Internet

▸ Communication
▸ Information
▸ Cat Pictures

Figure 4.1 Example of pretty bullets

```
ul.features li {
  background: url(/images/pretty-bullet.png) 5px 5px no-repeat;
  list-style-type: none;
  padding-left: 20px;
}
```

Though a simple approach, this does pose some headaches. First, you have to calculate the layout, taking into account the desired padding and image width. Your 5px 5px x and y values for the `background-position` portion of your background shorthand are the output of a couple of calculations:

```
# x = (padding - image width) / 2
# y = (line height - image height) / 2
```

Your second problem is implied by the first: you have to know the dimensions of your image. To get around these issues, Compass makes it easy to use a background image as a list item bullet using the `pretty-bullets` mixin:

```
ul.features {
  @include pretty-bullets('pretty-bullet.png')
}
```

With the pretty-bullets mixin, Compass does the heavy lifting, determining the size of the image from the image itself, performing the calculations, and creating the same CSS you saw in the previous listing. If you need more control, you can pass in the desired $height, $width, $line-height, and $padding as either named or ordered parameters:

```
ul.features {
  @include pretty-bullets('pretty-bullet.png',
          $padding: 10px,
          $line-height: 22px)
}
```

Note that in each of the Compass examples, we didn't specify the full path to the image, only the filename and extension. This is because the pretty-bullets Compass mixin uses the image-url helper to determine the full path and will return the appropriate path for your development and production environments. Now that you've seen how to make pretty, cross-browser bullets, let's take a look at how to opt out of bullets for list items.

DISARMING LISTS USING NO-BULLET AND NO-BULLETS

Compass also provides some quick ways to remove list styles from <li> elements. You might be thinking, *why not just use* list-style: none *and call it a day?* For IE8 and above (as well as the rest of the world), you could do that. If you need to support browsers crafted in Redmond prior to version 8, you need to use this instead:

```
li.no-bullet {
  list-style-image: none;
  list-style-type: none;
  margin: 0px;
}
```

With Compass, you don't have to remember to do that; you can just use the no-bullet mixin:

```
li.no-bullet { @include no-bullet }
```

If you want to turn off bullets for an entire list, you can use the plural form of the mixin, no-bullets:

```
ul.no-bullet { @include no-bullets}
```

This form will mix in the singular no-bullet mixin for every <li> in the list. Now that you've seen how to add some pop to your lists with custom bullets and remove bullets entirely, let's look at how to teach your lists to lie flat and play dead.

EASY HORIZONTAL-LIST

By default, browsers display lists vertically and style them with margins and padding. While this is all well and good for listing most items, designers often prefer to style lists of navigational links horizontally (see figure 4.2).

Home Services Blog Contact

Figure 4.2   **Example of a horizontal list**

Consider the following markup:

```
<ul class="nav">
  <li><a href="/">Home</a></li>
  <li><a href="/services">Services</a></li>
  <li><a href="/blog">Blog</a></li>
  <li><a href="/contact">Contact</a></li>
</ul>
```

How do you apply some CSS origami to turn this list into a horizontal nav bar with a nice 8-pixel split between items? A common approach usually looks something like the CSS in the following listing.

Listing 4.4   CSS for creating navigation out of <ul>

```
ul.nav {
  border: 0;
  margin: 0;
  overflow: hidden;
  padding: 0;
}
ul.nav li {
  display: inline;
  float: left; /* make the menu horizontal */
  margin-left: 0px;
  padding-left: 4px;
  padding-right: 4px;
}
```

As with most tasks in this chapter, not incredibly difficult, but monotonous if you do it enough. With Compass, you can get all of this (and then some) simply by including the horizontal-list mixin:

```
ul.nav { @include horizontal-list }
```

In addition to the CSS in the previous listing, Compass also provides some hooks for styling the first and last list elements specially. Here's the full CSS output.

Listing 4.5   CSS output from Compass horizontal-list helper

```
ul.nav {
  margin: 0;
  padding: 0;
  border: 0;
  overflow: hidden;
  *zoom: 1;
}
```

```
ul.nav li {
  list-style-image: none;
  list-style-type: none;
  margin-left: 0px;
  white-space: nowrap;
  display: inline;
  float: left;
  padding-left: 4px;
  padding-right: 4px;
}
ul.nav li:first-child, ul.nav li.first {
  padding-left: 0;
}
ul.nav li:last-child {
  padding-right: 0;
}
ul.nav li.last {
  padding-right: 0;
}
```

.first for older browsers

.last for older browsers

For browsers that support `:first-child` and `:last-child`, we can omit the padding on the outside-facing edge of those elements. For older browsers, we can use the `.first` and `.last` class names.

Up until now, you may not have seen the point of this mixin (other than saving a lot of typing). As with most things Compass, the real power comes in leveraging the dynamic nature of Sass that powers this mixin. The `horizontal-list` mixin takes two arguments—a `$padding` value, and a `$direction`. Since these are optional, you can omit them and get a left-to-right, eight-pixels-between-elements list. (The actual default `$padding` is 4px. Four pixels on the right plus four pixels on the left equals eight pixels between items.) What if you want to reverse the item order and widen the space between list items? It's as simple as supplying these two arguments to the mixin:

```
ul.nav { @include horizontal-list(7px, right)}
```

Now, items have seven pixels on either side (for a 14-pixel split) and are floated right, reversing the list item order. Here's the updated CSS of the relevant portion of the previous listing:

```
...

ul.nav li {
  ...
  float: right;
  padding-left: 7px;
  padding-right: 7px;
}
```

As you can see, Compass reduces horizontal navigation lists to a single line of code, but can it handle inline lists?

INLINING WITH INLINE-LIST

In an earlier section, you saw how to make links look like text. What if you want to do the same thing with lists? Consider the following example:

```
<ul class="giant-words">
  <li>Fee</li>
  <li>Fi</li>
  <li>Fo</li>
  <li>Fum</li>
</ul>
<p>are some words of giants with acute senses of smell
for Englishmen.</p>
```

This (contrived) example would read better if you could style the items as an inline list, separated by a comma (see figure 4.3). Compass makes it easy with its one-line-of-code approach:

```
ul.words { @include delimited-list }
```

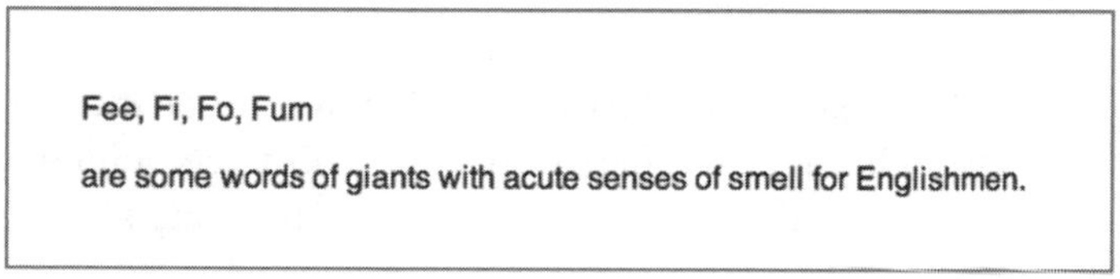

Figure 4.3   Example of a delimited list

Using a combination of :after and :last-child (to opt out of the trailing comma for the last item), Compass uses CSS to present the list as inline copy.

But wait, there's more! Since Compass also lets you supply the separator, you can make your list more intimidating:

```
ul.words { @include delimited-list("! ") }
```

That's a quick survey of Compass's list-styling prowess. In the next section, we'll look at how it can help bend stray text to your will.

4.2.3   Taming text with helpers

Unlike their print design counterparts, web designers spend a lot more time accommodating copy they didn't write and may never see. Design templates are fused with user-supplied, data-driven content that can often spill out of the intended container. Fortunately, Compass includes a few helpers to make working with text easier.

LEAVE THEM HANGING WITH ELLIPSIS...

A common problem web designers face is placing an unknown amount of text into a fixed-width container, such as cells within a table. In the past, designers have truncated content on the server before it's rendered as markup. With CSS, you can apply text-overflow: ellipsis:

```
td.dot-dot-dot {
  white-space: nowrap;
```

```
    overflow: hidden;
    text-overflow: ellipsis;
}
```

Now text that normally would wrap or spill out of its container will be truncated and an ellipsis will be appended. As you'd expect, Compass makes this even easier:

```
td.dot-dot-dot {
  @include ellipsis;
}
```

The added benefit of using the ellipsis mixin is the vendor-namespaced support for Opera and Microsoft browsers. Here's the full CSS output:

```
td.dot-dot-dot {
  white-space: nowrap;
  overflow: hidden;
  -o-text-overflow: ellipsis;
  -ms-text-overflow: ellipsis;
  text-overflow: ellipsis;
}
```

It's important to note that for text-overflow to take effect, it must be used in tandem with white-space: nowrap. Often, developers find it difficult to remember whether it's white-space or whitespace. Thankfully, Compass has your back, as you'll see in the next section.

PREVENT TEXT WRAP WITH NOWRAP

The nowrap mixin is nice and simple, and produces the following CSS:

```
td { white-space: nowrap}
```

It's simply called with the following:

```
td { @include nowrap }
```

Billed as a way to not have to remember that white-space does indeed contain a hyphen, it unfortunately can't help you if you read it (as many often do) as "now rap."

Now let's look at one more common task when dealing with text in web design—removing it altogether in favor of an image representation.

SWAP TEXT FOR IMAGES USING REPLACE-TEXT

Despite the best efforts of new features such as @font-face, Cufón, and other techniques, sometimes designers must resort to a traditional method to improve web typography—swapping text for an image representation. Often used for headlines and other core page elements, images can deliver complex design elements that sometimes you can't pull off with standard type. In those situations, many designers have felt the urge to plop an <img> tag on the page in place of the text and call it a day. For accessibility (and SEO) reasons, a much better approach is to handle this in CSS. Consider the example shown in figure 4.4, in which we'll secretly replace the headline the user is used to seeing with our own special blend of image-powered typographic magic.

Figure 4.4   Coffee text replacement

To achieve this with CSS, you could do something like this:

```
h1.coffee {
  text-indent: -119988px;
  overflow: hidden;
  text-align: left;
  background-image: url('/images/coffee-header.png');
  background-repeat: no-repeat;
  background-position: 50% 50%;
}
```

The first step is to hide the default text by negatively indenting it offscreen. (If you get a monitor that will do 119,988 pixels wide, call us; we want to be your friends.) You then swap out the text with the image using the `background` property. Compass makes this even easier with the `replace-text` mixin:

```
h1.coffee { @include replace-text("coffee-header.png") }
```

You'll notice that you didn't have to supply the `/images` portion of the image path. This is because internally, Compass uses an `image-url` helper which relies on a project's Compass configuration to write out image paths for you. As a result, you only have to supply the image's file name. You can read more about the image helper and other asset helpers in chapter 7.

Compass also supplies a specialized version of the `replace-text` mixin, `replace-text-with-dimensions`, which will set the dimensions of the element according to the height and width of the image passed in.

There you have it: a few handy helpers for dealing with text in Compass. Up next, we'll look at some tricks for handling common layout tasks.

4.3   Layout helpers

Outside of grids, layout patterns tend to be the most specialized parts of stylesheets. Compass does provide a couple of helpers for use with familiar layout scenarios: sticky footer and stretched elements. For the following examples to work, be sure to import the compass layout module with `@import "compass/layout";`.

4.3.1   Sticky footers

Imagine a scenario where you need the footer to fit flush to the bottom of the page. Your first instinct might be to use `position: fixed`. Unfortunately, if you need to support IE6, the CSS isn't this straightforward. Here's one approach, based on a technique developed by Ryan Fait. Consider the following markup.

Listing 4.6   Sticky footer markup

```
<body>
  <div id="content">
    Page content...
    <div id="bump"></div>
  </div>
  <div id="footer">
    Fix me to the bottom of the page.
  </div>
</body>
```

You can craft this into a layout with a sticky footer with the following CSS.

Listing 4.7   Sticky footer CSS

```
html, body {
  height: 100%;                          ←——— Hack for IE6
}

#content {
  clear: both;
  min-height: 100%;
  height: auto !important;
  height: 100%;
  margin-bottom: -40px;
}
#content #bump {
  height: 40px;
}

#footer {                                ←——— The footer
  clear: both;
  position: relative;
  height: 40px;
}
```

In this example, you can fashion a 40-pixel-tall footer, using the `#footer` selector. Setting a minimum height of 100% ensures the content area is at least as tall as the browser's screen height. Unfortunately, you have to use `height: 100%` for the `<html>` and `<body>` tags and `height: auto !important` on the `#content` element as min-height hacks for IE6. The `#bump` element is just an offset to provide enough padding at the end of the `#content` element to accommodate the footer.

Not only is this CSS more extensive than you'd like in order to play nice with IE6, it also falls down in that you have to set three values based on the height of the footer. With Compass, you can knock out the same footer using the `sticky-footer` mixin:

```
@include sticky-footer(40px, "#content", "#footer", "#sticky-footer");
```

Now, if you decide to make your footer taller or shorter, you change it in one spot and the rest of the CSS output falls in line. Now that you've seen how to make a footer stay put, in the next section, we'll look at how to stretch elements inside their parent elements.

4.3.2 *Stretching elements*

Flow layouts are considered one of the core strengths of web user interfaces, and web designers often take them for granted. Those coming from a desktop application background might miss the absolute positioning approach so common in frameworks like .NET WinForms, JavaSwing, Flash, and others. Of course, the web supports this approach via position: absolute:

```
a.login {
  position: absolute;
  top: 5px; right: 5px; bottom: 5px; left: 5px;
}
```

Compass provides a shorthand for this style of layout via the stretch mixin:

```
a.login { @include stretch(5px, 5px, 5px, 5px) }
```

This produces the same CSS as the previous code listing. The stretch mixin takes four arguments: $offset-top, $offset-right, $offset-bottom, and $offset-left. Compass also provides mixins to stretch only on one axis with stretch-x and stretch-y, which take only two arguments, $offset-left and $offset-right, and $offset-top and $offset-bottom, respectively.

4.4 *Summary*

In this chapter, we looked at some Compass time savers that take the monotony out of creating stylesheets. We used targeted resets to clear styles from a subset of elements in scenarios when a global reset is too heavy-handed. You saw how you can style links and lists with ease using mixins like link-colors, hover-link, no-bullets, pretty-bullets, and horizontal-list. We also looked at how Compass provides easy ways to handle text overflow and wrap, layout, colors, and even clearing floats.

In the next chapter, we'll look at some advanced CSS3 features of Compass that make it easier to create otherwise complex user interface themes.

CSS3 with Compass

This chapter covers

- Creating cross-browser CSS3 stylesheets with the Compass CSS3 module
- Supporting some CSS3 features in older versions of Internet Explorer
- Advanced CSS3 techniques with Compass

In the last three chapters, you saw how Compass makes creating stylesheets faster by removing much of the repetition, tedium, and even math from the process. Up until this point, we've focused on CSS techniques that use selectors and properties that have been available for over a decade. In this chapter, we'll look at more advanced approaches on the cutting edge of web design known collectively as CSS3.

5.1 What is CSS3?

CSS3, or *Cascading Stylesheets level 3*, builds upon the previous CSS2 spec. The first draft of what we now refer to as CSS3 first appeared in 1999 and contained more than two dozen modules, or groups of features, in varying states of completion. It's only been in the last couple of years that relatively recent browser support has enabled stylesheet authors to benefit from CSS3. So what does CSS3 give you? Nesting, variables, mixins? Sadly no, you'll need to use Sass for that. CSS3's innovations can be grouped into two main buckets—more powerful selectors for targeting markup elements and extensive new properties to change how those elements look. We'll take a brief look at the new selectors in CSS3 before we spend the rest of the chapter covering many of the new CSS3 properties.

5.1.1 *New properties: vendor prefixes got you down?*

Though we often speak of CSS3 as a well-formed tangible list of features, the truth is that it's a loose collection of CSS improvements in varying degrees of flux, ranging from suggestions to working drafts to recommendations. Since vendors have their own independent release cycles, browsers adopt new features at different rates, often while a proposed enhancement to the spec is under rapid iteration. For this reason, browser vendors often introduce support for new CSS3 properties under *vendor prefixes.* Consider an early example of using the `border-radius` property for native support for those coveted Web 2.0 rounded corners:

```
button, a.button {
  -webkit-border-radius: 5px;
    -moz-border-radius: 5px;
        border-radius: 5px;
}
```

Though the latest versions of popular browsers now support the `border-radius` property without the vendor prefixes, it wasn't always so. Support for rounded corners was introduced in Safari 3.2 using the `-webkit` prefix and in Firefox 3.5 using the `-moz` prefix. This meant that if you wanted to support Safari, Firefox, and Opera, you'd need to use all three properties. This is inconvenient enough when it's a copy-and-paste task in your stylesheet development, but when vendors implement different syntax, using CSS3 properties can become a real headache.

5.1.2 *Compass to the rescue*

As you saw briefly in chapter 1, Compass solves the pain of supporting each vendor namespace by doing the heavy lifting for you. You can now use a standard syntax and let Compass generate all of those CSS prefixes.

Listing 5.1 Faster vendor namespaces with Compass

```
@import "compass/css3";        ◁—❶ Import Compass CSS3 support

.notice {
  @include border-radius(5px);  ◁—❷ Add rounded corners with border-radius
}
```

Just by adding the Compass CSS3 module to your project ❶ and using the `border-radius` mixin ❷, you can quickly generate the CSS to target all modern browsers.

Listing 5.2   CSS output for Compass `border-radius` mixin

```
.notice {
  -moz-border-radius: 5px;
  -webkit-border-radius: 5px;
  -o-border-radius: 5px;
  -ms-border-radius: 5px;
  border-radius: 5px;
}
```

As the code listing indicates, you not only get support for Safari, Chrome, and Firefox, you also can easily target Opera and IE9. Though this is certainly convenient, what if you in your browser snobbery (er, pragmatism) don't wish to include every vendor prefix under the sun? After all, these do add some weight to your stylesheet. Compass provides an easy way to configure which vendor namespaces are created by setting some configuration values provided by the browser support module.

Listing 5.3   Configuring vendor namespaces in Compass

```
@import "compass/css3";

$experimental-support-for-opera: false;
$experimental-support-for-microsoft: false;
$experimental-support-for-khtml: false;

.notice {
  @include border-radius(5px);
}
```

Compass provides a number of configuration settings as experimental-support-for-xxxx-named variables. By overriding the default values for these with `false`, Compass will omit the appropriate vendor-namespaced versions in the CSS output.

In this first section, we've looked at new selectors in CSS3 and how to deal with some of the headaches of using CSS3 properties using Compass. In the rest of this chapter, we'll explore some concrete examples of using CSS3 to create modern design elements and how Compass makes that a snap.

5.2   Using CSS3 with Compass

You've seen how Compass abstracts away the ugliness of dealing with vendor prefixes and CSS3 properties. In this section, we'll survey the rather large CSS3 module in Compass and how to use it to tackle common design tasks with less work.

5.2.1   Rounded corners

Though we're certain no one has ever gotten injured on a sharp corner while reading a web page, designers (as well as managers and clients) love rounded corners. Buttons, tabs, sidebars, and tables aren't exempt from being cut off, sanded down, and smoothed. To this end, designers have resorted to such techniques as using multiple background images or employing extra markup. Thankfully, CSS3 brings some sanity

Figure 5.1 Buttons with rounded corners

back to your designs with the border-radius property. Let's look at the example shown in figure 5.1.

In the figure, we see three buttons (and a sidebar), all with nifty rounded corners. Note that each button has a different degree of roundness, or *border radius*. If you didn't care about Safari 4 and prior, Firefox 3.6 and prior, mobile Safari, or older versions of the Android browser, you could use the border-radius property in CSS3. But since you do care about these browsers, the CSS gets more messy, thanks to vendor namespaces.

Listing 5.4   Rounded corners in CSS

```
button {
  background: red;                          Base styles
  border: 0;                                for all three
  color: #fff;                              buttons
  line-height: 30px;
  width: 100px;
}

button.rounded {                            Firefox < 3.6
  -moz-border-radius: 5px;
  -webkit-border-radius: 5px;               Safari < 5,
}                                           Mobile Safari,
button.really-rounded {                     Android browser
  -moz-border-radius: 10px;
  -webkit-border-radius: 10px;
}
button.extreme-rounded {
  -moz-border-radius: 30px;
  -webkit-border-radius: 30px;
}
```

Since older browsers require vendor namespaces for this feature, you have to include the -moz and -webkit prefixes when using the border-radius property. This sort of tedium makes CSS feel more like a typing test at times than a design tool. Thankfully, Compass has a mixin to help you target multiple browsers when implementing rounded corners. Let's look at how you'd write the previous example using Compass.

Listing 5.5   CSS3 `border-radius` with Compass

```
button {              ◁——❶ Base button styles
  background: red;
  border: 0;
  color: #fff;
  line-height: 30px;
  width: 100px;
}

button.rounded {
  @include border-radius(5px)                    ◁┐
}

button.really-rounded {
  @include border-radius(10px)        ◁——❷ Set border radius
}

button.extreme-rounded {
  @include border-radius(30px)                   ◁┘
}
```

The CSS in this example is easy to follow. You set some base styles for all three buttons ❶ and then set the border radius for each ❷. It should be clear by now from the `@include` directive that `border-radius` in this context is a Sass mixin. You're back to a single line per rule set to round the corners of your buttons. Compass will include the required vendor namespaces (and more, based on the configuration variables discussed in section 5.1) in the CSS output.

Now that you've seen how to round corners in Compass, let's look at another common design element: drop shadows.

5.2.2   *CSS3 shadows*

Shadows are a common technique designers use to add depth to the page. Used subtly, they can add the illusion of texture or a third dimension to your two-dimensional designs, making it seem there's space between an element and the page behind it. Let's look at an example of some CSS3 shadows in figure 5.2.

How many shadows do you see in the figure? If you said two, then look again. You should see three shadows. Two should be obvious: the drop shadow on the first headline and the shadows around the box around the second. Unless you've used this technique before you might've missed the etching around the second headline. Though it's not really a *shadow* in that it conveys reflected light instead of obstructed light, you can still use the same CSS3 properties to achieve these different effects. Let's take a look at the CSS behind the example.

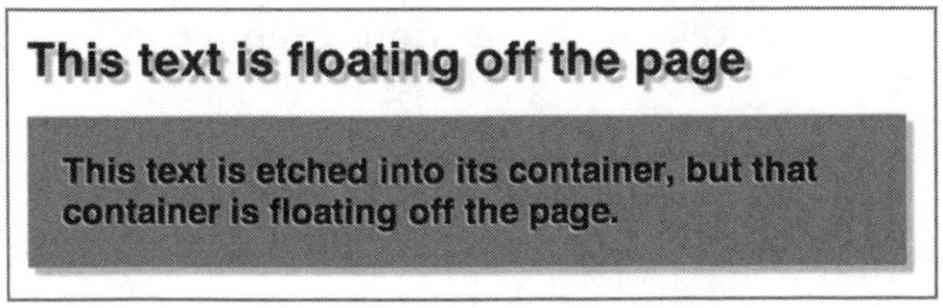

This text is floating off the page

This text is etched into its container, but that container is floating off the page.

Figure 5.2   CSS3 drop shadows

Listing 5.6   Creating shadows with CSS3

```
h1 {
  text-shadow: #cccccc 5px 5px 2px;                    ◁━❶  Text shadow
}

h2 {
  -moz-box-shadow: #cccccc 5px 5px 2px;                ◁━❷  Box shadow
  -webkit-box-shadow: #cccccc 5px 5px 2px;
  box-shadow: #cccccc 5px 5px 2px;
  text-shadow: #dddddd -1px 1px 0;                     ◁━❸  Etched text
  background: #999;
  padding: 1em;
}
```

You achieve the three shadows using CSS3 text-shadow ❶ and box-shadow ❷ for the drop shadows and text-shadow again ❸ for the etched text. If you're spotting the trend in this chapter, then you might guess that Compass provides mixins for box-shadow to save you from typing those vendor namespaces.

Listing 5.7   box-shadow mixin using Compass

```
h2 {
  @include box-shadow(#ccc 5px 5px 2px);
  text-shadow: #ddd -1px 1px 0;
  background: #999;
  padding: 1em;
}
```

Again, Compass abstracts away those pesky vendor namespaces behind a single mixin for box-shadow. You might be surprised to learn that Compass provides a mixin for CSS3 text-shadow even though no browser supports it using a vendor namespace. This is because both the box-shadow and text-shadow Compass mixins let you apply *multiple* shadows to elements. Let's look at an figure 5.3, which shows an example of applying multiple drop shadows using CSS3.

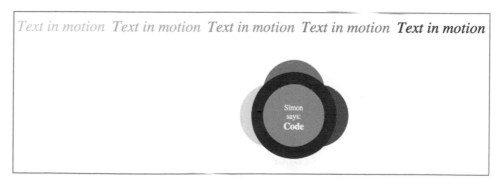

Figure 5.3   Applying multiple shadows to an element in CSS3

In the figure, you see how to apply multiple CSS3 shadows to achieve very different effects. In the first, we've set the text in motion. In the second, we've mocked up the old Simon Says game from the '80s. Let's look at the CSS to pull this off.

Listing 5.8　Applying multiple shadows using CSS3

```
.motion {
  text-shadow:                                    ①  Text in motion
    rgba(0, 0, 0, 0.5) -200px 0 0,
    rgba(0, 0, 0, 0.4) -400px 0 0,
    rgba(0, 0, 0, 0.3) -600px 0 0,
    rgba(0, 0, 0, 0.2) -800px 0 0;
  font-size: 2em;
  font-style: italic;
  text-align: right;
}
.simon {
  -moz-border-radius: 100px;
  -webkit-border-radius: 100px;
  border-radius: 100px;
  -moz-box-shadow:
   black 0 0 0 25px,                              ②  Black ring
    red 0 -50px 0,
    blue 50px 0px 0,                              ③  Colored buttons
    yellow 0 50px 0,
    lime -50px 0 0;
  -webkit-box-shadow:
    black 0 0 0 25px,
    red 0 -50px 0,
    blue 50px 0px 0,
    yellow 0 50px 0,
    lime -50px 0 0;
  box-shadow:
    black 0 0 0 25px,
    red 0 -50px 0,
    blue 50px 0px 0,
    yellow 0 50px 0,
    lime -50px 0 0;
  background: #999;
  color: #fff;
  height: 50px;
  margin: 100px auto;
  padding: 40px;
  text-align: center;
  width: 50px;
}
```

We achieve the text-in-motion effect by applying multiple `text-shadows` ① in graduated levels of opacity and position on the x-axis. For the Simon Says game, we apply a black offset shadow ② using a `spread` value of `25px` for the ring around the center of the game. We then use a series of colored shadows ③ each offset on the x- or y-axis for the buttons. As you'd expect, Compass *DRYs* up this code considerably.

Listing 5.9 Multiple CSS3 shadows with Compass

```
.motion {
  @include text-shadow(
    rgba(#000,.5) -200px 0 0,        ←① Multiple text shadows
    rgba(#000,.4) -400px 0 0,
    rgba(#000,.3) -600px 0 0,
    rgba(#000,.2) -800px 0 0
  );
  font-size: 2em;
  font-style: italic;
  text-align: right;
}

.simon {
  @include border-radius(100px);
  @include box-shadow(               ←② Multiple box shadows
    black 0 0 0 25px,
    red 0 -50px 0,
    blue 50px -0px 0,
    yellow 0 50px 0,
    lime -50px 0 0
  );
  background: #999;
  color: #fff;
  height: 50px;
  margin: 100px auto;
  padding: 40px;
  text-align: center;
  width: 50px;
}
```

The box-shadow ② mixin once again saves us from vendor namespaces. At first glance the text-shadow mixin ① doesn't appear to gain us much, since there are no vendor namespaces to deal with, but you can see the real power of this mixin if we push the example a bit farther.

Listing 5.10 Reusing text shadows with Compass

```
$shadow-1: rgba(#000,.5) -200px 0 0;
$shadow-2: rgba(#000,.4) -400px 0 0;      ←① Define text shadows
$shadow-3: rgba(#000,.3) -600px 0 0;
$shadow-4: rgba(#000,.2) -800px 0 0;
                                           ② Use all
.motion {                                      four
  @include text-shadow($shadow-1, $shadow-2, $shadow-3, $shadow-4);  ←  shadows
  font-size: 2em;
  font-style: italic;
  text-align: right;
}

.skipping {
  @include text-shadow($shadow-2, $shadow-4);   ←③ Use just two shadows
}
```

In this example, again we have two elements that use multiple shadows, but this time, one of the elements only uses two shadows. We can define the shadows once ❶ and then reuse them by passing them to the text-shadow mixin ❷, ❸. The text-shadow mixin gets even more interesting if you're creating shadows programmatically using Sass script and the techniques found in chapter 12.

Though each of the examples so far has shown you how to save time using Compass to create CSS3 shadows, perhaps the biggest time-saving features are setting shadow defaults with each mixin. Let's revisit the first example in the series, the simple text and box shadows as seen in figure 5.1.

Listing 5.11   Using default settings for shadows in Compass

```
$shadow-color: #ccc;                    ⬅—❶ Shared shadow settings
$shadow-h: 5px;
$shadow-v: 5px;
$shadow-blur: 0;

$default-text-shadow-color: $shadow-color;      ⬅—❷ Text defaults
$default-text-shadow-h-offset: $shadow-h;
$default-text-shadow-v-offset: $shadow-v;
$default-text-shadow-blur: $shadow-blur;

$default-box-shadow-color: $shadow-color;       ⬅—❸ Box defaults
$default-box-shadow-h-offset: $shadow-h;
$default-box-shadow-v-offset: $shadow-v;
$default-box-shadow-blur: $shadow-blur;

h1, h2 {font-family: sans-serif;}

h1 {
 @include text-shadow;                  ⬅—❹ Default
}

h2 {
  @include box-shadow;
  @include single-text-shadow(#ddd, -1px, 1px);  ⬅—❺ One-off text shadow
  background: #999;
  padding: 1em;
}
```

In raw lines of code, this refactor doesn't gain much. In fact, it's much longer than our original example. Before you pass judgment, let's walk through it step-by-step. First, we set some shared shadow settings in some Sass variables ❶. We can reuse those to set the Compass defaults for text-shadow ❷ and box-shadow ❸. We can now call these mixins without passing any values ❹. Additionally, we can add another text shadow via the single-text-shadow mixin, passing in the values we want to override ❺.

Granted, for a simple page with only two or three shadows, this is overkill, but consider a large-scale site with dozens of elements that need text or drop shadows with consistent values. Instead of creating special CSS classes, you can set some sensible defaults and get a great deal of reuse in your stylesheets.

Now that you've seen how Compass does text and box shadows, let's look at how it handles something tougher: CSS3 gradients.

5.2.3 Gradients

As you've seen already in our examples using CSS3 border-radius, text-shadow, and box-shadow, vendor namespaces are a pain. You've also seen how Compass saves you the monotony of typing -webkit, -moz, and the rest. With its support for CSS3 gradients, you'll see how Compass not only saves you typing, but saves brain cycles as well. Consider the real-world example shown in figure 5.4.

Figure 5.4   Television test pattern gradient

We've all seen the familiar television test pattern that networks broadcast when they go off air. This pattern is a vertical linear gradient of eight colors, with evenly distributed color stops every 12.5% of the width of the pattern. Let's look at the CSS involved to reconstruct this test pattern for the web.

Listing 5.12   Building the TV test pattern in CSS3

```
#pattern {
  background: -webkit-gradient(            <--❶ Older WebKit
    linear, 360deg, 360deg,
    color-stop(0%, #bfbfbf),
    color-stop(12.5%, #bfbfbf),
    color-stop(12.5%, #bfbf00),
    color-stop(25%, #bfbf00),
    color-stop(25%, #00bfbf),
    color-stop(37.5%, #00bfbf),
    color-stop(37.5%, #bfbf00),
    color-stop(37.5%, #00bf00),
    color-stop(50%, #00bf00),
    color-stop(50%, #bf00bf),
    color-stop(62.5%, #bf00bf),
    color-stop(62.5%, #bf0000),
    color-stop(75%, #bf0000),
    color-stop(75%, #0000bf),
    color-stop(87.5%, #0000bf),
    color-stop(87.5%, #000000),
    color-stop(100%, #000000));
  background: -webkit-linear-gradient(      <--❷ New syntax
    360deg,
    #bfbfbf 0%, #bfbfbf 12.5%,
    #bfbf00 12.5%, #bfbf00 25%,
    #00bfbf 25%, #00bfbf 37.5%,
    #bfbf00 37.5%, #00bf00 37.5%,
    #00bf00 50%, #bf00bf 50%,
    #bf00bf 62.5%, #bf0000 62.5%,
    #bf0000 75%, #0000bf 75%,
    #0000bf 87.5%, #000000 87.5%,
    #000000 100%);
  /* identical -ms, -o, -moz versions snipped /*
```

```
  height: 300px;
  margin: 100px auto;
  width: 400px;
}
```

It sure takes a lot of CSS to make eight vertical stripes, even with omitting the duplicate vendor-namespaced versions from the code listing! This is because linear gradients first came to CSS3 in 2008 with an earlier syntax ❶ adopted by Safari and WebKit-based browsers before the spec was simplified into the newer syntax now supported by the latest versions of almost all browsers ❷. Let's take a look at the same example using Compass.

Listing 5.13   TV test pattern using Compass

```
#pattern {
  @include background(
  linear-gradient(              ⊲—❶ Gradients with the background module
    360deg,
    #bfbfbf 0%,
    #bfbfbf 12.5%,
    #bfbf00 12.5%,
    #bfbf00 25%,
    #00bfbf 25%,
    #00bfbf 37.5%,
    #bfbf00 37.5%,
    #00bf00 37.5%,
    #00bf00 50%,
    #bf00bf 50%,
    #bf00bf 62.5%,
    #bf0000 62.5%,
    #bf0000 75%,
    #0000bf 75%,
    #0000bf 87.5%,
    #000 87.5%,
    #000 100%));
  height: 300px;
  margin: 100px auto;
  width: 400px;
}
```

That's it! Using Compass, you need only four lines in your stylesheet to pull off the same CSS written by hand a moment ago. Using the `background` mixin in the Compass CSS3 module, you can create linear (or radial) gradients using the standard CSS3 syntax ❶ and get vendor-namespaced and older browser syntax versions for free. Not only is this a lot less typing, it's a lot less thinking about syntax, letting you focus on your design.

So far in this chapter, we've looked at how Compass makes working with basic CSS3 features easier and more enjoyable. In the rest of this chapter, we'll dive into some more advanced, less-often-used CSS3 concepts and how Compass supports them.

5.2.4 *Embedding fonts with @font-face*

Think about your favorite magazine, newspaper, or other print publication. Consider how infused typography is with the brand. Great care is taken in choosing (or commissioning) fonts and in using them throughout the design. Unfortunately for web designers, we've been stuck with miserably small selections of fonts that can be depended upon to be installed on users' machines and used in our designs. We're used to defining *font stacks*, or lists of fonts in our order of preference that browsers should use for elements on the page:

```
font-family: Georgia, "Times New Roman", serif;
```

Though the @font-face rule has been around since CSS2, it was initially only supported through a proprietary format in Internet Explorer. Recently though, other browsers have added support for OTF, WOFF, SVG, and TTF so we can now serve up fonts *with* our designs. The trouble is that, just like the other emerging CSS3 modules, browsers still haven't agreed on a single format for web fonts and writing the CSS to support them all is tedious and easy to get wrong. Thankfully, Compass is here to help.

A quick warning: before using just any font with @font-face, be sure and check the license to see whether you have permission to do so. Font Squirrel and Google Web Fonts are great resources to find free, great-looking fonts that you can *legally* embed on your site. After selecting a font, you can download a zip archive with everything you need to serve up the font on your site, including multiple font files to support multiple browsers, as well as a stylesheet with the required CSS3 needed to render the font. For a demonstration, let's look at setting up our page to use Font Squirrel's extra bold ChunkFive for our headlines, as shown in figure 5.5.

Now that you have an idea of the end result, let's look at the CSS3 to make it happen.

This headline is Chunky

Figure 5.5 ChunkFive makes a great headline font

Listing 5.14 CSS3 for ChunkFive headlines

```
@font-face {
  font-family: 'ChunkFiveRegular';
  src: url('Chunkfive-webfont.eot');                          ❶ IE9

  src: url('Chunkfive-webfont.eot?#iefix')                    ❷ IE6-8
       format('embedded-opentype'),

      url('Chunkfive-webfont.woff')                           ❸ Latest browsers
        format('woff'),

      url('Chunkfive-webfont.ttf')          ❹ Safari, mobile browsers
        format('truetype'),

      url('Chunkfive-webfont.svg#ChunkFiveRegular')  ⊲
        format('svg');                                         Older iOS
  font-weight: normal;                                       ❺ browsers
```

```
    font-style: normal;

}

h1,h2,h3,h4,h5,h6 {
    font-family: 'ChunkFiveRegular'
}
```

It seems no slick new CSS feature is without its hacks for Internet Explorer, and @font-face is no different ❶, ❷. But this particular CSS3 feature requires a broad range of font formats to support the most popular browsers ❸, ❹ and older versions of some mobile browsers ❺. Though it's convenient that Font Squirrel provides the CSS along with the font files in their "font kits," the stylesheet assumes that you're serving your fonts from the same folder as your stylesheets. If your fonts are located elsewhere (like an asset host as outlined in chapter 7), you'll need to prepend that path for the url() location of each font in the declaration. Once again, Compass saves your fingers from a lot of typing, allowing you to create the same CSS with less code.

Listing 5.15   Using @font-face with Compass

```
@import "compass";
@include font-face("ChunkFiveRegular",
   font-files( "Chunkfive-webfont.woff", woff,
               "Chunkfive-webfont.ttf", ttf,
               "Chunkfive-webfont.svg", svg),
               "Chunkfive-webfont.eot", normal, normal);
```

Not only is this code more succinct, it's more robust. The font-files helper does a couple of things here. First, it provides a shorthand syntax for creating the url() and format() portions of the rule. Second, and perhaps more important, it builds the url() path based on your Compass configuration settings. This could be /fonts on your local machine while you're developing, or http://assets.example.com/fonts in production. We'll look a bit deeper at this Compass feature in the next chapter.

5.3   *Support for Internet Explorer with CSS PIE*

Many of the features we've discussed in this chapter enjoy broad support in Firefox- and WebKit-based browsers, but most of these CSS3 advancements didn't find support in Internet Explorer until version 8 or later. So what do you do if you need to support IE in an enterprise scenario that's locked into an older version of the browser? Frankly, it's all right to see some rough edges in older browsers, as figure 5.6, captured from dowebsitesneedtolookexactlythesameineverybrowser.com, indicates.

But while it's okay to live with differences, Compass does provide a way to give some love to users who can't let go of their classic browser. *CSS3 Progressive Internet Explorer*, or *CSS3 PIE*, is a project created by Jason Johnston that serves as a polyfill for many CSS3 features for older versions of IE. Using an old, proprietary feature in

Figure 5.6   Do web sites need to look exactly the same in every browser?

Internet Explorer known as an *HTC behavior,* PIE provides full or partial support for a number of CSS3 features, including these:

- Border-radius
- Box-shadow
- Border-image
- Multiple background images
- Linear-gradient background images

Let's take another look at a couple of CSS3 projects we discussed in section 5.2 and see how we could support rounded corners and linear gradients in older versions of Internet Explorer using PIE. Look at the buttons in figure 5.7.

As we saw earlier in the chapter, the cross-browser CSS for these buttons is simple but verbose.

Figure 5.7   Simple rounded corners and background gradients for buttons

Listing 5.16 Rounded corners and gradients using CSS3

```
.rounded {                              ◁── CSS3 rounded corners
  -moz-border-radius: 20px;
  -webkit-border-radius: 20px;
  -o-border-radius: 20px;
  -ms-border-radius: 20px;
  border-radius: 20px;
}

.gradient {                             ◁── CSS3 linear gradients
  background: -webkit-gradient(
    linear, 50% 0%, 50% 100%,
    color-stop(0%, #aaaaaa),
    color-stop(100%, #333333));
  background: -webkit-linear-gradient(#aaaaaa, #333333);
  background: -moz-linear-gradient(#aaaaaa, #333333);
  background: -o-linear-gradient(#aaaaaa, #333333);
  background: -ms-linear-gradient(#aaaaaa, #333333);
  -pie-background: linear-gradient(#aaaaaa, #333333);
  background: linear-gradient(#aaaaaa, #333333);
}
```

According to the PIE documentation, to extend your support for older IE, you need to make a few modifications. First, you need to download and add the HTC component to your website. See the PIE website for complete installation instructions, but for now let's assume you'll serve this file out of /stylesheets/PIE.htc. Next, you need to add some additional rules to your stylesheet.

Listing 5.17 Rounded corners and gradients with CSS3 PIE

```
.rounded, .gradient {                   ◁─❶ Apply the PIE behavior
  behavior: url("/stylesheets/PIE.htc");
  position: relative;
}

...

.gradient {
  background: -webkit-gradient(linear, 50% 0%, 50% 100%,
                               color-stop(0%, #aaaaaa),
                               color-stop(100%, #333333));
  background: -webkit-linear-gradient(#aaaaaa, #333333);
  background: -moz-linear-gradient(#aaaaaa, #333333);
  background: -o-linear-gradient(#aaaaaa, #333333);
  background: -ms-linear-gradient(#aaaaaa, #333333);
  -pie-background: linear-gradient(#aaaaaa, #333333);
  background: linear-gradient(#aaaaaa, #333333);
}
```

For PIE to jump into action, you need to apply it to the elements that need it ❶, along with position: relative to fix a bug in IE. Next, for your gradient, you have to use a nonstandard CSS property of -pie-background to tell PIE to add a gradient background to your button.

As you might expect, all of this is even easier with Compass, including installation. You can add the required PIE assets to your project and unfurl a well-documented example stylesheet right from the command line:

```
compass install compass/pie
```

With the PIE stylesheet and HTC component in place, you can now create the CSS in the previous listing with just a little Sass, using the Compass PIE mixins.

Listing 5.18 Using Compass PIE

```
@import "compass/css3/pie";                          ←—❶ Import PIE

.pie-element {
  // relative is the default, so passing relative
  // is redundant, but we do it here for clarity.
  @include pie-element(relative);
}

.rounded {
  @include pie;                      ←—❷ Extend pie-element class
  @include border-radius(20px);
}

.gradient {
  @include pie;
  @include background(linear-gradient(#aaa, #333));
}
```

That's it! You import the Compass PIE module ❶ and apply it to your buttons ❶. The rest of the CSS is the Compass CSS3 support we looked at earlier. It's clear that PIE is sweeter with Compass.

5.4   *Summary*

In this chapter, we looked at how Compass makes CSS3 quicker to write and more enjoyable to use. You saw practical ways to round corners, create drop shadows, apply gradients, and refresh your typography using Compass CSS3 mixins, all without writing a single vendor namespace. We explored how to target specific browsers using configuration properties as well as older versions of Internet Explorer using CSS3 PIE.

In the next chapter, we'll look at how Compass can increase site performance by replacing individual background images with automatically generated image sprites.

Part 3

Tuning for production

In the first two sections of this book, you've been introduced to Sass and Compass and looked at many practical ways they can transform your stylesheet authoring workflow. In chapter 6, we go deeper down the rabbit hole and explore the magic of spriting with Compass. We cover the reasons for using CSS sprites and take a look at simple and advanced use cases for spriting. You'll see how Compass completely automates the spriting process, from combining and measuring your images to writing your CSS. You'll also learn how to configure layout, spacing, position, class names, and more.

In chapter 7, you'll learn how Compass makes it easy to move from a locally developed prototype to a production website or web application. We discuss how to use Compass's asset helpers to make it easy to update all the URLs in your stylesheets with a simple configuration change. You'll see how Compass warns you when it can't find images referenced by your stylesheets, helping you avoid broken image links. We discuss approaches for designing in the browser and look at how to prepare your stylesheets for deploying to production.

Chapter 8 helps you get the best performance out of your stylesheets. You'll learn about stylesheet concatenation with @import, and how to use Compass's built-in stylesheet compression and configure it to use gzip compression to reduce download time. You'll learn how to use Compass's support for asset hosts to distribute downloads across different servers, and about Compass's inline image and font support for reducing HTTP requests. Finally, we cover selector performance and weigh the performance cost of over-nesting selectors in Sass.

By the end of this part, you'll have the big, end-to-end picture of how Sass and Compass fit into your web development workflow. You'll know how to smoothly move from a local development environment to a production web server and you'll be confident that you can squeeze the best performance out of your stylesheets. In the next section, we look at some more advanced features of Sass, and then we bring it all together by writing a Compass extension and sharing our stylesheets as an open source project.

Spriting

6

This chapter covers

- The history of and basic principles behind CSS spriting
- Automatic spriting with Compass mixins
- Advanced techniques for customizing sprite images and CSS output

In this chapter, we'll look at the purpose of CSS spriting, the challenges involved, and how Compass saves you from one of the most tedious jobs in web design.

If you've ever manually created your own sprites before, you're in for a treat! Spriting with Compass is remarkably easy. Compass creates the sprite maps, writes the CSS you don't want to write, and integrates smoothly into your stylesheet workflow. But this is just the beginning. Even when you need more control over how Compass creates sprite maps and generates CSS, the process is still incredibly simple.

In this chapter, we'll do an in-depth walk-through of a new Compass project, so if you haven't installed Compass on your computer yet, see appendix B for help.

6.1   *How do CSS sprites work?*

In the early days, CSS sprites were very simple. Designers would create images for the different states of a button and put them together as a single image, as shown in figure 6.1.

Then in CSS, they would set the height, width, and background image properties for the button, changing the background position for each state.

Figure 6.1   Example of a simple sprite map

Listing 6.1   CSS for simple sprites

```
.go-button {
  width: 75px; height: 45px;
  background: url('images/sprite-button-usage.png') top left;
}
.go-button:hover { background-position: center; }
.go-button:active { background-position: right; }
```

The dimensions of the button are smaller than the size of the sprite map, creating a viewport through which sections of the image are visible. When a user hovers or clicks, the background position changes and the viewport displays the next graphic (see figure 6.2).

Figure 6.2   CSS creates a viewport

This is a simple example of what CSS sprites looked like in the early days. Here in the enlightened future, we can create beautiful button styles in CSS3, and we don't really use sprites this way anymore.

When this technique was first becoming popular, most articles pitched it as a way to get rid of the annoying flicker when the browser went to fetch another image—as if that was the extent of it. But really, the flicker was just a visible pointer to one of the most critical performance issues on the web, and spriting needed to evolve to adequately address the real problem at hand.

6.2   *Why is spriting necessary?*

From the button sprite example, you've seen how spriting can combine three different button graphics into a single image while maintaining the same appearance. If you take this technique to the next level, you could build one giant sprite containing nearly every background image on your site, like in figure 6.3.

But why do this? Every image needs to be measured, and its position in the sprite map needs to be recorded in your stylesheets. Maintenance across redesigns is tedious work and requires a great deal of effort.

Figure 6.3   A more modern sprite map

If the problem being addressed is speedier downloads, why not just use really good image compression? Though that will help a bit, believe it or not, file size is only part of the problem. Sure, each file would load faster if you compressed them really well, but to understand what problems are solved by using sprites, you need to look at what your web browser has to do for each image it downloads.

6.2.1 The fewer HTTP requests, the better

When building a website locally on your own computers, your browser usually requests files directly from the hard drive, or from a web server running locally on your computer. In either scenario, you're experiencing nearly instant transfer of files and you won't see the pain of establishing network connections with a remote server and downloading files.

Every time your browser wants to download a file from a server, it has to go through a series of steps. Here's what that looks like in its simplest form:

1 *Browser*—Asks the server to open a socket for transfer
2 *Server*—Processes the request and responds
3 *Browser*—Acknowledges the server's response
4 *Browser*—Requests data from the server
5 *Server*—Processes the request
6 *Server*—Looks for the file
7 *Server*—Initiates the file transfer
8 *Browser*—Accepts the file transfer

Before your browser can get even a single bye of data, it has to go through all of this back-and-forth with the server. Even with small, properly compressed images, the time it takes to download the file may be a fraction of the time spent on the network overhead just to begin the download. More modern browsers try to download several files concurrently in an effort to avoid having to reestablish a connection for each file. But even then, this process can be significantly delayed by network congestion or high latency connections like cellular networks. Tally up all of the JavaScript, CSS files, and images a website requires, and it's easy to see how this could add up quickly.

This isn't only an issue for browsers. Web servers have to do a lot of work to process and answer these requests. Popular websites may process millions of requests every second. This means that your first request and your last request may be separated by hundreds of thousands of requests from other users, significantly delaying page load times. Each additional request puts more strain on a web server, reducing site performance and increasing operating costs.

Using CSS sprites is one way to significantly reduce the strain on a web server. It isn't just a good idea; it's a best practice and a necessary step for high-traffic websites. But what about the effort? Surely it takes a lot of work to combine images of different dimensions and maintain their positions in CSS!

6.2.2 *The soul-crushing tedium of doing it manually*

We're not going to lie to you. If you have to manually create and maintain large sprite maps and their corresponding stylesheets, you'll probably lose your mind. Okay, maybe that's a bit extreme, but at the least you'd probably rather do your taxes.

Sure, spriting images can seriously improve loading time for a website, but every time you change an image, you have to update the sprite map. If you need to change the dimensions of an image, that'll change the position of lots of other images, forcing you to move everything around, measure each image again, and update your stylesheets.

Clearly this is one of the more tedious jobs web designers and developers can be expected to do. As a result, many have refused to "eat their vegetables" and large-scale spriting has primarily been adopted out of necessity on websites with extremely high traffic, like Amazon.com (see figure 6.4).

What if this was easier? If someone would just melt some cheese on these vegetables, we'd all benefit from faster, more efficient websites.

When we consider this, measuring, combining, and compressing images and spitting out stylesheets is precisely the kind of work that automated software should handle. As it turns out, this has been a pretty popular problem to solve over the past several years.

With a simple web search, you can find lots of different spriting tools, ranging from command-line applications to browser-based web applications. Each tool offers different features and various levels of automation. Some of these are very nice, but they lack one critical feature: workflow integration. This is one area where the Compass solution is unbeatable.

Figure 6.4   A sprite map from Amazon.com

6.2.3 *The Compass solution*

Since Compass is already integrated into your stylesheet authoring workflow, it's ideally suited to generate CSS sprites. As you'll see in chapter 7, Compass has a configuration file that tells it where your site's images are located, and because it's generating your CSS, it's ideally suited to automate the spriting process.

This is what it's like when Compass generates your CSS sprites:

1 Point Compass to a folder of images to sprite.
2 Tell Compass to write the CSS for your sprites.
3 Compile your stylesheets.

With two lines of Sass, you can tell Compass to combine every image in a directory, measure each image, and write out the background positions under class names generated from each image's filename. When you make a change to an image, Compass will automatically update your stylesheets, generating a new sprite and updating background positions wherever necessary. This is as close to magic as it gets!

6.3 *Spriting with Compass*

In this section, we'll walk through a simple Compass spriting project. In the example code there's a starting-point project you can use to follow along. The project already has everything you'll need, including some icons from the free IcoMoon icon set (https://github.com/Keyamoon/IcoMoon-limited-) and the Compass logo. Figure 6.5 shows what we're starting with.

We use PNGs because at this time Compass can only generate sprites with PNG files. This shouldn't be a problem since PNG is an ideal image format for the types of images that need to be sprited. Now let's see what it takes to convert these into a sprite map.

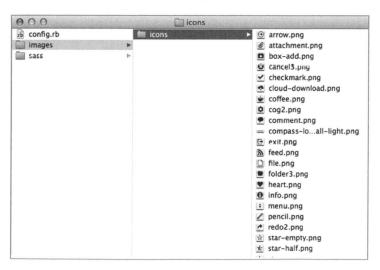

Figure 6.5 Example project setup

6.3.1   *Creating a sprite map*

To convert your folder of images into a sprite map, open up screen.scss and add the following.

Listing 6.2   Generating a sprite map with Compass

```
@import "compass/utilities/sprites";
@import "icons/*.png";
```

First, you import the Compass sprite module. Then, using a sprite import, you tell Compass to generate a sprite map from all of the PNGs in the images/icons/ directory. This will create an image with a name like icons-s0cad3f8f97.png in your images directory (see figure 6.6).

Figure 6.6   Generated sprite map (cropped)

By default, sprites are laid out vertically. Later on, we'll look at how to adjust sprite layout, spacing, and other settings for each sprite individually or for the entire sprite map. But first, let's look at how Compass generates spriting CSS.

6.3.2   *Generating spriting CSS*

Compass has two handy mixins that can automatically generate spriting CSS for you.

Listing 6.3   Sprite mixins

```
@include all-<map>-sprites;
@include <map>-sprite($name);
```

The <map> part is a placeholder and should be replaced with the name of the folder containing your sprite images. In this case, it would be icons. The *all-sprites* mixin will write all the necessary CSS for the entire sprite map, whereas the second mixin will output CSS for a single named sprite. Both of these mixins are created by the sprite import, and therefore they can only be used after the import.

We'll take a look at how these two mixins work. You can follow along with the code examples in all-sprites-mixin and single-sprite-mixin in the automatic-sprites directory.

THE ALL-SPRITES MIXIN

Let's take a look at what it's like to have Compass generate all the sprite CSS for you. Look in the example code under automatic-sprites/all-sprites-mixin to follow along.

Listing 6.4   Generating a sprite map with Compass

```
@import "compass/utilities/sprites";
@import "icons/*.png";
@include all-icons-sprites;
```

The `all-icons-sprites` mixin will write out the necessary CSS for every sprite in the sprite map.

Listing 6.5   Generated sprite CSS (shortened)

```
.icons-sprite,
.icons-arrow,
.icons-attachment,
.icons-box-add, ... {
  background: url('/images/icons-s0cad3f8f97.png') no-repeat;
}

.icons-arrow { background-position: 0 0; }
.icons-attachment { background-position: -16px -96px; }
.icons-box-add { background-position: 0 -64px; }
...
```

We've shortened the preceding CSS output to save space in this book, but it goes on for 91 lines. *Ugh.* Now, let's go over what this mixin has generated:

1 It created a base class `icons-sprite` for styling all sprites from images/icons/.
2 It created classes for each sprite using its directory and filename.
3 It added a background image for all sprites.
4 It added the background position for each sprite.

By default, Compass doesn't set the width or height for these elements. Compass can generate sprite dimension styles automatically (and you'll see how in a bit), but this isn't always desired.

To use this CSS in a project, you could add these sprite classes to your HTML markup, or you might prefer to use @extend (covered in chapter 2) to inherit properties from the sprite classes.

Listing 6.6   Using @extend to inherit sprite styles

```
.add-button { @extend .icons-box-add; }
```

If you decide to create more than one sprite map, you can add images to another directory, import them, include the all-sprites mixin, and you're done.

THE SINGLE-SPRITE MIXIN

This mixin will let you output the sprite CSS for each individual sprite. Look in the example code under `automatic-sprites/single-sprite-mixin` to follow along.

Listing 6.7   Using the single-sprite mixin

```
@import "compass/utilities/sprites";
@import "icons/*.png";

.add-button {
    @include icons-sprite(box-add);
}
```

This will only output the CSS necessary to style this element.

Listing 6.8   Generated single-sprite CSS

```
.icons-sprite,
.add-button {
  background: url('/images/icons-s0cad3f8f97.png') no-repeat;
}

.add-button { background-position: 0 -358px; }
```

With the single-sprite mixin, it's not necessary to generate a class name for the sprite styles because it's included inside of a selector. Compass uses that selector, in this case `.add-button`, when it adds styles for `background-image` and `background-position`. Whereas the all-sprites mixin is nice and easy, this approach generates less CSS and gives you more control of your output.

It's a nice start, but sometimes you need even more control of the spriting process. Next, you'll see how Compass gives you the control you need without making you do all the work.

6.4   *Configuring Compass sprites*

Even for advanced users, Compass still manages to make spriting delightfully simple. Remember that special sprite import? It does much more than generate a sprite image. When Compass evaluates this special import, it first checks for a list of configuration variables that you can use to influence how the sprite images and CSS are generated. The sprite import also creates several other mixins and functions for tweaking your sprites in Sass.

Compass uses the name of the folder containing the imported images to name these configuration variables, mixins, and functions. In the preceding example, you imported sprites from a folder named *icons*, which is where the `all-icons-sprites` mixin got its name. If you import sprites from nested folders, Compass uses the name of the last folder, the one containing the images. So `@import "sprites/social/ *.png";` would use the name *social* in its variables, mixins, and functions. This feature makes it easy to work with multiple sprite maps without naming conflicts.

6.4.1   *Customizing the sprite map*

You can customize a sprite map or its sprites individually by setting their configuration variables. Variables affecting the whole sprite map begin with the map name, whereas variables for changing an individual sprite use the map name followed by the file name for that sprite.

Listing 6.9   Variable naming scheme

```
$<map>-<property>: setting;
$<map>-<sprite>-<property>: setting;
```

In our example project, the sprite folder name is *icons*, so the variable for the changing spacing would be `$icons-spacing`. So in order to set the spacing variable for `icons/attachment.png`, you'd assign a value to `$icons-attachment-spacing`.

Remember, these variables must be defined before the sprite import or they won't take effect. Check out the configuring-automatic-sprites folder to find code examples for the following sprite configurations.

CONFIGURE SPRITE SPACING

Compass allows you to surround your sprites with padding by configuring the sprite spacing variables:

```
$<map>-spacing: 0px;
$<map>-<sprite>-spacing: 0px;
```

This defaults to `0px`, meaning each sprite is placed into the sprite map without any padding. Set this variable to add pixels of transparent space surrounding each sprite in the sprite map, or assign it to sprites individually. This example code can be found under configuring-automatic-sprites/spacing.

Listing 6.10   Configure sprite spacing

```
$icons-spacing: 4px;
$icons-arrow-spacing: 12px;
```

This is how you'd add 4 pixels of transparent space around each sprite in the icons sprite map and 12 pixels of spacing around the arrow sprite. Figure 6.7 shows how this changes your sprite map.

Spacing is especially useful in a design where small sprites are used as a background for larger elements. Without added spacing, adjacent sprites would show through.

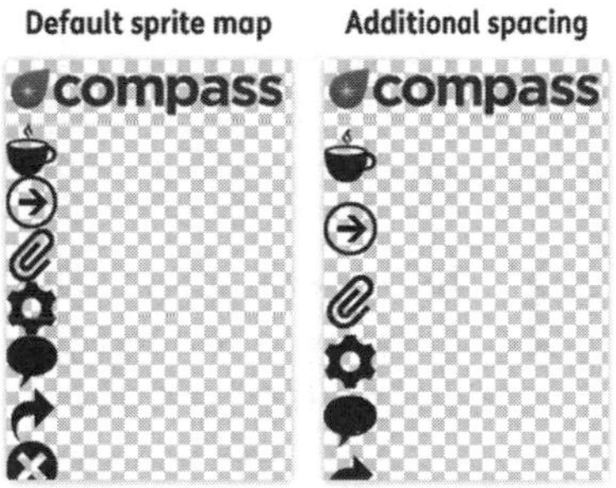

CONFIGURE SPRITE REPEAT

In some cases it may be helpful to have a sprite image repeat horizontally across the sprite map. For that, you can set the sprite repeat variables:

Figure 6.7   Sprite map spacing comparison

```
$<map>-repeat: no-repeat/repeat-x;
$<map>-<sprite>-repeat: no-repeat/repeat-x;
```

This defaults to `no-repeat`, but you can change it to `repeat-x` to make sprites repeat across the entire x-axis of the sprite map. This setting can be applied to the whole sprite map or an individual sprite. This example code can be found under configuring-automatic-sprites/repeat.

Listing 6.11   Configure sprite repeat

```
$icons-arrow-repeat: repeat-x;
```

This will cause the arrow icon to repeat for the entire width of
the image. By looking at the sprite map in figure 6.8, you can
see how the arrow icon repeats all the way across the sprite map
until it fits beneath the wide compass logo.

   At the time of publication, Compass doesn't yet support
repeating images across the y-axis.

   Next we'll look at how to configure the offset position

CONFIGURE SPRITE POSITION

Occasionally, it might be helpful to shift a sprite image's position. Compass allows you to move sprites horizontally by setting
the position variables:

**Figure 6.8   Repeating
arrow icon**

```
$<map>-position: 0px;
$<map>-<sprite>-position: 0px;
```

This variable adjusts the horizontal positioning of sprites in the sprite map. It defaults
to 0px, meaning that each sprite is aligned to the left. This value can be a percentage
or a pixel value. An example of the following configuration can be found in configur-
ing-automatic-sprites/position.

Listing 6.12   Configure sprite position

```
$icons-position: 4px;
$icons-arrow-position: 100%;
```

In this example, each sprite in the icons sprite map will be shifted
four pixels to the right, and the arrow sprite will be placed all the
way to the right, as in figure 6.9.

   Next, we'll cover ways to change the layout of the sprite map as
a whole.

CONFIGURE SPRITE MAP LAYOUT

Compass has several different sprite layouts to choose from:

```
$<map>-layout: vertical/horizontal/diagonal/smart;
```

**Figure 6.9   Sprite
positioning
example**

The default layout is vertical and affects the sprite map as a
whole, telling Compass how to arrange all of the sprites. In most
cases, you'll probably want to set this to smart, which tells Compass
to position sprites with the least amount of empty space. The following code example
is in configuring-automatic-sprites/layout.

Listing 6.13   Smart sprite layout

```
$icons-layout: smart;
```

If you used the smart layout in the example project from earlier, the sprite map would look like figure 6.10.

The position and repeat configurations will only apply to sprite maps with a vertical or horizontal layout. With a smart or diagonal layout, position and repeat will have no effect.

Next, we'll look at how to prevent Compass from removing out-of-date sprite maps.

Figure 6.10   Sprite map with smart layout

CLEAN UP OLD SPRITE MAPS

Whenever images are added, removed, or changed, new sprite maps are generated. Compass can automatically remove old sprite maps for you, or you can keep them around:

```
$<map>-clean-up: true/false;
```

By default, Compass automatically removes old sprite maps when new ones are generated. This keeps your hard drives from filling up with files you're not using anymore, and ensures that you never have to wonder which file your stylesheets are using. If you prefer to manually remove old sprite maps, you can set this to `false` instead.

Up to this point, we've looked at ways to modify the way Compass generates the sprite map. Next, we'll look at how to customize the CSS that Compass writes.

6.4.2   Customizing the sprite CSS

You've seen how simple it is to change the way Compass places sprites in the sprite map. Though these changes to the sprite map will necessarily affect the CSS generated by Compass, there are also ways you can directly customize the generated CSS.

OUTPUT SPRITE DIMENSIONS

If you want to assign dimensions to a specific sprite, you can use the sprite dimension helpers:

```
<map>-sprite-height($name)
<map>-sprite-width($name)
```

These are two functions that tell Compass to measure the size of the original sprite image and output its dimensions so you can use them in your stylesheets. Using these helper functions, you can set the width and height properties for an individual sprite. The following code example is in configuring-automatic-sprites/dimensions.

Listing 6.14   Include sprite dimensions

```
@import "icons/*.png";
.next {
  @include icons-sprite(arrow);
  width: icons-sprite-width(arrow);
  height: icons-sprite-height(arrow);
}

.add-button {
  @include icons-sprite(box-add);
}
```

Alternatively, if you wanted to automatically set the dimensions for every sprite in the sprite map, you could set a configuration variable for that sprite map:

```
$<map>-sprite-dimensions: true/false;
```

This configuration defaults to `false`, but setting it to `true` will measure each sprite image and assign the width and height to its sprite class.

Listing 6.15   Include sprite dimensions

```
$icons-sprite-dimensions: true;
@import "icons/*.png";
.next { @include icons-sprite(arrow); }
```

The resulting CSS would look like the following listing.

Listing 6.16   Generated CSS with sprite dimensions

```
.next {
  background-position: 0 -70px;
  width: 32px;
  height: 32px;
}
.add-button {
  background-position: 0 -358px;
  width: 32px;
  height: 32px;
}
```

Automatically generating sprite dimensions is really nice compared to the tedium of doing it manually. But if all of your icons are the same size, writing dimensions for each sprite would unnecessarily bloat your CSS. Instead, it would be better to manually set the dimensions on the sprite map's base class.

SPRITE BASE CLASS

Compass makes it easy to apply common styles to each of your sprites by generating a base class. You can choose your own class name by setting the base class variable:

```
$<map>-sprite-base-class: ".class-name";
```

When you use the all-sprites or single-sprite mixins, Compass outputs a sprite base class, followed by a chain of sprite selectors when setting the `background-image` property base class to the selector chain. The base class for each sprite map is chosen by the name of the folder. If the sprite folder is named *icons*, the sprite map's base class would be `.icons-sprites`. Let's take a look at how you'd change it. (This example is in configuring-automatic-sprites/base-class.)

Listing 6.17   Change the sprite's CSS base class

```
$icons-sprite-base-class: ".spritey-mcspriterson";
@import "icons/*.png";

.spritey-mcspriterson {
```

```
  overflow: hidden;
}
.next {
  @include icons-sprite(arrow);
}
```

Each sprite class extends the base class, so any styles you add to the base class will also affect each of your sprites.

Listing 6.18 Generated CSS with custom base class

```
.spritey-mcspriterson,
.next {
  background: url('/images/icons-s0cad3f8f97.png') no-repeat;
}
.spritey-mcspriterson, .next {
  overflow: hidden;
}
.next {
  background-position: 0 -70px;
}
```

Keep in mind that this will only change the base class in the CSS output. Variable names, functions, and mixins remain the same, deriving their names from the sprite map's folder.

MAGIC SPRITE SELECTORS

Compass can automatically generate sprite CSS with pseudo selectors, but you can disable that if necessary:

```
$disable-magic-sprite-selectors: true/false;
```

Magic sprite selectors are enabled by default, meaning Compass will automatically output CSS :hover, :active, and :target pseudo selectors for sprites with names ending in *_hover*, *_active*, or *_target*. The code for this section is in configuring-automatic-sprites/magic-selectors.

For example, if you want to have a different sprite for normal and hover states, you add arrow.png and arrow_hover.png to your sprite folder, and Compass will generate CSS sprite backgrounds for the hover pseudo class.

Listing 6.19 Generated CSS with magic pseudo selectors

```
.next {
  background-position: -32px 0;
}
.next:hover, .next.arrow-hover {
  background-position: -48px -96px;
}
```

If magic pseudo selectors interfere with the image-naming scheme you've chosen, set this configuration to true to disable this feature for all sprite maps.

6.5   *Mastering the magic with sprite helpers*

So far, we've looked at tools to automatically generate sprite maps and CSS, as well as some options for customizing their output. In most cases, those magical mixins will be all you need. But occasionally, you might want to slip behind the curtain and run the show yourself.

To perform its spriting feats, Compass relies on a number of helper functions. By wielding these directly, you'll have more flexibility and greater control over the spriting process.

6.5.1   *Creating sprite maps*

As we looked at earlier, creating a sprite map with the special sprite import, such as @import "icons/*.png"; doesn't just create a sprite map; it sets up mixins and variables for the sprite map and each of its sprites. If you're using sprite helpers, you won't use those variables or mixins, which makes the sprite import overkill. Instead, you'll use the sprite-map helper. See manual-sprites/sprite-helper for the code in this example:

```
sprite-map($glob, ...)
```

This helper accepts a glob, like "icons/*.png", and optional keyword arguments for configuring the sprite map or individual sprites. Here are a couple of examples.

Listing 6.20   `sprite-map` helper

```
$icons: sprite-map("icons/*.png", $layout: smart);
```

This will create a sprite map with a smart layout and assign the sprite map's image URL to the $icons variable. We'll use this variable later to generate CSS with other helpers, which we'll cover in a bit.

Listing 6.21   `sprite-map` helper—configuring an individual sprite

```
$icons: sprite-map("icons/*.png", $arrow-spacing: 5px);
```

Any property of the sprite map or properties of individual sprites can be configured like this. Simply use configuration variables we covered earlier without the <map> namespacing. To configure repeat, instead of $<map>-repeat, you'd use $repeat; or, instead of $<map>-<sprite>-repeat, you'd use $arrow-repeat, where *arrow* is the name of the sprite image you're configuring.

6.5.2   *Writing sprite CSS*

After Compass generates the sprite map for you, you still need to write out the CSS for each sprite. To do that, you'll turn to a few helpers and mixins.

THE SPRITE HELPER

The sprite helper makes writing sprite CSS simple:

```
sprite($map, $sprite, [$offset-x], [$offset-y])
```

The `sprite` helper requires the sprite map, the name of the sprite image, and option-ally accepts offset coordinates.

Listing 6.22 `sprite` helper

```
$icons: sprite-map("icons/*.png");
.next {
  background: sprite($icons, arrow) no-repeat;
}
.add-button {
  background: sprite($icons, box-add) no-repeat;
}
```

This will only output the background properties. There won't be a sprite base class or any other CSS you haven't asked for.

Listing 6.23 `sprite` helper CSS

```
.next {
  background: url('/images/icons-s943de15a54.png') 0 -70px no-repeat;
}
.add-button {
  background: url('/images/icons-s943de15a54.png') 0 -358px no-repeat;
}
```

One nice thing about the sprite base class is that you can assign the background image once; here, it's assigned to each class, which is unnecessary duplication.

SPRITE POSITIONING

To remove the duplication of the background image, you can use the `sprite-position` helper or the `sprite-background-position` mixin instead of the `sprite` helper. Example code for this these are in manual-sprites/sprite-position:

```
sprite-position($map, $sprite, [$offset-x], [$offset-y])
sprite-background-position($map, $sprite, [$offset-x], [$offset-y])
```

Both the helper and the mixin require a sprite map, a sprite name, and accept optional offset position values.

Listing 6.24 Sprite positioning

```
$icons: sprite-map("icons/*.png");
.sprite-base { background: $icons no-repeat; }
.next {
  @extend .sprite-base;
  background-position: sprite-position($icons, arrow);
}
.add-button {
  @extend .sprite-base;
  @include sprite-background-position($icons, box-add);
}
```

Both the `sprite-position` helper and the `sprite-background-position` mixin per-form the same duty, and it's a matter of preference which to use.

Listing 6.25   CSS for sprite positioning

```
.sprite-base, .next, .add-button {
  background: url('/images/icons-s943de15a54.png') no-repeat;
}

.next { background-position: 0 -70px; }
.add-button { background-position: 0 -358px; }
```

Here, you can see how nicely trim this CSS is. You have more flexibility, with no unnec-essary duplication. But it'd be nice to add sprite dimensions.

SETTING SPRITE DIMENSIONS

To include the sprite dimensions as well, you can use the `sprite-dimensions` mixin, which requires the sprite map and the sprite image name, and outputs the measured dimensions. Example code for this mixin is in manual-sprites/sprite-dimensions.

Listing 6.26   The `sprite-dimensions` mixin

```
$icons: sprite-map("icons/*.png");
.sprite-base { background: $icons no-repeat; }
.next {
  @extend .sprite-base;
  @include sprite-background-position($icons, arrow);
  @include sprite-dimensions($icons, arrow);
}
```

This helper will measure the sprite image and write out its width and height proper-ties in the generated CSS.

Listing 6.27   CSS for the `sprite-dimensions` mixin

```
.sprite-base, .next {
  background: url('/images/icons-s943de15a54.png') no-repeat;
}

.next {
  background-position: 0 -70px;
  height: 32px;
  width: 32px;
}
```

And that's all there is to it. With this power and flexibility at your disposal, you should have no trouble adding image sprites to any web design project.

6.6   *Summary*

In this chapter, we looked at where image sprites came from and how they found their way into web design. We looked at the performance impact of loading lots of images from a remote server and how spriting is an essential practice for any high-traffic site. We saw how Compass can fully automate the spriting process, and we explored ways to configure and control how Compass generates sprite maps and writes spriting CSS.

In the next chapter, we'll look at some advanced Compass features that help you prep your stylesheets to be served up in production.

From prototype to production

This chapter covers

- Best practices for generating URLs to your assets
- Authoring stylesheets without needing a web server
- Tips and tricks for designing in the browser
- How to compile and structure stylesheets for production

Websites can be so simple, a kid can build one in a few minutes with a text editor and a hosting account. Of course, websites can also be complex, have dynamic content, and need to scale to millions of visitors a day. It's safe to say that the web encompasses one of the broadest ranges of expertise of any software technology field. From your high school home page to Google, the web can be micro-optimized at every layer.

The complexity of the web isn't just limited to HTML markup. Due to their heavy reliance on external resources like images, other CSS files, and fonts, stylesheets can become a serious maintenance burden.

In this chapter, you'll learn how to use Compass helpers and configuration to generate URLs to your assets, making it easy to transition from prototype to production. By using these helper functions, you'll have the freedom to author your stylesheets and HTML without a web server and the usual headaches that would result from that approach; you'll also be setting the stage for some great performance optimizations that we'll cover in the next chapter.

Given the advancements in CSS3 coupled with the powerful abstractions of Sass and Compass, it's time to re-evaluate your design and prototyping tool chain. We'll cover some basic tips and tricks for designing in the browser so that you can decide whether tools like Photoshop are actually slowing you down in the long run.

With CSS, you've been fine-tuning your search-and-replace skills to manage the changes that are needed to shepherd your stylesheets from prototype to production. In chapter 3, you learned about some of Compass's configuration options describing where your assets are stored and how they're served. In this chapter, you'll learn how you can use those simple configuration options and some authoring best practices to make production deployment considerations virtually disappear, while simultaneously allowing you to simplify your development environment. You'll also learn how to deal with banal things like copyright notices and source control.

Then, in the next chapter, you'll learn about some performance optimizations like compression and image inlining to help you eke every bit of performance from your stylesheets. But first things first: let's look at the Compass best practices for generating URLs and then get prototyping.

7.1 Abstracting URLs

Where are your images? That might sound like a dumb question; your images are right there in your project folder! Sure, they're easy enough to find, but you're a human. If you were a web browser, you'd have a harder time tracking them down. Your images start their long and arduous journey in your project's images directory, but they may soon find themselves packaged, copied, deployed, unpackaged, URL-rewritten, compressed, cached, and finally served from one or more places on the internet.

It's not uncommon for a project to change where and how it stores and references its images three or more times. When you use Compass, you'll find it easier to generate and change where and how you store your images, but the benefits don't stop there. While Compass makes URLs for you, it also makes sure that images really exist and that stale images don't get stuck in the browser cache.

7.1.1 Generating URLs to assets

CSS provides the `url` function to denote URLs:

```
background-image: url('/logo.png');
```

URLs identify a resource anywhere on the internet, but when you refer to your own assets, you often use relative URLs and the browser resolves the missing pieces of

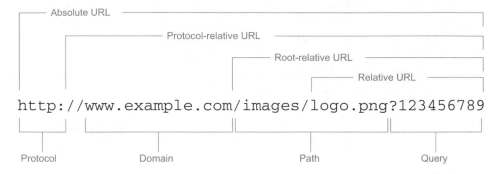

Figure 7.1   Breaking down the URL

information based on what it knows about the current request. Before we go on, let's review some terminology related to URLs in figure 7.1.

Recall that four kinds of URLs can be specified in CSS, depending on which parts of the fully qualified URL are omitted (see table 7.1).

Table 7.1   The four types of URLs

Example	Type	Description
`url('http://www.example.com/logo.png')`	Absolute URL	The details of the originating request don't matter in this case.
`url('logo.png')`	Relative URL	The browser resolves the URL relative to the request that served it, which in this case is the CSS stylesheet, not the web page. So if the stylesheet was at http://www.example.com/stylesheets/application.css, then this URL would point to http://www.example.com/stylesheets/logo.png.
`url('/logo.png')`	Root-relative URL	The browser resolves the URL against the protocol and domain of the CSS stylesheet. So if the stylesheet was at http://www.example.com/stylesheets/application.css, then this URL would point to http://www.example.com/logo.png.
`url('//imgs.example.com/logo.png')`	Protocol-relative URL	The browser resolves the URL using the domain specified, but with the same protocol as the originating request for the CSS stylesheet. This type of URL is especially useful when serving assets from a different domain than your main website. So if the stylesheet was at https://www.example.com/stylesheets/application.css, then this URL would point to https://imgs.example.com/logo.png.

Though you can still use any of these URL types in Sass, Compass best practices dictate that you use asset helper functions (http://compass-style.org/reference/compass/ helpers/urls/) to refer to your own assets. Compass provides three asset helpers, but to each of them you always pass a path that is relative to that asset class's directory—never relative to the stylesheet:

- `image-url('logo.png')`—References the file `logo.png` saved at the root of your images directory.
- `font-url('arial.ttf')`—References the file `arial.ttf` saved at the root of your fonts directory.
- `stylesheet-url('randomfile.xml')`—References the file `randomfile.xml` saved at the root of your `css` directory.

You might have noticed that there's no URL helper for JavaScript. The JavaScript configuration option exists so that Compass extensions can provide JavaScript files as part of their installation. Similarly, there's no URL generator for the `sass` directory because that's merely an aspect of development; the `stylesheet_url` will point to the location where your CSS files live.

The reason why Compass has chosen this approach is because it makes imports and refactoring much simpler. As you'll soon see, it's possible to generate all four kinds of the URLs that CSS supports using this single syntax.

Your project configuration tells Compass where to find your assets so that you can stop caring about how to refer to them in your stylesheets and leave that as an aspect of configuration that *will* change over time as your stylesheets move from prototype to production to scaling your website or application.

But wait, there's more! Compass will also check to make sure your URLs are *valid* and up to date during compilation!

7.1.2 Avoiding broken links

You're human; sometimes you make mistakes. Maybe a typo; maybe an image gets renamed but you miss a reference to it. It happens. Don't beat yourself up over it. When you refer to an image using the `image-url($path)` helper function, Compass will verify that the file exists; if it doesn't, it'll print out a warning to your console during compilation. Similarly, missing fonts will be noticed when you use the `font-url($path)` helper.

Observe the following output from a compass compilation run where an image isn't found. If this was in your console, the `WARNING` line would be colored red:

```
[~/Projects/my_compass_project] compass compile
directory stylesheets/
   create stylesheets/ie.css
WARNING: 'missing.png' was not found (or cannot be read) in images/
    create stylesheets/main.css
    create stylesheets/print.css
```

Of course, Compass can't actually ensure that you won't have broken links. A configuration error or a change that occurs after compilation will still break your site, but this simple check can save many hours of painful debugging due to common development mistakes (like why that image isn't showing up).

Speaking of common development mistakes, have you ever spent 10 minutes trying to figure out why an image isn't displaying correctly, only to discover that the browser was caching it? So have we, but not since starting to use Compass to generate our URLs. Read on to see why.

7.1.3 *Avoiding stale images with cache busting*

Another common problem during development and across production deployments is that browsers are lazy; they don't like to download things. Perhaps it's tedious for them. So they cache your images and other assets in case they need them later, and they often do. This is great for users; it makes their browsing experience much nicer. But it's a pain for web developers. If you change an image, those users who have recently downloaded it won't notice. And it's a shame, because the new image is clearly much better. To work around this, Compass adds a query parameter to the end of each asset based on its modification time. Your web server will still serve it just fine, but when the query parameter changes, it'll force the browser to ask for the image again.

For example,

```
#logo { background-image: image-url('logo.png'); }
```

might be compiled to

```
#logo { background-image: url('/images/logo.png?1298578273'); }
```

It's also possible for you to configure what cache-buster parameter gets created if timestamps aren't a good approach for your needs. For example, you could increment a deployment count before each deployment or you could use your source control's revision number for that file. Doing this requires that you write a little Ruby code. For example, adding this to your compass configuration file

```
# Increment the deploy_version before every
# release to force cache busting.
asset_cache_buster do |http_path, real_path|
  "v=1"
end
```

would cause Compass to now generate the following output for your logo image:

```
#logo { background-image: url('/images/logo.png?v=1'); }
```

Using a query parameter as a cache-busting strategy might interfere with some proxies' ability to cache your assets. (The query string makes them scared that the asset might be dynamically generated.) If this is a problem for you, it's possible to disable the cache buster by adding the following line to your Compass configuration:

```
asset_cache_buster :none
```

But if you want to maximize cacheability of your assets while also busting the cache, the best way is to rewrite the path to the asset. With some corresponding web server configuration, you can generate a URL more like this:

```
#logo { background-image: url('/images/logo-1307943914.png'); }
```

You'll need to configure your web server so that it knows how to map the timestamped path to the real path. How to do this is specific to your web server, but the Compass configuration looks something like the following.

Listing 7.1 Defining a path-based asset cache buster

```
asset_cache_buster do |path, real_path|       Always check if file
  if File.exists?(real_path)                  really exists

    pathname = Pathname.new(path)                             Path names
                                                              easier to work
                                                              with than strings
    modified_time = File.mtime(real_path)         Last modified time

    new_path = "%s/%s-%s%s" % [                     Construct new
      pathname.dirname,                             path from four
      pathname.basename(pathname.extname),          strings
      modified_time.strftime("%s"),
      pathname.extname
    ]
    {:path => new_path}              Special return format
  end                               for path-based assets
end
```

As you can see, arbitrarily complex logic can be used within the Compass configuration file because it's just a Ruby script. For example, some users integrate with their content delivery network (CDN) or generate MD5 fingerprints for each asset. But more complex logic is outside the scope of this book, so please contact the Compass mailing list (http://groups.google.com/group/compass-users) or your nearest Rubyist if you need help crafting custom code.

But long before you can start worrying about how to serve your assets from a CDN, you'll need to do some prototyping first. CSS best practices dictate that you should set up a web server before you write your first selector; let's find out why that is and why it's not necessary when you use Sass and Compass.

7.2   *Prototyping with Sass and Compass*

Whether you're working on a new concept or starting up a new project with some fresh mockups or wireframes, the start of a new project is the point in a project's life when Sass and Compass really shine. Some people think that Sass and Compass are for large sites with tons of CSS, but every large site starts small.

Additionally, at the start of a project when everything is in flux and subject to change, the capabilities of Sass and Compass to manage are indispensable. The CSS3 module and grid systems make designing in the browser easier than Photoshop. The

Sass color functions can make experimenting with your site's color theme so easy it's worth doing just for fun.

Of course, prototyping involves writing HTML too, but Sass and Compass stay out of the business of HTML, so we encourage you to investigate using a rapid prototyping framework like Serve (http://get-serve.com/) or Middleman (http://middlemanapp.com/), which include support for Sass and Compass out of the box.

In order to write CSS files with root-relative URLs during development, getting started with a new project with CSS used to mean setting up web servers, editing configuration files, and editing DNS host files. Let's explore how Compass can make your development environment simpler.

7.2.1 *Simplifying your development environment*

URLs relative to your stylesheet are a great starting point for your new application or website. They work without a web server, so you can use them when prototyping using plain old HTML, and they also work in any server environment where your assets are served from the same domain as your stylesheets. For many users, this is the beginning and end of their needs.

Figure 7.2   A simple project

Of course, one of the challenges that relative URLs present to the CSS developer is that they make it hard to reorganize your stylesheets. Consider the project structure shown in figure 7.2.

When using relative URLs, if you want to move some styles from main.css to header.css, then you have to change this,

```
#logo { background-image: url(../images/logo.png); }
```

to this:

```
#logo { background-image: url(../../images/logo.png); }
```

For this reason, it has long been considered a best practice to always use a simple web server and domain-relative paths even when prototyping. Even when you have a web server set up on your development environment, setting up a new site isn't always straightforward. Navigating the maze of configuration files, local host names, and server ports can be even more daunting than working with the command line to many front-end developers and designers.

But with Compass you're once again free to use local files by enabling relative assets. To use relative assets, simply add (or uncomment) the following line in your Compass configuration:

```
relative_assets = true
```

When enabled, Compass will generate relative paths whenever you use `image-url($path)`, `font-url($path)`, or `stylesheet-url($path)`. It's important to note that the paths generated are relative to the *compiled* stylesheet—not the Sass stylesheet.

This means that if you have a shared partial that's included by several different CSS files, the relative path to an image referenced in the partial will be correct in all cases. For example, consider the project structure shown in figure 7.3.

If _partial.scss is imported into both main.scss and header.scss, and _partial.scss contains this,

```
#logo { background-image: image-url("logo.png"); }
```

then the generated main.css will contain this,

```
#logo { background-image: url(../images/logo.png?1298578273); }
```

and the generated header.css will contain this:

```
#logo { background-image: url(../../images/logo.png?1298578273); }
```

You can now refactor your stylesheets to your heart's content; your relative URLs will always just work. With Compass you have a development environment set up in just a few minutes; if your next inclination is to open up Photoshop, stop and read the next section instead.

7.2.2 Designing in the browser

If you're a designer who writes your own stylesheets, you're probably used to first mocking up your website with Adobe's Photoshop or Fireworks and then building out your stylesheets when you have a design that you're happy with. Before CSS3 and progressive enhancement, the need to create image slices almost demanded this workflow. But with CSS3, Sass, and Compass, there's now tremendous efficiency to be had by designing your website in the browser.

From gradients to shadows, rounded elements to fancy fonts, modern browsers can now handle the most common design elements without images. In many cases, Compass's CSS3 module now makes it easier to write the code than to emulate the effect in Photoshop. And when you're done, if you really need to support legacy browsers, take screen grabs of your web page and slice the images from there.

This efficiency gain isn't only the result of doing it just once. When you design directly in the browser, it's more likely that you'll express the relationships between design elements clearly and explicitly. During the act of creation, you don't think, *Boy, what this design needs is some* #4F9942. You think, *I need to de-emphasize this header color.* At that instant it's easier to write adjust-color ($header-color, $saturation: -15%, $lightness: -25%) and then tweak the values a couple times until it looks right to you. But when you're authoring CSS from a mockup, the easiest thing to do is take out your color picker and copy the end-result value to your stylesheet,

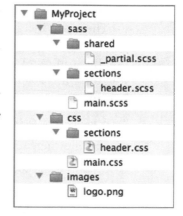

Figure 7.3 A project with a shared partial

thereby losing all the information that was in your head during the design step and making it much harder to change the header color than it should be.

Browsers are full of limitations. From time to time it's great to push the limits of what's possible in the browser, but most of the time, you just need to get the job done. Designing in the browser allows you to work within those limitations and embrace them as part of the design process. The way floats work, it's hard to imagine and emulate how floated elements will respond to browser window resizing. But when you're designing in the browser, it's easy to test and see how it'll work out.

Sure, you might find that it takes a little longer to build your initial design with this approach, but unless you have to throw the whole thing out, it's likely that designing and prototyping in the browser will yield a higher-quality product, in less time, that is easier to change in the future.

Now that you have a design that you like, it's time to share it with the world. Let's put this baby into production!

7.3   Deploying to production

Deploying CSS to production is actually easier than deploying Sass files to production. After all, CSS is a plain file so you simply need to copy the file to your web server and call it a day. With Sass and Compass, there's a compilation step and production configuration that must be taken into account. Though this might feel like a hassle at first, you'll soon realize that Compass is making you consider and do things that you *should* have been doing with your CSS anyway.

7.3.1   Surprise! It's moving time

Your client calls to inform you that the app you're building that was going to be deployed to http://example.com/fancy-app/ is now going to be renamed to http://example.com/super-fancy-app/. The client feels bad; they thought this was all approved, but the CEO *really* wanted the app to be super. Finally they get to *the question*: "So, how long will this take?"

There are literally hundreds of URLs in your stylesheets and if you had to change and test them all by hand, it would be at least an hour of mindless busywork and testing. But you're a Compass user who has been using all the URL helpers provided, so you know this will be a simple configuration change. You just have to change one line in your configuration from this,

```
http_path = "/fancy-app"
```

to the following, and then recompile:

```
http_path = "/super-fancy-app"
```

So now you have a small dilemma on your hands. Do you give them the real time estimate or not? We lean toward telling them it was a piece of cake and there would be no extra charge because we like to elicit good will and show off that we've thought ahead by using a stylesheet compiler. Isn't it great when we let these machines do all our busy work for us? In the next section, you'll see how Compass can make your life easier by targeting your production environment when it's time to deploy.

7.3.2   *Compiling for production*

Compass has two modes that you can use to manage your stylesheets differently when doing development and when you're serving them in production. Normally, Compass uses the development environment. To use the production environment you can compile your stylesheets like so:

```
compass compile --force -e production
```

Compass will use sensible defaults for production stylesheets. Your output will be compressed and most comments will be stripped out. It's also possible to set a specific configuration for the current mode. For instance, if you want compact output in production mode, you can add this conditional setting in your Compass configuration:

```
if environment == :production
  output_style = :compact
end
```

Using the preceding approach, it's possible to use the environment toggle to set up different asset configurations depending on whether you're on a development machine or in production.

7.3.3   *Generating domain-relative assets*

By default, Compass generates domain-relative URLs that assume you're viewing your web page via a web server. Now that you're about to deploy your website, you'll need to consider some configuration settings for Compass to correctly generate URLs for you. The first setting to consider is the http_path of your entire project—this defaults to /, but if your site is hosted within a directory, you should change this in your Compass configuration:

```
http_path - '/my-app'
```

If you have relative assets enabled, you should disable them now because you don't want the generated URLs to be relative to the generated CSS files, and the relative_assets setting will take precedence:

```
relative_assets = false
```

After the next compile, the logo's URL becomes

```
#logo {
      background: url('/my-app/images/logo.png?1240702589');
    }
```

Suppose that during deployment your images get copied to a folder called *imgs* that's relative to the site's root folder. In this case, you need to set the http_images_dir for your project:

```
http_path = '/my-app'
      relative_assets = false
      images_dir = 'images' #locally it's the images folder
      http_images_dir = 'imgs' #on the webserver it's different
```

After the next compile, the logo's URL becomes

```
#logo {
  background: url('/my-app/imgs/logo.png?1240702589');
}
```

But if your website is strange and decides to put its images in a place entirely different from the HTML, then you can set the http_images_path instead:

```
http_path = '/my-app'
relative_assets = false
images_dir = 'images'                    ⟵——— Locally it's the images  folder
http_images_path = '/somewhere-else/imgs'
```

After the next compile, the logo's URL becomes

```
#logo {
      background: url('/somewhere-else/imgs/logo.png?1240702589');
}
```

Compass has a lot of possible configuration options relating to assets. For common cases, it's easy to ignore them, but it's nice to know that if your needs are outside the norm, you can still accommodate them. Before your site goes live, it's important to dot your i's and cross your t's—small stuff like copyright notices might have been overlooked.

7.3.4 Adding copyright notices

Some sites choose to annotate their stylesheets with a copyright. If you do this, you'll be sad to find out that Sass strips out CSS comments when stylesheets are compressed. To work around this, Sass provides *loud comments*. Loud comments start with an exclamation mark immediately following the asterisk of a CSS comment:

```
/*!
  Copyright © 2012, Example Inc. All Rights Reserved.
*/
```

It's worth noting here that loud comments evaluate Sass script, so they can be used to set your copyright notice into a variable and reuse that across your site:

```
$copyright-year: unquote("2012");
$company-name: unquote("Example, Inc.");
/*!
  Copyright © #{$copyright-year}, #{$company-name}
  All Rights Reserved.
*/
```

That made the lawyers pretty happy, didn't it? Now it's time to put your site into production!

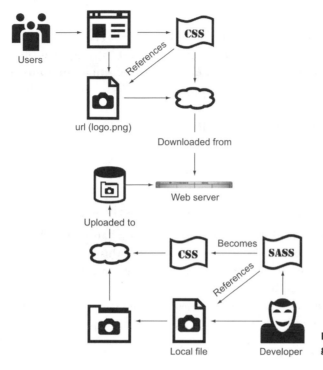

Figure 7.4   How Sass stylesheets get served

7.3.5   *Deploying CSS is simple*

If your deployment system for CSS was to copy stylesheets to your web server, then things won't change much for you. After you've recompiled your stylesheets for production, you have plain old CSS files just like you had before. From this point on, your process should be the same as it was. All that matters is that you get your stylesheets where they can be served to your users. In figure 7.4, you can see how a simple deployment process works.

If your website is a simple site and you're the only developer, this process likely works fine for you. But if you work on a team and have source control and/or deployment or build scripts, there's more to consider.

7.3.6   *Working with source control and the deployment process*

Source control best practices dictate that generated files that aren't hand-edited shouldn't be tracked in source control. Instead, you should ignore your generated CSS files and have a build step before or during deployment that prepares your stylesheets using a repeatable process.

But many websites don't have such a step and don't want to add one just because they use Sass. In these cases, many users do check their compiled CSS into source control. If you do this, merge conflicts will eventually occur; when they do, the best approach is to delete your generated stylesheets, resolve the merge conflicts (if any) in the source files, and then recompile.

If your application has a build step, it might be enough to compile the whole project with one command, but some build systems may want to compile a file at a time using a tool like make. In this case, you can either pass the single file to the Compass compiler or use the Sass command-line compiler, which has a more traditional interface that's expected by such tools.

This compiles a single file with the Compass command line:

```
compass compile my_sass_dir/application.scss
```

To compile a single file with the Sass command line, you can pass the --compass option:

```
sass --compass my_sass_dir/application.scss my_css_dir/application.css
```

If you don't understand your team's build process, don't be afraid to ask for help getting things set up. Most engineers would rather deal with this one-time setup than an ongoing risk of merge conflicts in generated files. Teams with complex build and deployment scripts usually have a staging environment where they practice deployments and do final testing before a release. Read on to learn some great strategies for managing more than two environments.

7.3.7   *Working with staging servers*

Some sites have a staging environment where code that's about to be put into production goes for final testing. Some websites even have three staging environments (edge, integration, and staging) where they test and integrate features of varying maturity.

Sometimes it's sufficient to deploy the same stylesheets into staging as production, but the staging environment is probably a little different—usually the hostnames are different, or maybe you don't use a CDN like in production. In these cases, you'll need to adjust your configuration accordingly.

There are two approaches you can use in this case. The first is to set an environment variable when you compile:

```
STAGING=true compass compile --force -e production
```

Then, in your configuration file, you can use Ruby to inspect this environment variable and vary settings accordingly:

```
if ENV['STAGING']
  relative_urls = true
  output_style = :compact
elsif environment == :production
  relative_urls = false
  output_style = :compact
else #development
  relative_urls = true
  output_style = :expanded
end
```

If your configuration is significantly different for each environment, then you can also create different configuration files:

```
compass compile --force -c staging_config.rb -e production
```

In order to keep things consistent and DRY, the `staging_config.rb` file should source the normal configuration file and then make changes:

```
eval(File.read("#{File.dirname(__FILE__)}/config.rb"))
relative_urls = true
output_style = :compact
```

Deployment to a staging server is a great practice for complex sites, and though not natively supported, you can see why the authors have chosen to use a Ruby file for configuration: it allows the less-common cases to be supported easily.

Congratulations on getting your website into staging. Next stop: production! We're sure it'll be a smashing success.

7.4 Summary

In this chapter, we looked at how Compass supports the full lifecycle of your project, from early rapid prototyping to production-ready deployment. We explored Compass asset helpers to hide the details of asset serving from your stylesheets, giving you a single configuration-driven approach to serving local assets during development while supporting multiple asset hosts for faster sites in production. You also learned some tips and tricks for working with Compass in the browser, and how your stylesheets should be treated in source control. Without knowing it, you've already laid a strong foundation for optimizing and scaling your website's performance by creating smart, well-abstracted stylesheets that don't assume any knowledge about how your assets will be served. In the next chapter, we'll take a look at the strategies employed by the busiest websites on the internet and how Compass supports them to help you scale the front end.

High-performance stylesheets 8

This chapter covers

- Stylesheet concatenation
- Stylesheet and asset compression
- Strategies for reducing and parallelizing image requests
- Selector performance and optimization strategies

In the last chapter, you learned how stylesheets, due to their heavy reliance on external assets, can become a serious maintenance burden. But even worse, stylesheets can be the source of myriad client-side performance issues and the dreaded "mixed content" warning.

But by following the best practices of client-side performance, you may be able to shave *seconds* off of your page load times. This can have a significant impact on your search engine rankings, user engagement, and goal conversion metrics. There are whole books devoted to this subject, but in this chapter we'll outline the unique features of Sass and Compass that enable you to quickly implement many web performance best practices.

By far, one of the best resources on the web regarding web page performance tuning is Google's PageSpeed documentation: http://developers.google.com/speed/pagespeed/. It's a must-read for anyone who's focusing on client-side performance. Though some of the tactics they suggest are simple enough to perform, many are very challenging to implement. When "doing it right" in CSS is hard, there's a good chance that you'll accept the trade-off and go with wrong and easy. With Sass and Compass in your tool chest, "doing it right" is so easy that we hope you'll take the small amount of time needed to optimize your stylesheets and do your part to make the web a faster, better place.

Optimizing stylesheets basically comes down to reducing how many bytes are transferred, ensuring they're maximally cached, and reducing the number of round trips between the browser and the server. There's no silver bullet that makes your website screaming fast, but Sass and Compass are used by some of the biggest sites on the internet because they provide the tools and a platform for tuning your stylesheets based on measurements and usage patterns relating to your specific needs.

But how can you make your website faster without first knowing just how slow it is? Measuring your client-side performance used to be a chore, but in the last couple of years it's become easy to measure load time speeds and identify the critical paths in your page's structure.

8.1 Measuring client-side performance

Performance optimization starts and ends with measurement. Before you make your first performance change, you need to know where you stand. A decade ago such measurements could only be done coarsely and the remedies weren't always obvious. Today there are some really great developer tools that can help you diagnose these issues. If you haven't used the following tools, you're missing out on a wealth of information about what's going on when your web page renders:

- *YSlow*—http://developer.yahoo.com/yslow/
- *Google PageSpeed*—http://developers.google.com/speed/pagespeed/
- *WebPagetest*—http://www.webpagetest.org/ (see figure 8.1)

The chart in figure 8.1 is a waterfall diagram from webpagetest.org. It's a free service that makes diagnosing performance issues straightforward. It's not a pretty site, but the information it provides is stunning. It allows you to see which requests block other requests and which requests are parallelized. It allows you to compare a cached experience to an uncached experience, and it breaks down the network time into DNS, time to first byte (how long the server takes plus round-trip time), and transfer time.

Now that you know how to measure page performance, you can get started optimizing. The first step along the way is to stop doing unnecessary things that cause slowness. There's nothing less necessary than CSS-based imports.

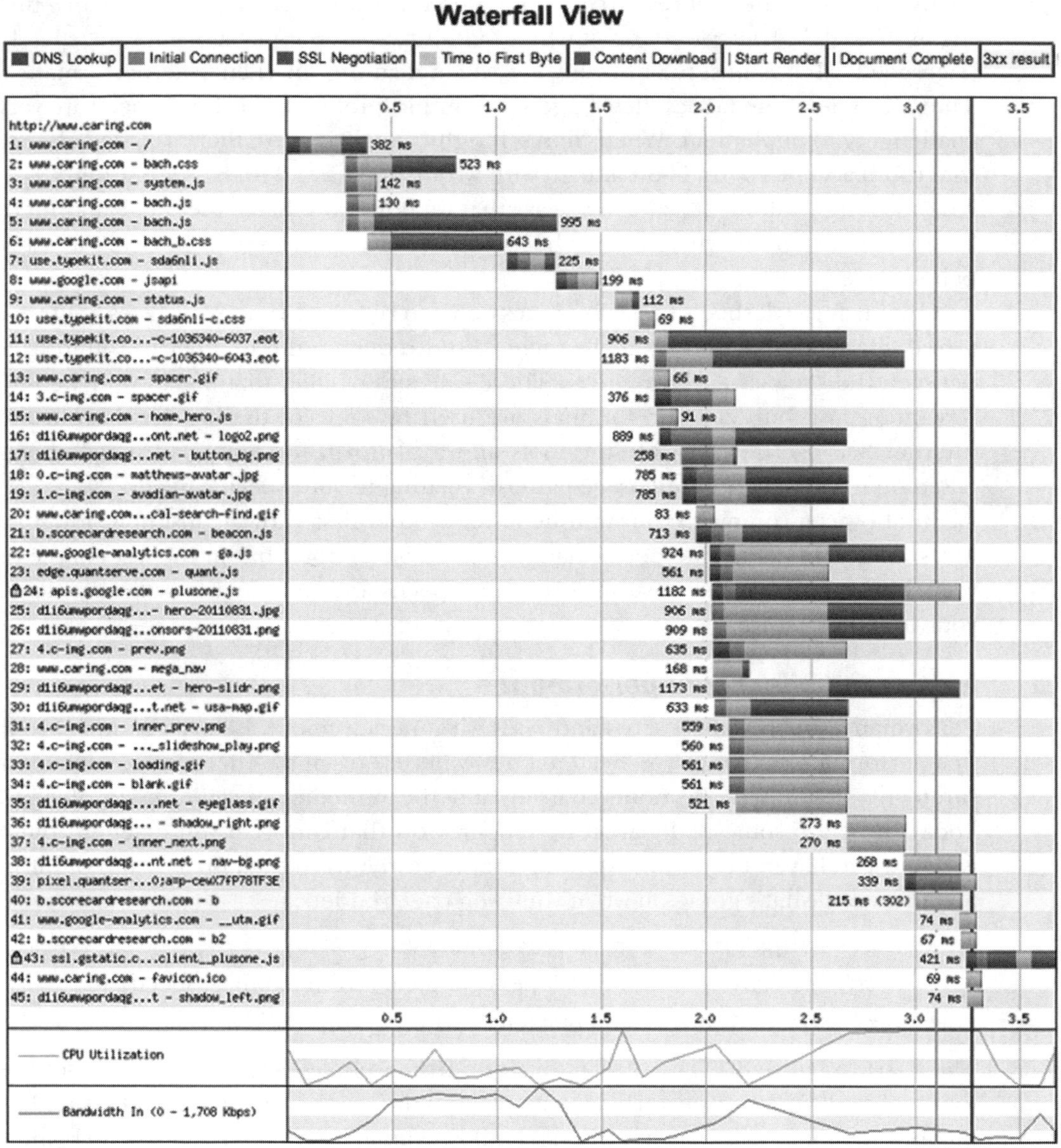

Waterfall View

| DNS Lookup | Initial Connection | SSL Negotiation | Time to First Byte | Content Download | Start Render | Document Complete | 3xx result |

Figure 8.1   Performance waterfall from webpagetest.org

8.2   *Avoiding HTTP requests with server-side @import*

As you've already seen in chapter 3, the @import directive is a helpful tool for organizing large stylesheets into smaller partials so that styles are easier to find and peruse. With CSS it's not uncommon to have a single stylesheet that imports many others:

```
@import url("blog.css");
@import url("forum.css");
@import url("article.css");
@import url("header.css");
@import url("footer.css");
```

This slows down the first page view because it requires users to make several HTTP requests in order to download the styles for the page (see figure 8.2).

The waterfall in figure 8.2 shows how browsers handle having a single stylesheet that imports three others, each of which imports another 10 stylesheets. This is a perfectly legitimate structure for a project, but as you see, each level of imports can't start until the CSS files are downloaded. Worse still, browsers have a limit on the number of files that can be downloaded at a time from a single server. The net effect is that @import in CSS adds unnecessary load time where it matters most: the first page view. For this reason, CSS best practices dictate concatenating your stylesheets into as few stylesheets as make sense for your website. This is why Sass provides server-side imports:

```
@import "blog", "forum", "article", "header", "footer";
```

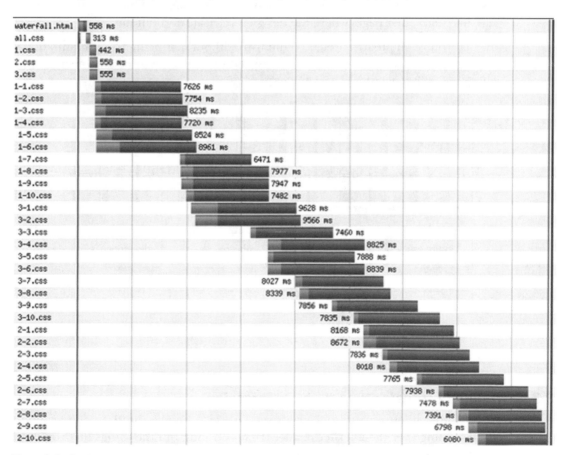

Figure 8.2 Performance waterfall from CSS-based `@import`

This will speed up the first page view because all the styles are downloaded with a single request.

But did you notice the caveat? Different websites and web applications have different visitor patterns. If your visitors come back often and some portions of your stylesheets rarely change, then it may make sense to serve some stylesheets as separate downloads. This will allow their browser to make better use of its cache when some stylesheets do change—otherwise, a small change to the stylesheets would require downloading the entire site's styles again. Similarly, if your visitors land and look at only a few pages in an isolated section of your site, then it may not make sense to make them download the styles for every template.

A strategy that works for many websites is to organize your CSS files into three levels (as in figure 8.3):

- *Core stylesheets*—Common styles needed on most every page.
- *Section stylesheets*—Common styles need by a large section of your application or website.
- *Single-page stylesheets*—Styles needed by only one page. These are usually things like marketing pages where the design is intricate and unique.

Now that you've eliminated useless round trips without sacrificing your organizational structure, you can start focusing on how to reduce the amount of time spent downloading assets like stylesheets and images.

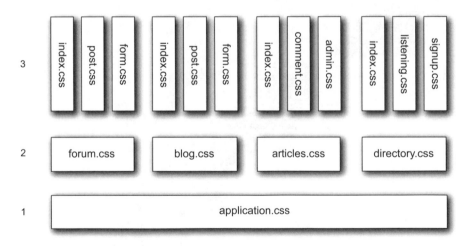

Figure 8.3 A common CSS structure

8.3   *Reducing transfer time with compression*

One of the simplest ways to make your site faster is to make the size of the content you're sending over the internet smaller. That's obvious, but the things that you need to do to accomplish this aren't so obvious.

If you're not already doing it, it's time to start compressing your Sass output. For most users, this is a simple matter of running the Compass compiler again with the -e production --force arguments set. The production environment default is set to use the compressed output format. But you can also accomplish this by setting the Compass configuration setting output_style to :compressed or by passing -t compressed to the Sass command-line tool.

Compressing the text of your stylesheets is a good start. Sass will eliminate comments and superfluous whitespace, and use the smallest representation of colors that it can. But that's just the start of what you need to do; gzip compression is a much bigger win.

8.3.1 gzip compression

Most modern browsers send a header with their requests, Accept-Encoding: gzip, which allows the response to be compressed as long as the response includes a header of Content-Encoding: gzip. Due to the verbose, repetitive nature of CSS, stylesheets can be compressed to about 10–15% of their original size—a huge reduction! By comparison, JavaScript files generally compress down to around 25% of their original size.

As a rule, one of the best things you can do for front-end performance is to make the over-the-wire size of your assets as small as possible. Compressing your textual assets using gzip and optimizing your images for the web are musts for any site that's focused on client-side performance.

Most web servers have a setting or plugin to enable on-the-fly compression. In many cases, the time spent compressing is more than covered by the time savings when transferring the content across the internet.

It's also possible to precompress your stylesheets and serve different files based on the request headers. The details of how to set this up are web server–specific, but if you need to do this, Compass provides a simple way to automatically generate a compressed stylesheet. You can register a callback with Compass and it'll run your code each time a new stylesheet is saved. Simply add the following code to your Compass configuration file:

```
on_stylesheet_save do |filename|
    # run the gzip tool on the file
    # generates a file of the same name
    # plus a .gz at the end.
    `gzip -f #{file}`
end
```

We encourage you to investigate how to enable gzip compression for your site. It'll take a little time, but it'll be well worth it for your users.

Unfortunately, stylesheets are only one small part of the amount of content you need to compress. Often, images are where the biggest improvements can be made.

8.3.2   *Image compression*

This section doesn't have anything to do with Sass or Compass, but we'd feel terrible if we didn't share with you some of the basics of image compression.

The first thing to know about images is that most formats have compression built in. As general rule of thumb, you should use the image format that's most appropriate for the content to achieve maximum compression. This means that you should generally use the following:

- GIF for small files with a small number of colors
- JPG for photographic images with a quality setting at the lowest value that doesn't cause obvious degradation in picture quality
- PNG for everything else

PNG is a complex format that can handle a range of image types. Be sure to remove the alpha layer unless you need transparency. We highly recommend that you install the free tool Pngcrush and run it on all your PNG images. You can download Pngcrush from http://pmt.sourceforge.net/pngcrush/.

Now that you've made your assets as small as possible, you can turn your attention to how these assets are loaded. For instance, did you realize that browsers limit the number of consecutive downloads from a web server? If you're running a load-balanced website, this should seem conservative to you—certainly you can handle more simultaneous connections than that. And you can, with a little trickery called *asset hosts*.

8.4   *Speeding up page loads with asset hosts*

HTTP/1.1 specifies that web browsers should play nice by limiting the number of simultaneous downloads from a single domain per page request. But load-balanced sites running many web servers can happily handle this burst of traffic, so you have to trick the web browser into being mean to you. A common strategy for this is to register several domains (or subdomains) that all resolve to the same place. The web browser will then download many more assets in parallel, resulting in a faster page load for your users.

For example, a site named example.com might set up img-1.example.com, img-2.example.com, img-3.example.com, and img-4.example.com. Each of these DNS names would actually be what's called a `CNAME` record, which means they're an alias to www.example.com.

Beyond the benefits of parallelization, it's also important to set up your assets hosts to use a *cookieless domain*—a domain that doesn't share cookies with your site. This will result in fewer bytes being sent to your web server with each image request. It's not a huge deal, but if you're going through the effort to set up new domains, it's a small but important savings that you can get basically for free. For more information on cookieless domains, see Google's PageSpeed documentation: http://developers .google.com/speed/docs/best-practices/request/.

Then the links to images, stylesheets, and JavaScripts are distributed evenly across the available asset hosts. When doing this, it's important that the same assets are always accessed via the same asset host; otherwise the assets might be downloaded several times. Clearly, this solution is only feasible if you have a framework at your disposal to take the busy work and human error out of the equation. Well, you're in luck! Compass makes using asset hosts super easy!

8.4.1 Generating URLs with asset hosts

By default, asset hosts are disabled in your Compass project, but you can enable them by teaching Compass how to distribute your assets across your asset hosts. For example, to distribute across four subdomains, you need to add a bit of Ruby code to your Compass configuration:

```
asset_host do |asset|
  host_number = (asset.hash % 4) + 1
  "http://img-#{host_number}.example.com"
end
```

Let's explain what's going on here. As you learned in the previous chapter, you should be authoring all your assets' references using Compass's asset URL helpers. If you're already following this best practice, then you're good to go with asset hosts. You still write this:

```
#logo {
  background-image: image-url("logo-small.png")
}
```

The `asset_host` function you've defined in your configuration takes an argument of `asset`, which will be the fully resolved absolute HTTP path to the asset. Depending on your other configuration settings, this will be something like `/images/logo-small.png`. The job of the `asset_host` function is to return the protocol and hostname for the asset's generated URL.

Though you're free to implement whatever logic suits your needs, the preceding example will usually suffice. First, the `asset.hash` gives you a number that fairly uniquely represents the `asset` string. Then, the modulo operator (`%`) returns the remainder after dividing by 4, which is an integer between 0 and 3 inclusive. Last, it's incremented by 1 to give a 1-based count. In the second line, the `host_number` is inserted into a string to construct the appropriate return value. The last value of the function is what is returned—no explicit `return` is needed here.

Compass then joins this asset host value with the path that was passed in and any cache buster to generate the full URL:

```
#logo {
  background-image:
    url('http://img-3.example.com/images/logo-small.png?1298578273');
}
```

Using asset hosts can shave significant time off of your client-side rendering. It's such a simple thing to do, there's no excuse for not doing it.

8.4.2   *Avoiding mixed content warnings with domain-based assets*

If your site supports SSL access and you'd like to use asset hosts, it's important to make sure that your users don't receive warnings about insecure assets from their browser. The best way to handle this is to use protocol-relative URLs:

```
#logo {
  background-image:
    url('//assets3.example.com/images/logo-small.png?1298578273');
}
```

You're probably thinking, *Where's the http: at?* It's not needed. When a protocol-relative URL is encountered, the browser will use the same protocol that was used to serve the original request (the request for the stylesheet, in this case). Protocol-relative URLs are supported in every major browser—even IE6. To configure Compass to use a protocol-relative URL with asset hosts, you can do something like this:

```
asset_host do |asset|
  host_number = (asset.hash % 4) + 1
  "//img-#{host_number}.example.com"
end
```

While we're on the subject, a word of caution if you decide to use protocol-relative URLs in your HTML markup. There's a bug in Internet Explorer 6 and 7 that causes a protocol-relative stylesheet `<link>` to be downloaded *twice*.

IE 6 and 7 also botch another kind of URL called a *data URI*. But that doesn't mean you can't give the performance benefits to those users with a decent browser. Sass and Compass make inline data URIs a breeze.

8.5   *Inline data URIs*

As fantastic as CSS3 is for allowing you to create nice effects without needing images, you still rely on images to spice up the design and call attention to the important aspects. When you're developing locally, it's easy to forget that each image doesn't load instantly. Whereas on desktops, low-latency broadband connections are increasingly common, the growing user base of international visitors and mobile devices is more like a throwback to the era of dial-up connections: low bandwidth and high-latency round-trip times are on the rise again.

Imagine if you served images embedded *within* your stylesheets. You could avoid the corresponding costs of an HTTP round trip. Fortunately, this is already possible using a mechanism called a *data URI*, shown in figure 8.4.

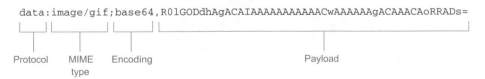

Figure 8.4   Data URI breakdown

The URI shown in figure 8.4 represents a 2 x 2 pixel solid black image. The 35 bytes in the original image have been transformed into a 70-byte data URI using base-64 encoding. If you were to type it into your browser's URL bar, a tiny image would be displayed.

With CSS, you might use a web service that lets you upload an image and have it spit out the corresponding data URI, and then repeat this process for each image that you need to embed, but this would be both laborious and difficult to maintain. With Compass, embedding images and other assets is a piece of cake:

```
.icon { background: inline-image("black-dot.png"); }
```

Compass knows the MIME type of the most-common image formats based on the image extension, but if it doesn't recognize the extension and the extension isn't the same as the second part of the MIME type, you can provide the MIME type explicitly:

```
.icon {
  background: inline-image("black-dot.bitmap", "image/bmp");
}
```

Given how easy Compass makes it to embed images and the benefits of avoiding all those extra round trips, why not do this all the time? It turns out there are a few reasons:

- *Bloat*—The base-64 encoding algorithm isn't as efficient as normal binary encoding. Binary data becomes about 20% larger when base-64 encoded. Even when compressing your stylesheets, if you have large amounts of inline data, the costs of encoding overhead outweigh the gains in HTTP overhead and latency. *As a rule of thumb, you should be wary of embedding data that's more than 1 KB.*

- *Caching*—Even though it may be faster, inlining images can cause your CSS file to get very large. Some user agents might decide to not cache a file that's too large. For example, the iPhone won't cache any single CSS file larger than 25 KB. Additionally, changing an inlined image will cause the entire stylesheet to change—whereas if each image was a separate request, only the image that changed would need to be requested again.

- *Browser support*—IE6 and IE7 don't support data URIs, and IE8 limits their length to 32 KB. To work around this, you can use hacks to support legacy browsers with a fallback image:

  ```
  background-image: inline-url("logo.gif");
  *background-image: image-url("logo.gif");
  ```

If you do this, those users will pay a performance penalty by downloading the image twice. If your browser support requirements include these legacy browsers, you might consider sending your data URIs in a separate stylesheet that's conditionally linked.

If inline images don't appear to be a good fit for your needs, another great strategy for speeding up image loading is to use sprites, as discussed in chapter 6.

So far, we've looked at ways to improve performance by shipping smaller files and requiring fewer HTTP requests. Next, we'll tackle the browser-rendering side of things and learn how to optimize Sass for better selector performance.

8.6   *Selector performance*

It's easy to see how a JavaScript file can slow down a page. Just make an infinite loop and you'll see your browser come to a screeching halt. CSS selectors have no loops and are very fast compared to JavaScript, so it's harder to see how a stylesheet impacts a web page's load time and general responsiveness. Beyond the time taken to transfer and parse your stylesheets, the number and structure of your selectors can have a small but measurable impact on the speed of your page. For a large website, this impact might measure a couple hundred milliseconds, and when this becomes your worst performance issue, your website is in a good place.

Most performance issues follow the Pareto principle: you get about 80% of the speedup with 20% of the work. Optimizing your selectors is a step you should take only after you've already gotten past the easy part. You can spend weeks of work and only save 100ms. For some sites, it makes sense to go through this effort, but if you do so, consider rolling it out with some kind of redesign or larger template reorganization to make it more cost effective.

You shouldn't even think about this aspect of performance until you've focused first on your web page load order, server response time, and network transfer costs.

8.6.1   *It all adds up*

Selectors are fast. Really fast. But when you get into thousands of selectors, the time spent calculating the cascade and inheritance of selectors and resolving properties for an element in a document can add up—especially if the document itself has many elements.

The selector performance battle is fought on two fronts: pruning and matching. In the pruning phase, the browser excludes all the selectors that it can say quickly and definitively won't match a particular element. At a minimum, the browser looks at the key selector (usually the rightmost selector component) to decide whether the selector can be pruned. Recently, browsers have started to introduce new pruning heuristics like ID scoping.

In the matching phase, the browser checks each selector that couldn't be pruned to see whether the entire selector matches the element's document context. This might mean looking up the document hierarchy in the case of descendant and child selectors or looking at sibling elements.

In general, a good approach with selectors is to keep the complexity of a selector low by keeping the number of HTML elements that have to be considered in order to decide whether the selector matches to a minimum.

8.6.2   *The danger of over-nesting*

Sass makes it easy to make slow selectors—and lots of them. Ugh. *Now* we tell you! All these lovely, presentation-free stylesheets that are possible with Sass are slowing down your page.

Sometimes Sass files that are compact and immensely readable can become behemoth CSS files, so it's important to keep the size and complexity of your generated CSS in mind when writing in Sass. In particular, there's a tendency for new users of Sass to begin to replicate their HTML structure using nested selectors. There's a certain purity to this approach. Ultimately, you end up in a world that's harder to maintain than inline styles—the smallest change in markup can break your design. What's more, since the default combinator when nesting is the descendant combinator (a.k.a. a space) and the key selector is usually an element selector, this means that your coding style is generating the most inefficient form of selectors that you can write.

To help you identify stylesheets that have become unsuspectingly bloated, Compass provides the stats command. To use the stats command, you must first install a Ruby gem called css_parser:

```
$ gem install css_parser
```

Then you can run the Compass stats command:

```
$ compass stats
```

You'll see all kinds of useful information about your Sass files. Here's the output from running compass stats on the Compass website's stylesheets. (Note: Some columns aren't shown here for formatting reasons.)

Filename	Sass Size	CSS Selectors	CSS Properties	CSS Size
home.scss	387	510	1579	41879
ie.scss	114	3	4	306
screen.scss	595	932	2846	68575
core/_base.sass	2052	--	--	--
core/_clearing.sass	382	--	--	--
core/_extensions.scss	192	--	--	--
partials/_ads.scss	666	--	--	--
partials/_blog.scss	84	--		
partials/_code.scss	4100	--	--	--
partials/_example.scss	483	--	--	--
partials/_home.scss	2508	--	--	--
partials/_install.scss	603	--	--	--
partials/_layout.scss	683	--	--	--
partials/_main.scss	1840	--	--	--
partials/_nav.scss	2085	--	--	--
partials/_sidebar.scss	550	--	--	--
partials/_theme.scss	9667	--	--	--
partials/_typography.scss	1824	--	--	--
Total (18 files):	28815	1445	4429	110760

As you can see, this makes it easy to see how many selectors are getting generated and how big the files are. The generated CSS files here are almost four times bigger than the source files. It's great that Sass and Compass do so much for you, but it's important to remember to wield their power responsibly.

8.7   *Summary*

One of the amazing things about working on the web is how many small ways there are to optimize just about anything that needs optimizing. Unfortunately, many of these approaches would take more effort than they're worth without a framework in place to help get the work done quickly. As you've seen, Compass has a broad array of tools to help you scale your website from thousands to millions of visitors.

As you've learned, there are dozens of things that you, the stylesheet author, can do to make your site much faster. Performance isn't just a server-side issue—quite the contrary, for many sites, client-side performance can end up being one of the hardest parts to optimize. Aren't you glad you have Sass and Compass to help you?

In the next chapter, you'll learn advanced Sass techniques for writing smarter, more powerful stylesheets. We'll look at how to write better, more flexible mixins, how to manipulate color and perform advanced math, and how to write your own Sass functions.

Part 4

Advanced Sass and Compass

In the first three sections, you've learned the basics of Sass and Compass and how they fit into your stylesheet authoring workflow. In this section, we explore some advanced features of Sass and Compass. In chapter 9, we start off looking at how Sass handles data types and expressions, allowing you to add strings and values, with intelligent unit conversions. We'll walk you through the many powerful functions for working with numbers, lists, and colors. You'll see how Sass can easily manipulate colors, giving you the ability to do dynamic theming right in your stylesheets. You'll also learn how to write your own Sass functions. Finally, we look at how to write loops with @for, @while, and @each and how to do conditional styling with @if and @else directives.

In chapter 10, we build on all you've learned so far to create a Compass extension. First, we discuss the various methods of sharing stylesheets and front-end code, their shortcomings, and how Sass and Compass make it easier for you to share great reusable stylesheets. You'll learn how to write an extension in its most basic form, followed by a thorough walk-through of the process for creating an advanced extension for styling beautiful CSS3 buttons. As you write and refactor your extension, we discuss design decisions and best practices for writing extension stylesheets. We discuss different ways to release your extension, and you'll learn how to easily create a Ruby gem to help you distribute your extension. Finally, we take a brief look at how to share and manage an open source project on GitHub.

When you've completed this book, you'll have a thorough understanding of how to use Sass and Compass to write smarter and more maintainable stylesheets. You'll be equipped to approach web design problems with a powerful set of new tools and a fresh perspective. You'll also know how to more easily participate in the design community by sharing your ideas and discoveries through open source. The tedium of writing stylesheets will be behind you, as new and exciting challenges await.

Scripting with Sass

In the last chapter. we looked at how to optimize your stylesheets to get the best performance out of the browser. In this chapter, you'll learn how to optimize Sass for readability and maintainability, and how to write smarter stylesheets that go way beyond the limitations of CSS.

You've already learned about the many benefits Sass adds on top of plain CSS. Variables, nested rules, and mixins all help to make CSS less repetitive. Mixins in particular are a good way to refactor repeated styles and patterns in a stylesheet and make them reusable.

But variables and mixins on their own can only go so far toward expressing patterns that you use in your stylesheets. Sometimes you want to avoid doing width

153

calculations over and over, or you want a mixin to have slightly different styles under different conditions. For this, you need Sass's more advanced scripting features, which we'll introduce in this chapter.

The core of advanced Sass use is the ability to manipulate CSS values (the sort that appear as property values). Sass supports all the arithmetic for numbers that you learned when you were seven: they can be added, subtracted, multiplied, and divided. It even understands units, so 5px + 10px = 15px.

Sass also understands all the other standard CSS data types like colors, names (like bold or center), and lists (like 1px solid black or font, font, font). It also has a data type of its own for representing true and false; this is used for making decisions about which styles to use.

Other than arithmetic, which is mostly used with numbers, the main way CSS values are manipulated in Sass is with functions. In addition to built-in CSS functions like rgb or hsl, Sass adds a whole slew of its own functions that do all sorts of useful things. Many of these are useful primarily in the context of complex scripting, but some are useful in isolation as well, especially the functions that manipulate colors. These are powerful enough to allow an entire theme's worth of colors to be generated from one or two base colors.

Sass also allows CSS values and Sass variables to be used outside of properties. They can be included in selectors and property names using a special syntax. This is useful for passing selectors or property names as parameters to a mixin.

The most advanced use of CSS values is in control structures. Control structures allow you to control whether styles are actually used and to produce many variations of one style without using mixins. They'll likely be familiar if you've used JavaScript or another programming language, but if you haven't, don't fret; despite being advanced, they're very straightforward.

9.1   *Using expressions*

Expressions are the most common way to manipulate CSS values in Sass. What's an expression? It's anything that can show up to the right of a property. In plain CSS, this is usually a simple value like bold or 5px, or a list of values like 1px solid black. In Sass, it can include not only variables, but mathematical operators, which we'll cover in this chapter.

Although all types of values can be used in expressions, they're most useful with numbers. Numeric expressions work just like the arithmetic you're used to: you can add, subtract, multiply, and divide, using the +, -, *, and / characters. The order of operations is the same, too: * and / happen before + and -, and expressions in parentheses happen first. In the following styles, we use multiplication and subtraction to create a simple grid system.

Listing 9.1 Using Sass expressions

```
$grid-cells: 20;
$cell-width: 25px;
#main {
  $main-width: $grid-cells * $cell-width;
  $main-padding: 10px;
  width: $main-width;
  padding: $main-padding;
  .sidebar {width: ($main-width - $main-padding*2)/4}
}
```

Expressions can occur anywhere in a property or variable value; they don't have to take up the entire thing. This is useful for combined properties, like border or background, that take multiple values separated by spaces. Take the following property, for example:

```
border: ($something - $something-else) solid blue
```

Since $something - $something-else is 5px, the property becomes 5px solid blue. The parentheses aren't required, but they make it easier to read.

Now that you've seen how expressions work, let's go over the data types CSS and Sass use and look at what they can do in Sass expressions.

9.2 Understanding data types

Every value in a CSS property or a Sass variable has a type, and, depending on this type, it works in different ways. Values like #abcdef or violet represent colors and are used to color things like text, backgrounds, and borders. Values like 100% or 5px represent numbers and are used to set widths, margins, and padding. Values like center or auto can represent a lot of different things, usually a choice among alternatives or a special value.

Sass understands all these types and more besides, and uses this understanding to allow them to be manipulated in expressions. The way they're manipulated differs from type to type, but all of them support the arithmetic operators (+, -, *, and /) to some degree. In this section, we'll examine each type and how it uses the operators in depth.

9.2.1 Strings and names

Strings are the most common data type in CSS. They're so called because they're just strings of letters. Anything that's just a name—bold, auto, center, and so on—is a string, as is anything with quotes around it, like "Helvetica Neue". The former is an *unquoted string*, whereas the latter is a *quoted string*.

The main difference between quoted and unquoted strings, other than the quotes themselves, relates to which characters are allowed as part of the string. Quoted strings can contain any character other than ", whereas unquoted strings can't begin with numbers or special characters, and can't contain spaces and some special characters like * or &.[1]

---

[1] There are exceptions to this rule, but they're part of CSS and outside the scope of this book.

There are also a few special constructs that Sass considers strings. The most straightforward is !important, which would not normally count as an unquoted string (because it begins with !), but Sass counts it as one anyway. url() values are also considered to be unquoted strings, even though (,), and special characters commonly found in URLs aren't normally allowed. But url($variable) is *not* considered to be a string; it instead wraps the contents of $variable in url().

The Internet Explorer–specific filter values are also considered to be strings, because they're technically invalid syntax according to the CSS spec (which is what Sass's parser follows). Thus, progid:DXImageTransform.Microsoft.gradient (startColorstr=#550000FF, endColorstr=#55FFFF00) is considered to be one big unquoted string. Similarly, the CSS3 calc() function is currently considered to be a string as well.

The most common operation on strings is +. When adding a string to any other value, string or not, the two values get joined together as a new string (see table 9.1). If the string was quoted, the result is quoted; otherwise, it won't be. If both values are strings, and one is quoted and the other isn't, then the resulting string will have the same quotation as the string on the left.

Table 9.1   Using the + operator with strings

Expression	Result
foo + 1	foo1
"foo" + 1	"foo1"
foo + bar	foobar
"foo" + "bar"	"foobar"
"foo" + bar	"foobar"
foo + "bar"	foobar

Most other operations are unsupported for strings. For historical reasons, - and / actually join the strings together like +, except that the operators themselves are included in the result (see table 9.2).

Table 9.2   The - and / operators working like + on strings

Expression	Result
foo - bar	foo-bar
foo / bar	foo/bar

Like strings, numbers are a common data type in CSS and Sass.

9.2.2 *Numbers*

In Sass, as in CSS, a number has two parts: the actual numeric value and (optionally) the unit. Commonly used units include px, em, and %.

Since Sass understands numbers with units, all the operations work with units as well. This follows the rules for handling units in science: when multiplying and dividing numbers with units, the units are multiplied and divided along with the numeric values.

This means that 5em * 4px is 20em*px, whereas 99px/1in is 99px/in.[2]

This unit arithmetic is useful for doing conversions between units. For example, if you set $pixels-per-em: 16px/1em, then you can calculate the pixels for 5em by doing 5em * $pixels-per-em. The result is 80px*em/em; both ems cancel out, and you get 80px. Sass handles all this automatically.

When adding or subtracting, there's not always an appropriate unit for the result. For instance, 5px + 10% doesn't make sense, since Sass doesn't know how to convert between pixels and percentages.[3] In these circumstances, Sass will throw an error. But if Sass knows how to convert between the units (such as in and cm), it will.

Most of the operations that can be done on numbers are just the familiar grade-school arithmetic operations that we've already talked about. There's one additional (slightly more complicated) operation for numbers: *modulo*. Modulo, written as %, gives the remainder of division of two numbers. So $num1 % $num2 is the remainder of $num1 / $num2. This operator is infrequently useful.

There's one complexity that arises when using / with numbers. CSS allows certain values to be separated by a forward slash (/), which in that case doesn't mean division. This is rarely used in practice, but since Sass expressions are a superset of CSS, they need to support this syntax without actually dividing the numbers.

The way Sass handles this is to use a few simple rules to determine whether to divide or to use a plain / (forward slash). If either value is a string, the result will use a plain forward slash. Otherwise, Sass will divide if and only if any of the following three conditions are met:

- Either side of the / uses a variable.
- The entire value is surrounded by parentheses.
- The value is used as part of another arithmetic expression.

For example, in the following expression, division isn't performed:

```
1px/2px => 1px/2px
```

But in these three, it is:

```
$var: 1px; $var/2px => 0.5px
(1px/2px) => 0.5px
1 + (1px/2px) => 1.5px
```

---

[2] Note that the px*em and px/in notation isn't valid Sass syntax; in order to get these values, you must multiply and divide by numbers.

[3] The CSS3 calc() function, which Sass supports, can do this, but only because it's calculated by the browser, which knows how everything is laid out.

Although numbers are used more often, colors are one of the most interesting of Sass's data types.

9.2.3   *Colors*

Colors in CSS can be written in a number of different ways. The most common is using the hexadecimal representation of the RGB channels: #abcdef represents 171 red, 205 green, and 239 blue. You can also represent the same information using a function: rgb(171, 205, 239). Then there are named colors like blue and violet, which are more descriptive but limited in selection. The hsl() function works similarly to rgb(), but with more useful dials to turn. Finally, rgba() and hsla() work like rgb() and hsl(), respectively, but also allow an alpha transparency value for the color to be specified. Sass understands all of these forms.

Internally, Sass keeps track of both the RGB and HSL values for a color, regardless of what form it was originally written in. This is useful for the color manipulation functions that we'll cover in section 9.3.2, many of which operate on the HSL properties of a color.

Colors used to support +, -, *, and / with numbers and other colors. But the way these operations worked was neither straightforward nor very useful, so they were deprecated in favor of the color functions we'll discuss in section 9.3.2.

The next data type we'll address is lists. Although lists, like colors, pop up a lot in CSS and Sass, you may not be used to thinking of them as their own entities. They're useful in cleaning up repetitive styles.

9.2.4   *Lists*

Lists are the sequences of values that are used for compound properties like border or background. For example, 1px solid black is a list of three values that you might use for the border property. Values in lists can be separated by either spaces, as in this example, or commas, as in font, font, font.

Precisely speaking, lists in Sass must contain more than one item. But individual values count as lists containing a single item for everything that cares about lists, including list functions and control directives like @each, which we'll cover later in this chapter.

Although in CSS lists can only contain individual values, in Sass lists can contain other lists as well. The clearest way this is done is by including space-separated lists within comma-separated lists. For example, the list foo bar, baz bang, bip bap contains three elements: foo bar, baz bang, and bip bap. Each of these in turn is a list containing two elements: the individual words.

Lists can be nested within other lists of the same type using parentheses as well, as in (foo bar) (baz bang) (bip bop) and (foo, bar), (baz, bang), (bip, bop), which are both lists of three two-element lists. When lists containing lists are converted to CSS, the parentheses are removed in order to make them valid CSS syntax.

Arithmetic operations don't do anything particularly useful for lists; they're allowed, but the lists are simply converted to unquoted strings, and then the corresponding string operation is used.

The real usefulness of lists is twofold. One use is for making code more concise with the @each directive, covered in section 9.5.2. The other use is as a way to pass more-complex arguments to mixins, which can then be accessed using Sass functions, covered in section 9.3.3.

The final data type in Sass is one that's not from CSS, but was added to allow mixins to use logic and make choices.

9.2.5 *Booleans*

Booleans, named after logician George Boole, represent truth values. There are only two of them: true and false. They're used (along with @if, which we'll cover in section 9.5.3) for making decisions in Sass about which styles to use.

Booleans don't use arithmetic operators. Instead, they have their own: and, or and not. These operators are straightforward: $bool1 and $bool2 is true if both $bool1 and $bool2 are true, whereas $bool1 or $bool2 is true if either one of $bool1 and $bool2 is true. not only operates on one value: not $bool is true if $bool is false, and false if $bool is true.

In fact, and, or, and not can be used with any value, although they're most useful with Booleans. Numbers, colors, strings, and lists all count as true for the purpose of and, or, and not. When using non-Boolean values, the result of and and or will be non-Boolean as well: $val1 and $val2 will return $val2 unless $val1 is false, whereas $val1 or $val2 will return $val2 only if $val1 is false.

There are also operators that work on other types but return Booleans, as in table 9.3.

The less-than and greater-than operators only apply to numbers, whereas the == operator applies to all types.[4] All of these operators return Booleans.

For many data types, operators don't do nearly enough to allow the user to make full use of those types. Because of this, Sass exposes much of its scripting functionality through functions.

Table 9.3 Operators that return Boolean values

Operator	Meaning
<	Less than
<=	Less than or equal to
>	Greater than
>=	Greater than or equal to
==	Exactly equal to

---

[4] Recall that Sass knows the RGB and HSL values for all colors, so blue, #0000ff, and hsl(240, 100, 50) all count as the same color for the purposes of ==.

9.3   *Functions*

Sass functions perform special operations on one or more values (called *arguments*). They use the familiar syntax of CSS functions like rgb() or hsl(), but they're evaluated as part of Sass expressions and they return Sass values.

Unlike CSS functions, Sass functions can have keyword arguments. This means that instead of using the order of arguments to a function to figure out which argument is which, some or all of the arguments can be explicitly named. The syntax for this is $name: value; the names of the arguments are listed along with the functions. This is especially useful for functions with many arguments, so you don't need to remember which goes where:

```
rgb($green: 127, $blue: 127, $red: 255)
```

One important aspect of Sass's design philosophy is that it's not possible to always have up-to-date information about which browsers support what, so it's better not to try. Thus, if you use a function that Sass doesn't recognize, it'll assume it's meant to be a plain CSS function and pass it through unchanged (except for evaluating the arguments). This can be annoying if you've made a typo in the function name, so it's important to keep it in mind.

Most of Sass's built-in functions are designed to be widely useful in many different circumstances. But they can't account for everything that anyone might want to do to a color or a set of numbers. Thus, Sass allows users to define their own functions in a manner similar to defining mixins. User-defined functions will be covered at the end of this section.

A substantial number of Sass's functions are designed to make it easier to define your own functions and mixins. Many of Sass's number functions aren't terribly useful in day-to-day design, but are good to have around when writing, say, a function to figure out grid width. Similarly, there's a collection of functions that provides information about values so that functions and mixins can make decisions based on that.

In this section, we'll go over the most commonly used built-in Sass functions, and then wrap up by discussing how to write your own. We'll begin by looking at the number functions. Then we'll move on to the color functions, before examining the list functions and finally concluding with a brief overview of the miscellaneous functions that don't fall into any of the other categories.

9.3.1   *Number functions*

Sass has a few functions that make it easier to deal with numbers, especially in situations that come up frequently when writing stylesheets with Sass. Currently there aren't any functions for relatively complex mathematical operations like exponentiation, logarithms, or trigonometry, since these are almost never useful for stylesheets. If they *are* necessary, they can be easily added through the Ruby extension API. Table 9.4 lists the functions we'll discuss.

Table 9.4 Functions for working with numbers

Function	Description
abs($number)	Takes the absolute value of $number
ceil($number)	Rounds $number up
comparable($number-1, $number-2)	Returns whether $number-1 and $number-2 can be compared
floor($number)	Rounds $number down
percentage($number)	Converts a decimal $number to a percentage
round($number)	Rounds $number to the nearest whole number
unit($number)	Returns the unit of $number
unitless($number)	Returns whether $number has no unit

Three of the Sass number functions have to do with rounding numbers to whole numbers. Unlike some programming languages, in Sass when you divide two numbers, the result is a decimal rather than always being a whole number. This is usually the desired result, but sometimes you do want a whole number. The rounding functions are for that. ceil($number) (for *ceiling*) rounds up, floor($number) rounds down, and round($number) rounds to the nearest whole number.

Similar to the rounding functions is abs($number), which returns the absolute value of a number. If $number is positive, abs returns it unchanged; if it's negative, abs returns the positive version of $number

percentage($number) is a different sort of function. It takes a decimal number (like 0.6, 0.33, or 1.3) and turns it into a percentage. So 0.6 becomes 60%, 0.33 becomes 33%, and 1.3 becomes 130%. This is the same as $number * 100%, but somewhat easier to read.

There are also a couple of number functions that provide information about one or more numbers. unit($number) returns the unit of the number as a string; this can be useful for printing error messages when the unit for a mixin argument is incorrect. unitless($number) returns true if a number has no units and false otherwise. comparable($number-1, $number-2) returns whether two numbers can be added and compared, based on the units. For example, comparable(13in, 5cm) is true since inches and centimeters can be converted back and forth, but comparable(5px, 10%) is false because pixels and percentages aren't measured on the same scale.

Whereas Sass's number functions are, by and large, normal mathematical operations, the functions Sass provides for dealing with colors are much richer and more interesting.

9.3.2   *Color functions*

The Sass color functions can be roughly divided into two categories: functions that return information about colors, and functions that transform old colors into new ones. Table 9.5 lists all these functions and divides them into *informative* and *transformative* categories.

Table 9.5   Functions for working with colors

Function	Type	Description
alpha($color) / opacity($color)	Informative	Returns the alpha channel of $color
blue($color)	Informative	Returns the blue channel of $color
green($color)	Informative	Returns the green channel of $color
hue($color)	Informative	Returns the hue property of $color
lightness($color)	Informative	Returns the lightness property of $color
red($color)	Informative	Returns the red channel of $color
saturation($color)	Informative	Returns the saturation property of $color
adjust($color, ...)	Transformative	Adjusts properties of $color by fixed amounts
complement($color)	Transformative	Returns the color wheel complement of $color
grayscale($color)	Transformative	Returns a grayscale version of $color
invert($color)	Transformative	Returns the negative version of $color
mix($color-1, $color-2, [$weight])	Transformative	Returns $color-1 and $color-2 mixed together, weighted by $weight
scale($color, ...)	Transformative	Scales properties of $color by percentages
set($color, ...)	Transformative	Sets properties of $color to fixed values

You learned in section 9.2.3 that all Sass colors know their RGB and their HSL values, regardless of how they were created. The information functions give you direct access to the individual components of these values: the red, green, blue, hue, saturation, or lightness of a function, as well as the alpha channel (which is 1, indicating a completely opaque color, unless the color was created with rgba(), hsla(), or certain Sass functions). These functions are named after the component they return: red($color), green($color), blue($color), hue($color), saturation($color), lightness($color), and alpha($color) (also known as opacity($color)).

Each of these functions returns the component in the same form as would be passed to either the rgb() or hsl() functions. Thus, red(), green(), and blue() return numbers from 0 to 255; hue() returns a number from 0deg to 359deg;[5] saturation() and lightness() return numbers from 0% to 100%; and alpha() returns a number from 0.0 to 1.0.

The transformation functions are more widely used than the information functions, since they make it easy to make nice-looking color themes quickly. Two of the most useful ones are adjust($color) and scale($color). Both of these take a color as the first argument, followed by a set of keyword arguments that describe how to transform specific components of that color. Both functions take a keyword argument for each component (such as $red, $saturation, $alpha), but what they do with these arguments differs.

adjust($color, ...) increases or decreases the value of the component or components by the amounts given. Thus, adjust($color, $red: 20, $alpha: -0.5) increases the red component of $color by 20 and decreases the opacity by 0.5. Similarly, adjust($color, $lightness: 15%, $hue: 10deg) increases the lightness by 15% (the new lightness is the old lightness plus 15%) and the hue by 10 degrees.[6]

scale($color, ...) is similar, but it takes percentages for all components. Rather than increasing or decreasing the components by a set amount, it scales them fluidly by the percent given. Thus, scale($color, $lightness: 30%) will make $color 30% lighter (30% closer to pure white) regardless of what the lightness already is. This can be better than adjust() for colors that are light to begin with: if a color already had 80% lightness, adjust() would make it pure white (100% lightness) whereas scale() would only make it 86% lightness. Like adjust(), scale() can have as many keywords as you want as long as it doesn't have both RGB and HSL components specified. scale() also doesn't support $hue, since the color wheel is a circle and so scaling it doesn't make a lot of sense.

Another useful color function is mix($color-1, $color-2, [$weight]).[7] This mixes two colors together by taking the average of their components. In addition, you can optionally choose how much one color or the other affects the mix using the $weight argument. The closer $weight is to 100%, the more $color-1 is used; the closer it is to 0%, the more $color-2 is used. The mixing is also affected by how opaque the colors are; a more opaque color will have a greater effect on the resulting color.

The set($color) function works similarly to adjust() and scale(): it takes a keyword for each component of a color. But its behavior is much simpler (and somewhat less useful): rather than modifying the existing components, it sets them to the new

---

[5] The CSS spec says that the unit for the hue component of HSL colors is deg. Using it is optional, so it's usually omitted.

[6] You aren't allowed to use RGB keywords at the same time as HSL keywords; otherwise, you may use as many keywords as you want.

[7] The square brackets around $weight indicate that it's an optional argument.

value. So set($color, $red: 120) will set the red component of $color to 120 and be done with it.

Finally, there are a few convenience color functions. These functions' effects are possible to achieve without the functions themselves, but the functions make it easier and more explicit. grayscale($color) sets the saturation of $color to 0%, making it a shade of gray. complement($color) rotates the hue by 180 degrees, making the color wheel complement of the original color. And invert($color) flips all the RGB components, returning the negative version of the original color.

Sass provides three built-in list functions, which we'll examine next.

9.3.3   *List functions*

Using the Sass list functions, it's possible to do whatever you need with lists, although it may be useful to define your own functions for some repetitive operations.

The most useful list function is nth($list, $n), which returns a single item (the nth one) in a list. Unlike in languages like JavaScript, Sass lists start counting items at 1. Thus, nth(foo bar baz, 2) returns bar, and nth(a b c, 1) returns a.

The join($list1, $list2, [$separator]) function is used to create new lists. It joins two lists together. Since a single value counts as a list with a single item, this function can also be used to make lists out of individual items. The optional $separator argument says which type of list it should be; it can be either space or comma. If it's left out, then the type of $list1 is used.

The length($list) function is simple. It returns the number of items in $list. So length(1 2 3) is 3, whereas length(foo) is 1.

Sass also has some miscellaneous functions that are mostly useful for doing advanced scripting.

9.3.4   *Other Sass functions*

Sass's miscellaneous functions are mostly used for writing mixins to be used in many projects. The type-of($value) function returns an unquoted string representing the type of the value in question. This type can be number, string, color, bool (for Boolean), or list.

The if($condition, $if-true, $if-false) chooses between two values based on a Boolean value. If $condition is true, then it returns $if-true. Otherwise, it returns $if-false. Like the Boolean operators, any non-Boolean values count as true for if().

You may also define your own Sass functions using the @function directive.

9.3.5   *User-defined functions*

The @function directive for defining your own function is useful when you have some repetitive math calculation or color transformation that you're using in many contexts. @function works much like @mixin, except that only a few things are allowed within a @function and every @function must return a result:

```
@function grid-width($cells) {
  @return ($cell-width + $cell-padding) * $cells;
}
```

The @return directive is the heart of a @function. It works much like return in JavaScript: it takes a Sass expression and returns the value as the result of the function. It will also end the function immediately, although this won't be very useful until you learn about control directives.

It wouldn't make sense to have a CSS rule inside a function, nor a property. In fact, a @function may only contain a few things: @return, naturally, as well as variable declarations, comments, and control directives (which we'll cover in section 9.5).

9.4   *Using expressions in selectors and property names*

CSS properties aren't the only place where CSS values can be used in Sass. Sass adds a special syntax for using CSS values, as well as variables and expressions, in many additional contexts, like selectors and property names. This is useful for mixins, especially those that are made to be widely used, and thus need to be as generally applicable as possible.

You can wrap an expression in #{ and } anywhere in selectors or property names, and the result will be included in the CSS output in place of the #{...}. The result will appear just as it would if it were the value of a property, except that quotes will be removed from quoted strings. This is known as *interpolation*.

In the following example, a mixin is created that uses interpolation to use its arguments in a selector and a property name.

> **Listing 9.2   Replacing an expression with its end value**

```
@mixin thing($class, $prop) {
  .thing.#{$class} {
    prop-#{$prop}: val;
  }
}

@include thing(foo, bar);
```

#{$class} is replaced by foo, and #{$prop} is replaced by bar, so the resulting CSS looks like the following:

```
.thing.foo {
  prop-bar: val;
}
```

Interpolation allows mixins to be used for more than packaging up a few styles. For example, it can be used to remove the repetition of writing the vendor prefixes for properties that are common when using the latest CSS facilities provided by browsers. In the following example, the experimental mixin uses interpolation to avoid having to write browser prefixes for every cutting-edge CSS property.

Listing 9.3   Using interpolation to add vendor prefixes for CSS properties

```
@mixin experimental($property, $value) {
  -moz-#{$property}: $value;
  -webkit-#{$property}: $value;
  -ms-#{$property}: $value;
  #{$property}: $value;
}
```

Although CSS hacks to target specific browsers are distasteful, sometimes they can be necessary. Interpolation can be useful there as well. The following example uses interpolation to avoid having to write out a property name twice when giving it an IE6-specific value.

Listing 9.4   Using interpolation for CSS browser hacks

```
@mixin bang-hack($property, $value, $ie6-value) {
  #{$property}: $value !important;
  #{$property}: $ie6-value;
}
```

Interpolation can also be used in expressions, although this is less useful since expressions themselves already allow variables and other expressions to be used. But it does allow variables to be inserted into strings and string-like expressions (like `calc()` or Internet Explorer's `filter` syntax).

Listing 9.5   Inserting variables into strings

```
content: "This element is #{$color}";
width: calc(10% + #{$padding});
filter: progid:DXImageTransform.Microsoft.Alpha(
          Opacity=#{$opacity * 100}
      );
```

As you can see, interpolation can be very useful for writing dynamic stylesheets. It may not be something you'll use every day, but it's a good technique to have in your arsenal.

9.5   *Control directives*

In some ways, *control directives* are the most advanced aspect of scripting with Sass. They certainly bear great similarity to programming languages, unlike most of the rest of Sass, which is based more on CSS than anything else. But even if you're a pure designer with no experience coding, don't let this intimidate you: all of Sass's control directives are straightforward. They're also useful for making designs and making mixins to help make designs (they'd have to be, or they wouldn't be part of Sass).

A control directive is a special type of directive that controls the way a chunk of Sass styles becomes CSS. Control directives take the form `@directive { ... }` and control the styles within their block. How this works differs from directive to directive. We'll look at all three of Sass's control directives in this section. The first two, `@for` and @each, cause a chunk of styles to be used multiple times with variations each time; @for does so for a specific number of times, whereas @each does so for each item in a list. Finally, @if controls whether a chunk of styles is used at all.

Control directives work for more than just styles. When writing complex mixins or functions, it can sometimes be useful to have only variable assignments within control directives. This allows you to choose the definition of a variable using @if, or build the value up using @for or @each.

Let's begin by looking at the @for directive.

9.5.1 *Repeating styles for a range of numbers*

The @for directive counts from one number to another, using a chunk of styles for each number on its way. It has two syntaxes, which are similar to one another: @for $i from 1 to 5 { ... } and @for $i from 1 through 5 { ... }. For both of these, the variable $i is first set to 1 and then increases by 1 each time the styles in the block are used. The two syntaxes differ in where $i stops: for 1 to 5, it stops at 4, whereas for 1 through 5, it stops at 5.

The following style is compiled to five different rating classes, each with a different background image. These images presumably contain one through five stars, thumbs-up, or something like that:

```
@for $i from 1 through 5 {
  .rating-#{$i} {
    background-image: url(/images/rating-#{$i}.png);
  }
}
```

You don't have to use 1 and 5 for your start and end numbers. You could use -5 and 15, or 22 and 379. You could even use variables and count from $a to $b (this can be useful for mixins or user-defined functions). Similarly, you can name the counting variable ($i in this example) whatever you want.

@for can't do everything, though: it can't count down, or count by twos, or count fractions. But with a little cleverness, you can mimic this by doing some math on $i.

Listing 9.6 Mimicking counting backward or by twos

```
// count backwards from 10 to 0
@for $i from 0 through 10 {
  $i: 10 - $i;
  ...
}

// count to 20 by twos
@for $i from 0 through 10 {
  $i: $i * 2;
  ...
}
```

Although counting is useful, often you just want to make styles for each of a list of values. For this, you use the @each directive.

9.5.2   *Repeating styles for a list of values*

The @each directive, like @for, repeats a chunk of styles multiple times. But instead of just counting, @each uses the chunk for each item in a list. The syntax is @each $item in foo, bar, baz { ... }, and it assigns $item to each of foo, bar, and baz, in turn. The following example uses @each to style a link for each section of a website:

```
@each $section in home, about, archive, projects {
  nav .#{$section} {
    background-image: url(/images/nav/#{$section}.png);
  }
}
```

The list for @each can be space-separated as well as comma-separated, although comma-separated lists tend to be easier to read. It can also be a list in a variable, or even a variable containing some other type of value (since nonlist values count as single-element lists).

9.5.3   *Conditional styling*

The @if directive controls whether a chunk of styles is used at all. It's less useful in day-to-day styling than @for or @each, but it comes up a lot when writing mixins and functions that are going to be used across many projects. These mixins and functions need to accept a broad range of parameters, and sometimes they need to behave differently based on these parameters. @if provides the means to do that.

The syntax is @if condition { ... }, where condition can be a Boolean variable, an expression with a Boolean value (such as one using == or >), or even an expression with any other value (since such values count as true). If the expression is true, then the block of styles is used; otherwise, it's ignored. The following example uses @if to add browser prefixes to a style if the $use-browser-prefixes variable is set.

Listing 9.7   Conditional styling with @if

```
.rounded {
  @if $use-browser-prefixes {
    -moz-border-radius: 5px;
    -webkit-border-radius: 5px;
  }
  border-radius: 5px;
}
```

You can optionally include the @else directive after the @if block as well. This allows you to use a different block of styles if the first one isn't used. The @else directive can either have its own condition, as in @else if condition { ... }, in which case the block is only used if that condition is true; or it can just be on its own, as in @else { ... }, in which case the block is always used. Any number of @else ifs can be used for each @if, along with one @else. The following example uses an @else if and an @else to scale a background color based on an alpha channel value.

Listing 9.8   Combining @if and @else for advanced conditions

```
@if $alpha < 0.2 {
  background-color: black;
} @else if $alpha < 0.5 {
  background-color: gray;
} @else {
  background-color: white;
}
```

This is the sort of thing that you'd expect to see in a mixin that takes $alpha as a parameter, but probably not in any non-mixin styles.

9.6   *Summary*

Now you've been introduced to the full range of Sass's functionality. Using these tools properly, you'll be able to create powerful, reusable styles that will dramatically increase the ease and expressiveness with which you design. You'll even be able to write styles that can be used across many projects by yourself and others, improving the broad world of design.

In this chapter, you've learned how Sass expressions work, including how to use arithmetic operations and variables in them. We've covered the various data types that Sass supports, including operations on those types.

We've gone over the many useful functions that Sass provides for dealing with these data types, and you've learned to write custom functions. You've learned to use the result of these functions and expressions in selectors and properties via interpolation. Finally, we've talked about how to use control directives to control how, and how often, blocks of styles are used in the compiled CSS.

So far, in this book you've learned a lot about Sass and Compass. You've seen the power of Sass as an expressive dynamic language, and seen how Compass integrates with your development and production environments and provides a fantastic library of Sass tools. In the next chapter, we'll bring it all together and learn how to use Compass extensions to create a modern stylesheet framework.

Creating and sharing
a Compass extension

10

This chapter covers

- Sharing Sass stylesheets and why Compass extensions are needed
- An introduction to simple extensions
- A detailed walk-through on writing an advanced extension
- Creating templates to bootstrap or demonstrate an extension
- A brief overview of different methods of sharing extensions

---

Up to this point, each chapter has focused on helping you get acquainted with different features of Sass and Compass and how they enhance working with stylesheets. This chapter brings it all together, building on your knowledge of Sass and Compass to help you take the next step and write a Compass framework. We'll discuss sharing code with the community and walk through the process of writing an extension for styling CSS3 buttons. We'll explore the design decisions that go into building this extension, and discuss the principles and best practices that create truly excellent code.

10.1 Sharing and reusing stylesheets

Those of us who've been writing stylesheets for some time know the joy of watching a tricky bit of CSS finally come together. We save our stylesheets and refresh our browsers in anticipation. Then our creation blinks into existence in all its glory. Success! A victory dance is in order. But what comes next?

Empowered with the expressiveness of Sass, our stylesheets can be smarter, and these moments of discovery can come far more frequently than when we used vanilla CSS. Also, Sass and Compass make it easier than ever to share our triumphs and epiphanies.

10.1.1 Sass is easier to share than CSS

Sharing stylesheets used to mean writing a blog post with CSS snippets and downloadable demos. The more ambitious the solution, the more challenging it was for readers to use. Helpful authors would explain how to properly customize and reuse their stylesheets, meaning that more complex and interesting CSS stylesheets were a greater burden to share and were harder for readers to use. Also, with CSS frameworks, any included stylesheet automatically affects a website's style. This means that users must be careful what class names they use, or they must edit the CSS framework to pick and choose what they want.

On the other hand, Sass users can share incredibly useful stylesheets that don't output a single line of CSS. A stylesheet full of mixins and functions will have no direct impact on a site's style. Instead, Sass provides tools to help designers build something that's completely their own. Sass stylesheets aren't limited to selectors, properties, and values. With variables, @if, @else, @for, and @while, as well as custom functions and mixins, Sass is inherently more expressive than CSS.

A critical flaw in CSS frameworks is that, beyond inheritance, they have no concept of reuse. When a Sass author writes @mixin button-style($color), they define a purposed block of code, and every time this mixin is included, it indicates to the reader that this element belongs to an organized framework of design. Vanilla CSS can't do this. A block of CSS styles can't be reused, only copied. CSS has no way to preserve its integrity as it's used across a series of stylesheets.

Expressiveness and abstraction are two key characteristics that make Sass easier to explain and easier to share.

10.1.2 Share-ready Sass

If you've ever used a CSS framework before, you're no doubt familiar with the frustration of having to become acquainted with new class names and design patterns. Though some frameworks are better documented than others, in general, if you don't want exactly what they offer, you could wind up spending hours digging through their code to remove parts you don't like while trying to preserve what you do. It's awful. When sharing Sass stylesheets, be careful to avoid this painful and outdated practice.

Though you can package up your favorite designs for buttons, lists, tables, and typography just like the CSS frameworks of the past, the features of Sass guide you toward a different kind of sharing. Instead of writing out the style for a certain type of button, it's much nicer to encapsulate that style inside of a mixin. Packaging your styles as a series of mixins is a terrific opt-in way to share a stylesheet framework, helping the user retain full control of their site's design. Also, you could wire up your mixins to accept a set of variables, allowing users to customize attributes of your framework.

Sass functions can also be a great resource. If your framework offers customizable color schemes, it can be awfully challenging to ensure quality results. For example, if a user is able to choose a background color for a button, the text for that button should still be easily readable. Here's a snippet of Sass that can help out. It uses the color functions built right into Sass to pick a higher contrast text color to go with the given background color. The following code is in color-helpers.scss in this chapter's code examples.

Listing 10.1   Helpful color functions

```
// Returns true if the color is brighter than 50% lightness
@function is-bright($color) {
    @return (lightness($color) > 50%);
}

// Returns the $light value if bright, $dark value if dark
@function if-bright($bg, $light: true, $dark: false) {
    @return if(is-bright($bg), $light, $dark);
}

// Picks the color with the highest contrast
@function text-contrast($bg, $dark-text: #000, $light-text: #fff) {
    @return if-bright($bg, $dark-text, $light-text);
}
```

This is a great example of how Sass addresses a broader range of problems in web design, transforming what designers and developers can do with stylesheets. Here you can see how sharing Sass differs from sharing CSS. It's also a picture of how authoring stylesheets has finally joined the world of web development as authors are sharing and reusing tools rather than implementations. But simply posting a Sass file or snippet on the web isn't enough. With Compass extensions, you can do much better.

10.1.3   *Sharing Sass isn't enough*

As you've seen, Sass is much more sharing-friendly than CSS, but when you have a handy Sass snippet you'd like to share, what's the best way to get it out there? You could blog about it, or even release it as an iterative demo on CodePen (http://codepen.io).

Others can simply copy your code into their projects and start enjoying your work. But what if you want to release something that's more than just a snippet?

What if you need to include companion assets like images, fonts, JavaScript, or HTML? This would require users to move all of these files to their proper locations in order to integrate your work into their project. The more elaborate the solution, the more effort it takes for someone to begin using it.

10.1.4 Why use a Compass extension?

Compass extensions are a great way to share Sass scripts (and related assets), making it easy for others to use your work. They also make a great building block for a personal or company-wide framework. Rather than copying snippets of Sass from project to project, you should really be writing Compass extensions.

When someone installs your Compass extension, you can be sure they have access to the same library of mixins, functions, and other features provided by Compass. This makes it easy to build against the solid library included with Compass. If you want to do something with sprites or CSS3, you can confidently leverage Compass's tools without worrying about adding complexity to your extensions.

Compass extensions can include multiple project templates to show users the different features of your extensions, and give them a starting point to begin playing around with working examples. Based on its configuration file, Compass knows where assets belong so your templates can easily install stylesheets, images, or JavaScript in the right place.

If it sounds like extensions take a lot of work, fear not. Creating your own extension is simple.

10.2 A simple extension

For this example, we'll take the color functions we looked at earlier and package them up as a simple extension called color-helpers. If you want to take a peek, you can find this simple extension in this chapter's code examples. The directory structure looks like the following.

> **Listing 10.2 The simplest extension**

```
color-helpers/
  stylesheets/
    color-helpers.scss
```

It's a directory named after the color-helpers extension that contains a stylesheets directory and a Sass file, which is also named after your extension. This is an extension in its most basic form. You could share this as a project on GitHub or upload a zip file to your website. This is generally referred to as an *ad hoc extension*. You can also distribute an extension as a Ruby gem, which allows users to download, install, and update your extension from the command line. We'll look at that more in a bit.

10.2.1 Installing ad hoc extensions

To install this extension, a Compass user would copy the color-helpers directory into their project's extensions folder. After the extension is in the proper directory, the extension's Sass files can be imported just as if they were in the project's sass directory.

For standalone projects, extensions belong in an extensions directory in the root of the project, for example project_root/extensions/color-helpers/. In Rails projects, ad hoc extensions are installed to vendor/plugins/compass_extensions. Compass doesn't automatically create these directories by default, so extension users will have to add them manually.

10.2.2 Testing your extension

To take your new extension for a spin, you'll create a new Compass project and install the color-helpers extension. Either run the following commands in a terminal, or check out the test-color-helpers directory from the code examples:

```
compass create test-color-helpers --bare
```

Now you'll add a sass/screen.scss and create an extensions directory. Copy the color-helpers extension into the extensions directory, and your project will look like figure 10.1.

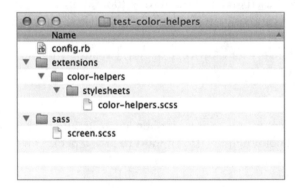

Figure 10.1   Color helpers project setup

Now you'll add @import "color-helpers"; to screen.scss, and you can begin using these color functions in your project. In the example code, you'll find a couple of examples of the color-contrast function in use. Admittedly, this isn't an exciting extension. Two color functions aren't going to get you very far and, as we covered earlier, extensions can be more than just stylesheets, so let's work on something more fun: CSS3 buttons!

10.3   Creating an extension demo project

As you've seen, an extension isn't a fully formed Compass project, but a library of files that are intended to be used within a Compass project. The best way to begin developing an extension is to create a Compass demo project. In a bit, we'll begin working on an advanced extension, but first we'll walk through setting up a demo project.

The demo will serve two purposes. First, it'll help you develop and test your extension, and second, after you're done, you can use this demo as a project template for your extension. Users will be able to easily install this demo into their own Compass projects, giving them a quick way to try out your extension.

Our goal for this extension is to help users generate beautiful CSS3 buttons with little effort. We'll call this extension nice-buttons, because who doesn't love a nice button? The directory structure for your demo project is shown in figure 10.2.

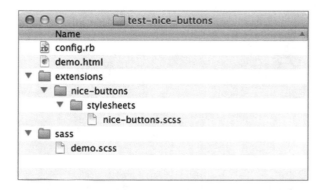

**Figure 10.2   Nice-buttons
demo project setup**

Just like for the color-helpers extension, you have a basic Compass project with an extensions directory named after your extension, containing a stylesheets directory with a Sass file which is also named after your extension. The only real difference here is that you have a demo.html file, which you'll use to preview your styles in the browser. The demo HTML doesn't have to be anything fancy. You just need a button and a link for your extension to style.

Listing 10.3   demo.html file

```
<!DOCTYPE html>
<html>
  <head>
    <title>Nice Buttons - Demo</title>
    <link href="stylesheets/demo.css" rel="stylesheet"
                                        type="text/css">
  </head>
  <body>
    <h1>Button Test</h1>
    <button>Click Me!</button>
    <a class="button" href="#">Click Me!</a>
  </body>
</html>
```

You may be wondering why we're using `<button>Launch</button>` instead of `<input type="submit" value="Launch">`. Historically, input buttons are hard to consistently style across browsers and operating systems. Modern browsers tend to be easier to work with, but the HTML 4.01 specification (http://www.w3.org/TR/html401/interact/ forms.html#h-17.5) states that the `<button>` element was created to offer richer rendering possibilities. As a result, we tend to use input buttons when we want to use the default style for an OS or a browser. When we want to do some custom styling, we know we can count on the <button> element to be consistent.

Next, in demo.scss you'll import the nice-buttons extension and add a bit of Sass to get started.

Listing 10.4   demo.scss file

```
@import 'nice-buttons';
html {
  font-family: Helvetica, Arial, sans;
  background: #f4f4f4;
}
body {
  text-align: center;
  position: absolute;
  top: 30px; left: 30px; bottom: 30px; right: 30px;
  padding-top: 20px;
  background: #fff;
  border: 1px solid #e5e5e5;
}
```

Since you haven't yet written styles for the button or link, figure 10.3 shows what you have after compiling demo.scss.

Figure 10.3   Nice-buttons demo—before styling

Now that your demo project is all set up, you can begin writing the extension.

10.4   *Writing an advanced extension*

Before we get to the fun CSS3 part, it's a good idea to write some simple button reset styles. Depending on the operating system and the browser, buttons have different default styles, and since links are commonly styled as buttons, you want to be sure that your styles will apply consistently to both of them. For that, you'll add the nice-button mixin to nice-buttons.scss.

Listing 10.5   nice-buttons.scss file

```
@import "compass/css3";

@mixin nice-button() {

    // reset styles
    font: normal 16px/18px "Lucida Grande", Lucida, Arial, sans-serif;
    margin: 0;
    text-decoration: none;
    cursor: pointer;
    padding: .5em 1.2em;
    @include border-radius(.3em);
    &:active, &:hover { outline: none }

    // Normal styles
    background-color: #eee;
    border: #bbb 1px solid;
    color: #333;
}
```

Since you'll rely on the CSS3 mixins in Compass, you need to make sure to import Compass's CSS3 module at the top. If users are already importing the CSS3 module, this import will be ignored. Now you just have to include this mixin in demo.scss:

```
button, .button { @include nice-button }
```

A trip to the browser shows you that you're on the right track (see figure 10.4).

The button and the link now appear identical, but they're far from beautiful. You should fix that.

10.4.1 *Automating the hard parts*

You've laid the groundwork; now it's time to work on the valuable part of this extension. You want users to be able to create a nice button by simply telling your mixin what color it should be. To help automate some of the styling, you'll rely on the brilliant color transformation functions in Sass as well as the two color functions we looked at earlier in this chapter.

Figure 10.4   Consistently styled buttons

Go ahead and create _color-helpers.scss in extensions/nice-buttons/stylesheets/, and then add the three color functions and import that file at the top of nice-buttons.scss with `@import "color-helpers";`. Next, you'll change your mixin to accept a background color and pick related colors.

Listing 10.6   nice-buttons.scss

```
@mixin nice-button($bg: #eee) {
    ...
  // Normal styles
  background-color: $bg;
  color: text-contrast($bg, $dark-text: mix($bg, #000, 25%));
  border: scale-color($bg, $lightness: -20%) 1px solid;
}
```

Now this mixin lets users set a background color (which defaults to #eee if they don't pass anything), and then, using the `text-contrast` function, you pick a good text color to go with it. You're mixing the dark text with a bit of the background color to help it blend more nicely with the rest of the button. Finally, the border color is chosen by darkening the background color. Make a quick update to the demo.scss.

Listing 10.7   demo.scss

```
button { @include nice-button } // default mixin background
.button { @include nice-button(#494e57) } // a dark blue gray
```

Figure 10.5 shows your progress.

Figure 10.5   Starting to automate color choices

Those color functions are doing a nice job of simplifying things, but these buttons need gradients. To keep this mixin simple, you'll generate the gradient in a separate "support" mixin.

Listing 10.8   nb-gradient—nice-buttons.scss

```
@mixin nb-gradient($bg) {
  // scale main color to pick
  $top:      scale-color($bg, $lightness: 40%);
```

```
$middle-1: scale-color($bg, $lightness: 10%);
$middle-2: scale-color($bg, $lightness: -5%);
$bottom:   scale-color($bg, $lightness: -20%);

@include background-image(linear-gradient(
  $top, $middle-1 50%, $middle-2 50%, $bottom));
}
```

With these variables, you can create a nice gradient with a top shine, a bottom shadow, and a faint center line, giving the button a three-dimensional appearance. When creating support mixins like `nb-gradient` it's nice to namespace them with the initials of the extension. It's a way of keeping mixin names short, while also telling those who read the source code, *This is an internal mixin; you're probably not going to use it.* Add `@include nb-gradient($bg);` to the `nice-button` mixin, and you get something like figure 10.6.

The dark button looks good, but the gradient on the light button seems a bit high-contrast. To address that, you'll treat light and dark backgrounds differently.

Listing 10.9   Color assignment in `nb-gradient` mixin

```
// scale main color to pick
$top:      scale-color($bg, $lightness: if-bright($bg, 80%, 40%));
$middle-1: scale-color($bg, $lightness: if-bright($bg, 20%, 10%));
$middle-2: scale-color($bg, $lightness: if-bright($bg, -2%, -5%));
$bottom:   scale-color($bg, $lightness: if-bright($bg, -10%, -20%));
```

Now your gradient mixin can tune its color transformations to improve the final gradient. The `if-bright` function looks at `$bg` and uses the first percentage if it's brighter than 50%, the second if it's darker. This is far simpler than writing separate gradient code for bright and dark colors. It took some fiddling to settle on the percentages, but it's a nice improvement (see figure 10.7).

The difference here is subtle, but this level of care helps you make a great extension. You can take the same approach to color manipulation when adding a text shadow and a box shadow.

Figure 10.6   Initial gradient styling

Figure 10.7   Improvements from tuning the color transformation

Listing 10.10   `text-shadow`—nice-buttons.scss

```
text-shadow: scale-color($bg, $lightness:
    if-bright($bg, 25%, -25%)) 0 1px 1px;
@include box-shadow(rgba(#fff,
    if-bright($bg, .6, .2))    0 0 1px 1px inset);
```

For the text shadow, the `if-bright` function is deciding whether to darken or lighten the color, and on the box shadow it chooses the correct transparency. You can see how powerful this simple automation can be. Figure 10.8 shows what you have so far.

**Figure 10.8   Added `text-shadow`
and inset `box-shadow`**

Now let's refine what you have and add some interactive styles and a nice CSS3 transition.

When styling a button's focus, hover, and active states, it's common to lighten, darken, and add shadows. There are many ways to achieve these effects, but as you begin to layer on the CSS3, you should consider the size of the generated CSS. At the time of publication, you still need to use CSS3 vendor prefixes, and though Compass takes care of that for you, the output can be pretty large. Generating a new brighter or darker gradient for hover and active states adds a lot of CSS to the output. If people use this extension to style many different buttons, the impact could be significant.

To add these interactive styles while keeping your output lean, you'll use a clever trick. When including the `nb-gradient` mixin, you'll use a partially transparent color. This means your gradient will show through to the background color of the button. Now you can change the background color of the button behind the gradient, and the change will show through. Here are the main button styles so far.

Listing 10.11   Normal button styles in `nice-button` mixin—nice-buttons.scss

```
// Normal styles
background-color: $bg;
border: scale-color($bg, $lightness: -20%) 1px solid;
color: text-contrast($bg);

@include nb-gradient(rgba($bg, .7)); // alpha shows color transitions
@include transition(background-color,box-shadow .15s);
```

```
text-shadow: scale-color($bg, $lightness:
    if-bright($bg,25%,-25%)) 0 1px 1px;
@include box-shadow(rgba(#fff,
    if-bright($bg,.6,.2)) 0 0 1px 1px inset);
```

Now add the button state styles.

Listing 10.12 Styling `:hover` and `:focus`—nice-buttons.scss

```
// State styles
&:hover, &:focus {
  background-color: scale-color($bg,
    $lightness: if-bright($bg, 85%, 25%)
  );
}

&:active {
  background: scale-color($bg,
    $lightness: if-bright($bg, 55%, 15%)
  );
  border-color: rgba(#000, if-bright($bg, .4, .8));
  @include box-shadow(
    if-bright($bg,
      rgba(mix($bg, #000, 25%), .4),
      rgba(mix($bg, #000), .9)
    ) 0 2px 12px inset
  );
}
```

Basically, you're adjusting the background colors and adding a deep inset box shadow while the button is being pressed. In the active state, instead of setting `background-color`, you set the `background` property, removing the gradient background image so that you're left with the background color and an inset box shadow, creating a depressed look. Figure 10.9 shows all three states back to back.

Figure 10.9 Interactive button states—nice-buttons.scss

With a screenshot, it's hard to get a sense of how this button feels when you click it, so be sure to check out the demo in the example code. The styling part of this extension is done, but you can still do some refactoring.

10.4.2 *Refactoring your extension*

Right now, your extension's main mixin, `nice-button`, consists of three different sections:

1 The reset styles
2 The normal button styles
3 The button state styles

The reset styles are the same for every button, and each button uses the same CSS3 transition. So each time the `nice-button` mixin is included, you duplicate eight lines of Sass. Add the extra CSS generated for vendor prefixes, and this is clearly something you need to fix.

This is a great use case for `@extend`. You could add these styles to a base class and have each button extend them like this:

```
.button-reset {
  // Reset styles
  ...
}
@mixin nice-button {
  @extend .button-reset;
  ...
}
```

But you're not going to do this.

This is a situation where writing an extension probably differs from how you might write the same styles in your own project. Even though .button-reset is probably a safe class name to use, this violates a key principle of extension design: *An extension shouldn't output any CSS unless asked to do so.* As much as possible, styles in your extension should live inside mixins. Otherwise, you make assumptions about which elements or class names people will use, and importing your extension's stylesheets could cause elements in their design to automatically inherit your styles.

You can achieve the same goal by putting your reset styles inside of a mixin, and then include the reset mixin under a placeholder selector:

```
@mixin nice-button-reset() {
  // reset styles
}
%nice-button-reset { @include nice-button-reset; }
```

As you saw in chapter 2, if placeholders are never extended, the styles inside of them will never be compiled to CSS. This is great for extension authors, since it allows your extension to enjoy the benefits of selector inheritance without generating any unnecessary styles or class names.

Why use a reset mixin instead of just writing styles underneath the placeholder? The reason is because a mixin stores your reset styles so they can be reused anywhere. It's possible that in someone's project, their styling could override your reset styles. With a mixin, they can easily include the styles to fight back against the cascade.

Applying this principle, the outline for your extension looks like the following.

Listing 10.13 Extension overview

```
@mixin nb-reset() {
  // Reset styles
}
%nb-reset { @include nb-reset }

@mixin nb-gradient($bg) {
  // Gradient styles
}

@mixin nice-button($bg: #eee) {
  @extend %nb-reset
  // Normal styles
  // Button state styles
}
```

With all the duplication removed, your extension is in great shape. It generates beautiful buttons and beautiful CSS. Take a look at the full 62 lines of Sass that make up your extension.

Listing 10.14 Extension directory pattern

```
@import "compass/css3";
@import "color-helpers";

// Button style reset and basic styles
@mixin nb-reset() {
  font: normal 16px "Lucida Grande", Lucida, Arial, sans-serif;
  margin: 0;
  text-decoration: none;
  margin-bottom: .3em;
  cursor: pointer;
  padding: .5em 1.2em;
  display: inline-block;
  border: { width: 1px; style: solid }
  @include border-radius(.3em);
  &:active, &:hover { outline: none }
  @include transition(background-color,box-shadow .15s);
}

%nb-reset { @include nb-reset; }

// Automate the gradient picking with simple color shifting
@mixin nb-gradient($bg) {
  $top:      scale-color($bg, $lightness: if-bright($bg,80%,40%));
  $middle-1: scale-color($bg, $lightness: if-bright($bg,20%,10%));
  $middle-2: scale-color($bg, $lightness: if-bright($bg,-2%,-5%));
  $bottom:   scale-color($bg, $lightness: if-bright($bg,-10%,-20%));
```

```
  @include background-image(linear-gradient(
    $top, $middle-1 50%, $middle-2 50%, $bottom));
}

@mixin nice-button($bg: #eee) {
  @extend %nb-reset;

  // Normal styles
  background-color: $bg;
  border-color: scale-color($bg, $lightness: -20%);
  color: text-contrast($bg);
  @include nb-gradient(rgba($bg, .7)); // alpha shows color transitions

  text-shadow: scale-color($bg, $lightness:
    if-bright($bg,25%,-25%)) 0 1px 1px;
  @include box-shadow(rgba(#fff,
    if-bright($bg,.6,.2)) 0 0 1px 1px inset);

  // State styles
  &:hover, &:focus {
    background-color:
                scale-color($bg, $lightness: if-bright($bg, 85%, 25%));
  }

  &:active {
    background: scale-color($bg,
      $lightness: if-bright($bg, 25%, 10%));
    border-color: rgba(#000, if-bright($bg, .4, .8));
    @include box-shadow(
      if-bright($bg,
        rgba(mix($bg, #000, 25%), .4), rgba(mix($bg, #000), .9)
      ) 0 2px 12px inset
    );
  }
}
```

Figure 10.10 shows a sample of what this extension can do.

Now with this extension, any Compass user can create nice CSS3 buttons with a single line of Sass. But you still have work to do. It's time to learn how to package up this demo as an example project, and then we'll look at ways to share this extension.

Figure 10.10   nice-buttons color trial

10.5 Creating a template

Now that your extension works, it's time to prepare it for release. Since you already have a nice working demo, you can include it to show new users how the nice-buttons extension works. Compass allows extension authors to include templates to help users get started quickly. For the type of extension you're building, this is just a demo, but for larger, more ambitious extensions, you might use templates to bootstrap a sophisticated framework. Here's how the directory structure for an extension might look if it was using templates and Sass extensions.

Listing 10.15 Extension directory pattern

```
my-extension/
  stylesheets/
    my-extension.scss
  templates/
    project/
      manifest.rb
      test.html
      test.scss
  lib
    my-extension.rb
    my-extension/
      sass_extensions.rb
```

For your nice-buttons extension, you have no need to write a Sass extension, but making your demo an installable template would be nice. To convert your demo into a template, you'll need to copy demo.html and demo.scss into nice-buttons/templates/ project. Then you'll need to create a `manifest.rb`, which helps Compass locate and identify its assets. The `manifest.rb` belongs in the templates/project directory and lists the assets for the template. You can also add a project description, help text (which is displayed when someone runs `compass help nice-buttons`), and a welcome message that's displayed when the extension is installed. Here's what the `manifest.rb` looks like for nice-buttons.

Listing 10.16 `nice-buttons/templates/project/manifest.rb`

```
stylesheet 'demo.scss', :media => 'screen, projection'
html 'demo.html'
image 'screenshot.png'

description "Create beautiful CSS3 buttons from a single color"
help "This will install a demo (HTML and Scss) to show you how to use
  nice-buttons"
welcome_message %Q{
Example usage: button { @include nice-buttons(#444) }
See demo.html and demo.scss for example usage.
See screenshot.png for a screenshot of the rendered demo.
Enjoy!
}
```

It's probably a good idea to include documentation and support URLs with the welcome message and help text if your extension has them.

With the demo added as a template, the directory structure for your extension looks like the following.

```
nice-buttons/
  stylesheets/
  _color-helpers.scss
    nice-buttons.scss
  templates/
    project/
      demo.html
      demo.scss
      manifest.rb
```

If a user has the nice-buttons extension in their project's extensions directory, they can run this command to install the default template:

```
compass install nice-buttons
```

This will use the project's Compass configuration to copy the assets from templates/ project to the appropriate locations. If you create a second template in the templates/ warm-cookies directory, a user could install it by passing the directory name:

```
compass install nice-buttons/warm-cookies
```

Before release, it'd be good to add a README file describing what the extension does, how to use it, and how to install it. But for the purposes of this walk-through, this extension is done. It has a nice demo and it's ready to be shared. Next, we'll look at how to publish this extension so others can begin using it.

10.6   *Distributing extensions*

Historically, the majority of sharing in the web design community has happened in blog posts, using zip files. Though developers have enjoyed releasing software through sophisticated versioning and distribution channels, designers have relied on far simpler methods. Today, though, more and more designers are participating in open source, and it's time to learn how to do this the right way.

This is a deep topic, so this section only introduces the concepts of different release methods. This isn't intended to be a walk-through of how to release open source software.

10.6.1   *Distributing extensions in an archive*

The simplest method for distributing your Compass extension is to zip it up in an archive and post it on a server somewhere. This takes almost no time, but it has its drawbacks.

For one, updates require users to manually replace old code. When files belong in more than one location, this can be a pain. Also, without sophisticated version control, trying to maintain older releases can be challenging when you have to work with different historical states of a project. Though version-controlled systems keep the full history for every file and offer features like tagging, an archive is merely a snapshot of your extension at one point in time. That can be limiting.

10.6.2 *Distributing an extension as a Ruby gem*

Ruby gems are a sophisticated way to package and distribute code. For our purposes, one of the most useful aspects of releasing a gem is the built-in dependency management. You can require users of your extension to have specific versions of other gems like Sass and Compass. Of course, with any release you can add a README file that states the minimum supported version, but with a gem, simply installing your gem will also fetch and install the correct versions of any gems you rely on.

With an ad hoc extension, users have to copy all of the extension's code into their project's extensions directory, but with a gem, the extension code will live in a centralized location, allowing multiple projects to point to the same extension code.

CONVERTING AN AD HOC EXTENSION TO A GEM

To distribute your extension as a Ruby gem, you'll need to add a couple of files to your project, as shown in figure 10.11.

At a minimum, a gem needs to have a `gemspec` and a lib directory with a Ruby file named after the gem. You'll use `nice-buttons.rb` to register your extension with Compass and tell it where to find your extension's directories. The next listing shows what the code for the `nice-buttons.rb` looks like.

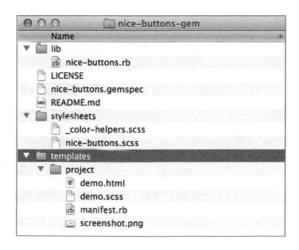

Figure 10.11 Gem project setup

Listing 10.18   `nice-buttons.rb`

```ruby
require 'compass'

Compass::Frameworks.register('nice-buttons',
  :stylesheets_directory => File.join(File.dirname(__FILE__), '..',
    'stylesheets'),
  :templates_directory => File.join(File.dirname(__FILE__), '..',
    'templates'))
```

That's not as pretty as the Sass you're used to looking at, but basically you're telling your gem it requires the Compass gem. Then you use a Compass function to register an extension called nice-buttons and you tell it where to find the stylesheets and templates directories.

Now, let's look at the `nice-buttons.gemspec`. There are lots of different ways to construct a gemspec, but we'll keep this one simple.

Listing 10.19   `nice-buttons.gemspec`

```ruby
# -*- encoding: utf-8 -*-
Gem::Specification.new do |gem|
    gem.name          = "nice-buttons"
    gem.version       = "1.0.0"
    gem.authors       = ["Brandon Mathis"]
    gem.email         = ["brandon@imathis.com"]
    gem.description   =
                        "Easily create beautiful CSS3 buttons with Compass."
    gem.summary       = "Nice and easy CSS3 buttons for Compass users"
    gem.homepage      = "http://github.com/imathis/nice-buttons"

    gem.files         = %w(README.md LICENSE)
    gem.files         += Dir.glob("lib/**/*")
    gem.files         += Dir.glob("stylesheets/**/*")
    gem.files         += Dir.glob("templates/**/*")

    gem.add_dependency  "sass", ">= 3.2"
    gem.add_dependency  "compass", ">= 0.12"
end
```

In this file, there are two sections. The first is made up of metadata about your gem, its name, version number, authors, and so forth. The second section includes the gem's files and sets up dependencies on other gems. Since your extension relies on some more recent features of Sass and Compass, you'll require users to have at least Sass 3.2 and Compass 0.12.

With all this set up, you can tell Ruby gems to generate your gem file by running this command in your terminal:

```
gem build nice-buttons.gemspec
```

This will generate the gem file `nice-buttons-1.0.0.gem` in the root of your project.

PUBLISHING A GEM

To publish this gem, you'll need to create an account at RubyGems.org (a free central repository for hosting gems) and follow their setup process. When you're ready, you can publish your gem by running the following command:

```
gem push nice-buttons-1.0.0.gem
```

With that, anyone can immediately install your gem and begin using your extension.

INSTALLING A GEM

You can install your gem manually by running this command from the terminal:

```
gem install nice-buttons
```

This will fetch the gem from RubyGems.org and, if you don't have the right versions of Compass or Sass, they'll automatically be installed for you. Clearly this is nicer than shipping a zip file.

To begin using your gem with a Compass project, you'll need to add a line to the top of your Compass configuration file:

```
require "nice-buttons"
```

Now Compass knows about your gem and you can import the nice-buttons stylesheet and begin using it in your project. If you like, you can also install the demo project you created earlier by running this from the command line:

```
compass install nice-buttons
```

This will unpack your demo files into the Compass project and recompile your stylesheets. Historically, this has been the most common way to install a gem and use it with Compass, but recently many developers have adopted a different technique using a gem called *Bundler* to install and manage gems.

INSTALLING A GEM WITH BUNDLER

Bundler (http://gembundler.com) is a gem that helps you install and manage Ruby gems in your projects. Bundler uses a *Gemfile* to list the gems your project is using. Here's how you add your gem to the list.

Listing 10.20 Add nice-buttons to the Gemfile

```
source :rubygems

group :assets do
  gem 'nice-buttons'
end
```

After you've updated the Gemfile, you'll install your gems with a simple command:

```
bundle
```

This will connect to RubyGems.org and find the latest version of the nice-buttons gem and all of its dependencies and install them to your system. It'll also create a file called

Gemfile.lock, which contains the full set of gems that your project is using, their version numbers, where they were downloaded from, and the hierarchy of gem dependencies. This detailed record keeping ensures that you don't run into problems using incompatible versions. It's a pain to do this manually, so the popularity of Bundler is no surprise.

To use Compass with Bundler, prepend your Compass commands with `bundle exec`, like this:

```
bundle exec compass compile
```

This gives Compass access to the Gemfile's assets group where it'll find your extension and make it available to your project. If you want to install the demo project you created, you can run this command:

```
bundle exec compass install nice-buttons
```

After your gem is installed, users can import your nice-buttons stylesheet and start using your code.

Distributing an extension as a Ruby gem is easy, and the benefit it provides over merely sharing an archive is worth the effort. But after you've shared your code with others, it's possible they'll find bugs or offer to make improvements. This introduces a new challenge. Communicating with other developers and dealing with code contributions can be a challenge, especially if your extension becomes popular. For this, we'll turn to GitHub, an excellent resource for collaborating with the open source community.

10.6.3 Social coding on GitHub

There are other open source communities out there, but GitHub is by far the most popular. GitHub will host your project on a nicely designed website where others can browse and download your code. It also gives you tools to manage contributors, publish a project website, and edit a wiki. Other GitHub users can fork your projects, make improvements, and offer their changes back to you. With GitHub's issue tracker, you review and accept code contributions, merging them into your projects right from the website. GitHub offers all of this freely to open source projects.

To publish your extension on GitHub, you need to add a new repository and follow their simple instructions for committing and pushing up your extension. If you add a README to your project, GitHub will show it on your project's home page. You can see the nice-buttons gem on GitHub right now at http://github.com/imathis/nice-buttons, and figure 10.12 shows what it looks like.

If you've published an ad hoc extension, users can download nice-buttons from the project website or install it from the command line by running this command from their extensions directory:

```
git clone https://github.com/github_user_name/nice-buttons.git
```

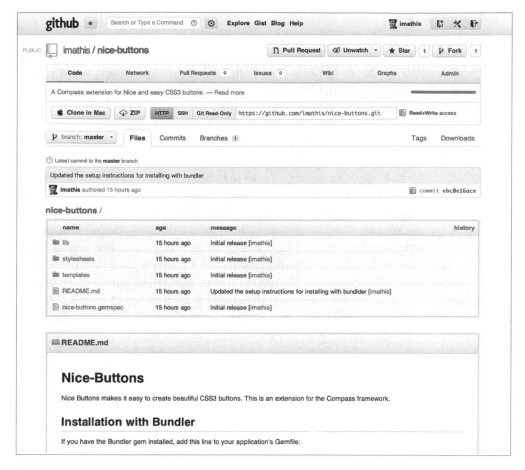

Figure 10.12 nice-buttons project page

Later they can update to the latest version by running the following command from their extensions/nice-buttons directory:

```
git pull
```

This will download the latest version of your extension, but if your extension requires an updated version of Sass, Compass, or another gem, the user will have to manually update those to the correct version. GitHub is an excellent place to host and collaboratively work on open source code, but if you want dependency management, you should distribute your code as a Ruby gem.

There's a great deal more to learn about how to release and manage open source software, but this section should provide a good starting point. As it goes with most things, the best way to learn is to try.

10.7 *Summary*

In this chapter, you saw that although Sass and Compass expand your ability to solve problems with stylesheets, they also let you share your knowledge and experience, and participate in the design community like never before. We explored ways of writing stylesheets that are designed to be shared with others. We discussed principles of good extension design as we walked through the steps to create, refactor, and package up a nice Compass extension. We also covered different methods of distributing your extensions, and looked at ways you can share your code and collaborate with others.

Over the course of this book, you've seen the power of Sass as a dynamic stylesheet language and how it empowers you to write readable, maintainable stylesheets. You've seen how Compass provides a solid library, integrates smoothly into your development environment, and a gives you a great platform for building and sharing your knowledge. You've seen Sass and Compass defeat the tedium of writing CSS, giving you new and interesting challenges and greater rewards. Whether you're new to Sass and Compass or you've been using them for years, we hope this book has enabled you to see stylesheets with new eyes, equipped you with new tricks and greater understanding, and emboldened you to stretch yourself and to attempt great things.

appendix A
Installing Sass
and Compass

Both Sass and Compass are command-line tools built on top of the Ruby programming language. To use them you'll need to have Ruby installed as well as a basic understanding of your computer's command line. Sass and Compass can be installed on Windows, Mac OS X, and Linux.

A.1 Installation on Windows

Windows doesn't come with Ruby, so unless you have previously installed it, you'll need to do so now. It only takes a few minutes.

A.1.1 Opening the Windows command prompt

On Windows 7, you can launch the command prompt from the Windows start menu by selecting All Programs > Accessories > Command Prompt. Alternately, you can type command into the search box and then select Command Prompt from the results.

On earlier versions of Windows, you can launch the command prompt by selecting All Properties > Accessories > Command Prompt. Alternatively, you can select Run and then enter cmd and press Return.

When the command prompt is running, you should see a window like figure A.1.

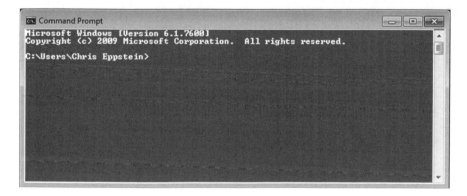

Figure A.1 Windows command prompt

A.1.2 *Installing Ruby on Windows*

From the command prompt, type ruby -v and then press Return. If Ruby isn't installed, the command prompt will tell you 'ruby' is not recognized as an internal or external command, operable program or batch file. If Ruby is installed, it'll print out the version of Ruby you have installed. The version should be greater than or equal to 1.8.7 (if 1.8.6 or below, please install Ruby with the following instructions).

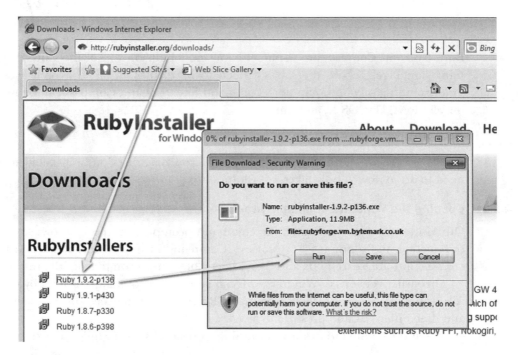

Figure A.2   Downloading the Ruby installer

Go to http://rubyinstaller.org/downloads/. Click on the most recent Ruby version and click Run. Walk through the guided installer's steps. When you get to the third screen, it'll ask you where to install Ruby; check the two check boxes before continuing.

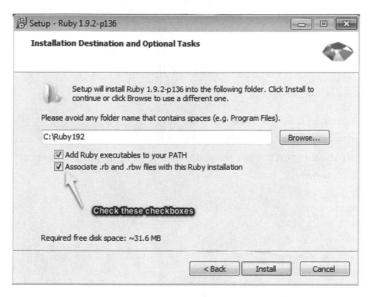

Figure A.3   Configuring the Ruby installer

Now close your command prompt and launch it again, and verify that Ruby is installed by typing `ruby -v` and pressing Return.

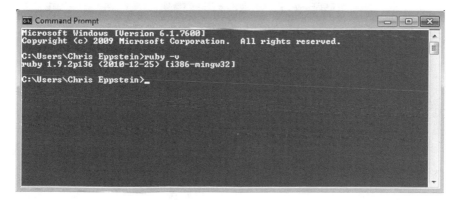

Figure A.4   Ruby installed

A.1.3   Installing Sass and Compass on Windows

Ruby comes with a system for installing Ruby-based software called *RubyGems*. Both Sass and Compass can be easily installed using this system. To install the latest version of Sass:

```
$ gem install sass
$ gem install compass
```

In each case, you should see output that looks like this:

```
Successfully installed sass-3.1.0
1 gem installed
Installing ri documentation for sass-3.1.0...
Installing RDoc documentation for sass-3.1.0...
```

After installing, you should verify that the applications are installed correctly by running the following commands:

```
$ sass -v
Sass 3.1.0 (XXX NAME ME)

$ compass -v
Compass 0.11.0
Copyright (c) 2008-2011 Chris Eppstein
Released under the MIT License.
```

A.2   Installation on Mac OS X

Mac OS X has come with Ruby installed by default for some time now, so it's likely that you don't need to install Ruby.

A.2.1   Opening the Mac OS X Terminal

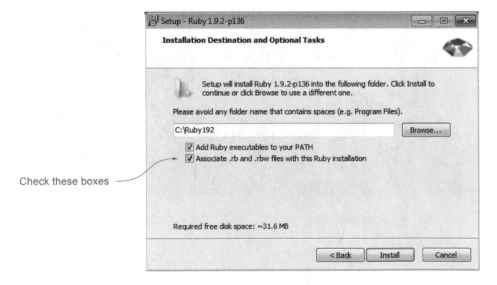

Check these boxes

Figure A.5   Launching the Mac OS X Terminal

You can launch the terminal application from the Finder by going into Applications > Utilities and double-clicking the Terminal application.

If you're unfamiliar with the Mac OS X Terminal, we recommend that you read the Terminal tutorial written by John Long, which can be found at http://wiseheartdesign .com/articles/2010/11/12/the-designers-guide-to-the-osx-command-prompt/.

A.2.2 Installing Ruby

From the command prompt, type `ruby -v` and then press Return. If Ruby isn't installed, the command prompt will tell you `bash: ruby: command not found`. In this unlikely scenario, please follow the instructions for installation found at http:// rubyosx.rubyforge.org/. Be sure to restart the Terminal after installing.

A.2.3 Installing Sass and Compass on Mac

Ruby comes with a system for installing Ruby-based software called *RubyGems*. Both Sass and Compass can be easily installed using this system. To install the latest version of Sass and Compass:

```
$ sudo gem install sass
$ sudo gem install compass
```

In each case, you should see output that looks like this:

```
Successfully installed sass-3.1.0
1 gem installed
Installing ri documentation for sass-3.1.0...
Installing RDoc documentation for sass-3.1.0...
```

After installing, you should verify that the applications are installed correctly by running the following commands:

```
$ sass -v
Sass 3.1.0 (XXX NAME ME)

$ compass -v
Compass 0.11.0
Copyright (c) 2008-2011 Chris Eppstein
Released under the MIT License.
```

A.3 Installation on Linux

Please follow your Linux distribution's instructions for installing Ruby if it's not installed.

A.3.1 Opening the Linux Terminal

It's assumed that as a Linux user you know how to access your terminal.

A.3.2 Installing Ruby

If Ruby isn't installed, install it using your Linux distribution's software installation mechanism.

A.3.3 *Installing Sass and Compass on Linux*

Ruby comes with a system for installing Ruby-based software called *RubyGems*. Both Sass and Compass can be easily installed using this system. To install the latest version of Sass:

```
$ sudo gem install sass
$ sudo gem install compass
```

In each case, you should see output that looks like this:

```
Successfully installed sass-3.1.0
1 gem installed
Installing ri documentation for sass-3.1.0...
Installing RDoc documentation for sass-3.1.0...
```

After installing, you should verify that the applications are installed correctly by running the following commands:

```
$ sass -v
Sass 3.1.0 (XXX NAME ME)

$ compass -v
Compass 0.11.0
Copyright (c) 2008-2011 Chris Eppstein
Released under the MIT License.
```

appendix B
Getting started
with Compass

B.1 Create a new project

To start using Compass in a new project, open up your terminal and run the following:

```
$ compass create my-project
```

This will create the my-project directory if it doesn't already exist and fill it with the following files:

```
my-project/
  config.rb
  - sass/
    - ie.scss
    - print.scss
    - screen.scss
  - stylesheets/
    - ie.css
    - print.css
    - screen.css
```

If you don't pass a directory to the compass create command, it'll use your current directory.

In config.rb, you'll make changes to Compass configurations like asset locations and compression level (more on that in a moment). The sass directory contains some starter stylesheets that you can edit, rename, or toss out completely, but this is where your Sass stylesheets will live. Finally, there's a stylesheets directory where compiled CSS files are written.

B.1.1 Configuring options during setup

There are several options you can use with the compass create command to configure your project:

```
--bare               (Install without default stylesheets)
--syntax sass        (Use the indented syntax for default stylesheets)
--sass-dir "cool"    (Use the `cool` directory for Sass)
--css-dir "style"    (Use the `style` directory for CSS)
--images-dir "img"   (Use the `img` directory for images)
```

```
--fonts-dir "type"      (Use the `type` directory for fonts)
--javascripts-dir "js" (Use the `js` directory for javascripts)
```

Adding several options looks like this:

```
$ compass create my-project --bare --sass-dir "cool" --css-dir "style"
```

You may be wondering why you can set a JavaScript directory. This is because Compass extensions can also package relevant JavaScript files, and this setting lets you tell Compass where to put them when you install extensions.

B.1.2 Adding Compass to a Rails project

To install Compass within a Rails project, `cd` into your project directory and add this to your Gemfile:

```
group :assets do
  gem 'compass-rails'
  # Add any compass extensions here
end
```

Then run the following command from the terminal:

```
$ bundle
$ bundle exec compass init rails
```

With Rails, the Compass configuration file is stored in `config/compass.rb`.

If your project is on Rails 2.3 or 3.0, you need to follow some additional steps, outlined in the `compass-rails` README: https://github.com/Compass/compass-rails/blob/master/README.md.

B.2 Installing Compass extensions

Compass extensions are distributed in two ways: as Ruby gems or ad hoc extensions. Both are easy to install and work fine together in any project. If you're curious about how to develop an extension, you can read about that in chapter 10.

B.2.1 Installing extensions released as Ruby gems

You can install the extension to your system gems like this:

```
$ sudo gem install extension-name
```

If you use Bundler, add this line to your Gemfile:

```
gem 'extension-name'
```

Then install the gem from the terminal:

```
$ bundle install
```

Now that you have the gem downloaded to your system, you'll need to install it into your project.

B.2.2 Install extensions for an existing project

Now that you have the gem, tell Compass about it by adding the following to your `config.rb`:

```
require 'extension-name'
```

Then, from your project directory, run this in the terminal:

```
$ compass install -r extension-name -f extension-name
```

Now you can begin using the extension with your project. You can install several extensions at the same time with this command by being sure to add `-r` and `-f` with each extension.

INSTALL EXTENSIONS FOR A NEW PROJECT

If you already have the extension's gem installed, you can create a new project using that extension with the following command:

```
$ compass create my-project -r extension-name --using extension-name
```

This will create a new Compass project and configure it to use your extension.

B.2.3 Installing ad hoc Compass extensions

Ad hoc extensions are simply directories containing Sass stylesheets and a few files to tell Compass how they work. If your project doesn't already have an extensions directory, create one and then copy the extension's folder into it. Your project's directory structure might look like this:

```
my-project/
  config.rb
  extensions/
    some-extension/
  sass/
  stylesheets/
```

To install ad hoc extensions on a Rails app, create an extensions directory in vendor/plugins/compass_extensions.

You can customize the extensions directory by setting `extensions_dir` in your project's configuration file.

B.2.4 Installing an extension's patterns

Most extensions ship with a default pattern consisting of a stylesheet or an asset to be used with the extension. These patterns get installed automatically with the `compass install` script. But some extension authors create additional patterns that provide usage examples or give you a boost with assets and boilerplate code. The command for installing an extension's pattern looks like this:

```
$ compass install extension-name/pattern-name
```

Compass will display the author's included instructions (if any) along with a list of new files installed with the pattern.

UNPACKING EXTENSIONS AND FRAMEWORKS

For some of you, using extensions installed as Ruby gems might feel unusual. Sometimes it's helpful to be able to read the source for an extension, but with Ruby gems the source code is stored elsewhere on your computer. To help with that, Compass offers the ability to unpack an extension—or even the Compass framework itself—right into your project directory. Here's how you do it:

```
$ compass unpack extension-name
$ compass unpack compass
```

This will extract the files for the extension and the Compass framework right into your project's extensions directory. So now your project might look like this:

```
your-project/
  extensions/
    compass-13.0/
    extension-name-1.0/
```

Compass will also output a nice warning essentially telling you to look but not touch. It may be tempting to alter the code you've just unpacked, but it's a bad idea and will prevent you from being able to update that extension without losing your customizations. The best use for this feature is to read the source for education or troubleshooting.

B.3   Configuring your Compass project

Compass is a library for Sass, a platform for extensions, and a system for integrating with your project environment. The Compass configuration ties all of these parts together to give you a smooth workflow and lots of flexibility.

B.3.1   Working with assets

Stylesheet authors frequently work with images, fonts, and JavaScripts in addition to writing stylesheets, and these files often have a codependent relationship. For example, in order to show a background image, the stylesheet needs to tell the browser exactly where to find that image. If you've ever reorganized a project or changed a directory name, you know the pain of having to update those URLs.

Compass aims to help you keep everything in sync by writing asset URLs for you. In your configuration file, you can tell Compass where to find your project's assets and what URLs you want to generate. Compass will even output a warning if it can't find something when you compile your stylesheets.

B.3.2   Configuring asset locations

To tell Compass where to find assets on your filesystem, you'll need to set these configurations:

- images_dir—Defaults to <project>/images
- sass_dir—Defaults to <project>/sass
- css_dir—Defaults to <project>/stylesheets
- fonts_dir—Defaults to <project>/<css_dir>/fonts
- javascripts_dir—Defaults to <project>/javascripts

These are relative to your project directory, so setting your images_dir = img will tell Compass to look at your-project/img/ to find your project's images. Then, in your stylesheets, you can reference an image by using the image-url() helper function:

```
#logo { background: image-url('logo.png') }
```

Compass will look for your image in your-project/img/logo.png and then compile the following CSS:

```
#logo { background: url('/img/logo.png') }
```

If your project will be deployed to a subdirectory on your web server, you can customize the URL by setting the http_path configuration. You can also set URL configurations for CSS, images, JavaScripts, and fonts.

If you want to know what value Compass is using for a configuration, you can ask it like this:

```
$ compass config -p sass_dir
app/stylesheets
$ compass config -p css_dir
public/stylesheets
```

For a deeper look at configuring Compass, flip back to chapter 8.

B.4 The command line

The primary commands for Compass are as follows:

- compass create—Create a new Compass project
- compass init—Add compass to an existing project (Rails)
- compass clean—Remove generated files and caches
- compass compile—Generate your stylesheets
- compass watch—Watch Sass files and regenerate on change

Some other useful commands are these:

- compass stats—See statistics about your stylesheets
- compass unpack <extension> —Unpack extensions into your project
- compass validate—Validate your generated CSS
- compass version—Display the version, license, and so on
- compass interactive—Enter a console for testing SassScript with Compass

B.4.1   *Getting help*

There's a lot to remember when working with Compass, but it's nice to know that you can ask the command line for help. Running `compass help` will list the following information:

- Commands with descriptions
- Available frameworks and extensions
- Global options for the `compass` command

You can also get detailed help for an individual subcommand like this:

```
$ compass help watch
```

Run this and you'll get a nice description of what `compass watch` will do, its syntax, and a full list of options with descriptions.

You can also get help with an extension or an extension's pattern:

```
$ compass help extension-name
$ compass help extension-name/pattern
```

If an extension author hasn't included help text for their extension, this will show the default Compass help screen.

appendix C
The Sass syntaxes

C.1 Indented Sass versus SCSS

Most of this book demonstrates the SCSS syntax, which stands for *Sassy CSS*. SCSS is a superset of CSS, meaning that any valid CSS file is also a valid SCSS file. This means that you can change the CSS file screen.css to screen.scss and begin adding Sass features without needing to make any other changes. As a result, though the SCSS syntax is newer, it has become the most popular syntax for Sass.

Originally, Sass only had one syntax, called the *indented syntax*, or at that time, just *Sass*. To illustrate the differences between these syntaxes, we'll look at the same code example written in each syntax.

First we'll look at the SCSS syntax.

Listing C.1 SCSS syntax example

```scss
/* Compass makes CSS3 easy!
   Especially CSS3 gradients. */

@import "compass/css3";

// This mixin gives us easy gradients
// It picks colors for us, how nice.

@mixin easy-gradient($bg, $alpha: false) {
  @if ($alpha) {
    $bg: rgba($bg, $alpha);
  }
  $top: lighten($bg, 5);
  $bottom: darken($bg, 5);
  @include background-image(
    linear-gradient($top, $bottom)
  )
}

nav {
  margin: 20px { left: 0; right: 0 }
  @include easy-gradient(#ccc);
  a { color: blue; text-decoration: none }
}
```

Now let's see the same code in the indented syntax.

Listing C.2   Indented syntax example

```
/* Compass makes CSS3 easy!
   Especially CSS3 gradients.

@import compass/css3

// This mixin gives us easy gradients
   It picks colors for us, how nice.
=easy-gradient($bg, $alpha: false)
  @if ($alpha)
    $bg: rgba($bg, $alpha)
  $top: lighten($bg, 5)
  $bottom: darken($bg, 5)
  +background-image(linear-gradient($top, $bottom))

nav
  margin: 20px
    left: 0
    right: 0
  +easy-gradient(#ccc)
  a
    color: blue
    text-decoration: none
```

There are some immediately obvious differences, and some subtle differences. Let's break them down.

C.1.1   *Whitespace versus braces and semicolons*

The most striking difference is the lack of curly braces and semicolons in the indented syntax. Whereas SCSS uses the familiar curly braces, the indented syntax uses, well, indentation. Also, rather than using semicolons, the indented syntax uses newlines to separate properties.

Those who prefer the indented syntax claim that with the noisy characters removed, their Sass is cleaner and easier to read. Those who are fond of SCSS enjoy having the freedom to use whitespace however they like, putting multiple properties on a single line or even splitting long functions up across several lines. They also like how they can begin using standard CSS without having to remove characters and reformat them to the strict whitespace requirements of the indented syntax.

Though the use of whitespace instead of characters is the most obvious difference, there are several others as well.

C.1.2   *The @import directive*

In SCSS, the `@import` directive requires the target to be surrounded with quote characters, but in the indented syntax, the quotes are unnecessary. It's also important to note that with the `@import` directive, file extensions aren't needed. You can use file extensions, but by avoiding them, you can import either .scss files or .sass files. With the directive @import "some-file";, Sass will look for some-file.sass and some-file.scss. Because of this, both syntaxes can easily coexist, and you can write your stylesheets in SCSS while importing extensions written by someone else in the indented syntax.

C.1.3 *Mixins*

The way mixins are created and used is also different. In SCSS the @mixin and @include directives are used to define and make use of mixins:

```
@mixin easy-gradient($bg, $alpha: false) { ... }
@include easy-gradient(#ccc);
```

The indented syntax can actually use these directives in the same way as SCSS, or it can use = instead of @mixin and + rather than @include:

```
=easy-gradient($bg, $alpha: false)
+easy-gradient(#ccc)
```

Fans of the indented syntax like to point out how minimal their mixin directives are, though some prefer the obviousness of writing out @mixin and @include, which is why they can also be used in the indented syntax.

C.1.4 *Comments*

In Sass, there are three kinds of comments. Comments beginning with // won't appear in the generated CSS, comments that begin with /* will appear in uncompressed CSS, and comments beginning with /*! (loud comments) will appear in compressed and uncompressed CSS. In the indented syntax, all of these comments can be multiline comments if the author indents each line beneath the comment markers, like this:

```
// some comment
   which spans
   multiple lines

/* This comment
   spans multiple
   lines too

/*! As does
   this one
```

In SCSS, the // comment is a single-line comment, and the two multiline comments must be closed with the matching close comment characters like this:

```
// some comment
// which spans
// multiple lines

/* This comment
   spans multiple
   lines too */

/*! As does
   this one !*/
```

C.1.5   *Which is better?*

There are Sass enthusiasts on both sides of this debate, and even some who admit to using both syntaxes for different purposes. Thankfully, you don't have to decide. The maintainers of the Sass project have committed to keeping both syntaxes, and you can even convert between the two using the `sass-convert` command-line tool. Thanks to the flexibility of the `@import` directive, you can easily use both syntaxes alongside each other within the same project; you just can't use both syntaxes within the same file.

index

HTML5 in Action
by Rob Crowther, Joe Lennon, Ash Blue,
  and Greg Wanish

ISBN: 978-1-617290-49-7
375 pages
$39.99
August 2013

Hello! HTML5 & CSS3
A user-friendly reference guide
by Rob Crowther

ISBN: 978 1 935182-89-4
560 pages
$39.99
October 2012

For ordering information go to www.manning.com

MORE TITLES FROM MANNING

Secrets of the JavaScript Ninja
by John Resig and Bear Bibeault

ISBN: 978-1-933988-69-6
392 pages
$39.99
December 2012

Third-Party JavaScript
by Ben Vinegar and Anton Kovalyov

ISBN: 978-1-617290-54-1
288 pages
$44.99
March 2013

For ordering information go to www.manning.com

Single Page Web Applications
JavaScript end-to-end

by Michael S. Mikowski
and Josh C. Powell

ISBN: 978-1-617290-75-6
325 pages
$44.99
July 2013

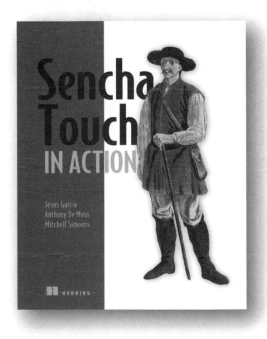

Sencha Touch in Action

by Jesus Garcia, Anthony De Moss,
and Mitchell Simoens

ISBN: 978-1-617290-37-4
320 pages
$44.99
July 2013

For ordering information go to www.manning.com

MORE TITLES FROM MANNING

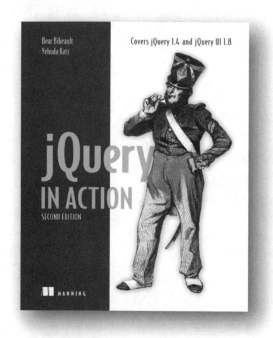